Basic Spanish Grammar

Basic
Spanish
Grammar

ANA C. JARVIS
San Bernardino Valley College

RAQUEL LEBREDO
California Baptist College

FRANCISCO MENA
California State University, Chico

D. C. HEATH AND COMPANY
Lexington, Massachusetts   Toronto

Credits

On the cover:

The set of gold earplugs shows 2 warriors running or dancing. Each of these earplugs is inlaid with turquoise, lapus lazuli, and other precious stones. The Moche, who flourished from 150 to 700 A.D. on the northwest coast of Peru, wore ornaments of this type.

Cover photograph by Lee Boltin.

All interior photographs by Stuart Cohen except: page 97: Mimi Forsyth/Monkmeyer Press; page 119: David Kupferschmid; page 135: Katherine A. Lambert; page 155: David Kupferschmid; page 165: Harriet Gans/The Image Works, Inc.; page 203: Peter Menzel; page 209: David Kupferschmid; page 217: Bernard P. Wolff/Photo Researchers, Inc.

International Standard Book Number: 0-669-10945-2

2 3 4 5 6 7 8 9 0

Preface

Basic Spanish Grammar provides a clear, concise review of the structures covered in the first and second levels of Spanish and introduces those that are appropriate for the third level. Each grammatical concept is illustrated by means of brief conversational exchanges. This method first exposes students to a specific point of grammar and demonstrates its correct usage in a natural, everyday situation.

The lessons of the Workbook correspond to those of the grammar and provide challenging opportunities for using the structure of the lesson. A Tape Program on cassettes accompanies the Workbook.

Basic Spanish Grammar includes:

1. An introductory lesson that consists of useful words and expressions, such as greetings and farewells, days of the week, and vocabulary for personal data
2. Twenty-four lessons, containing:
   Grammatical structures
   Conversational exchanges illustrating each grammatical point
   Exercises to practice and reinforce each concept
   A study of cognates
   A list of active vocabulary of the lesson. Every effort has been made to include high-frequency words and expressions
3. A self-testing section after lessons 5, 10, 15, and 24
4. The following appendices:
   Rules governing Spanish pronunciation
   Pronoun charts
   Verb paradigms
   Glossary of useful grammatical terms
   List of careers and occupations
   Answer key for self-testing sections

5. An end vocabulary including:
     Spanish-English vocabulary
     English-Spanish vocabulary
6. Index

The *Workbook for Basic Spanish Grammar* contains 24 lessons that correspond to the lessons of the student text.

The lessons contain:
 1. Dialogues presenting realistic situations in authentic Spanish, followed by English versions in smaller type
 2. Study of cognates
 3. Active vocabulary
 4. Grammatical structure exercise
 5. Question-answer exercise
 6. Dialogue completion
 7. Exercise based on visuals
 8. Translation in a situational format
 9. Situations to act out
10. Class activities

There are also eight reading comprehension activities based on simulated realia from the newspapers. Vocabulary Review sections occur after lessons 5, 10, 15, 20, and 24.

Spanish-English and English-Spanish vocabularies are provided for student reference.

The cassettes include the dialogues, the cognates, and the new vocabulary from the Workbook. Students hear the dialogue once at a normal conversational speed. It is then read with pauses for student repetition. The cognates and the new words and expressions are presented with pauses for student repetition.

We would like to express our appreciation to Professors Milton Azevedo, University of California, Berkeley, and T. Bruce Fryer, University of South Carolina, for their constructive criticism. Special thanks are due the members of the editorial staff of D.C. Heath and Company for their many valuable suggestions, which have substantially enhanced the quality of the manuscript.

Contents

LESSON 16

LESSON 17

LESSON 18

LESSON 19

LESSON 20

VOCABULARY

INDEX

BASIC SPANISH GRAMMAR

No.	Periodo	Lunes	Martes	Miércoles	Jueves	Viernes
1	8:05-9:00	Biología	Educación física	Biología	Educación física	Biología
2	9:05-10:00	Inglés	Inglés	Inglés	Inglés	Inglés

HORARIO   Colegio Cristóbal Colón

Marta Ruiz

Useful Expressions

1. PERSONAL DATA

¿Nombre y apellido?	*Name and surname?*
María Valdés.	*María Valdés.*
¿Estado civil?	*Marital status?*
Casada.	*Married.*
¿Apellido de soltera?	*Maiden name?*
Rivas.	*Rivas.*
¿Nacionalidad?	*Nationality?*
Argentina.	*Argentinian.*
¿Lugar de nacimiento?	*Place of birth?*
Buenos Aires.	*Buenos Aires.*
¿Edad?	*Age?*
Veinte años.	*Twenty (years old).*
¿Ocupación?	*Occupation?*
Estudiante.	*Student.*
¿Dirección?	*Address?*
Calle Magnolia,[1] número veinte.	*Number twenty, Magnolia Street.*
¿Ciudad?	*City?*
Riverside.	*Riverside.*

VOCABULARY: PERSONAL DATA

los años	years	divorciado	divorced (*masculine*)
el apellido	surname	la edad	age
el apellido de soltera	maiden name	el estado civil	marital status
la calle	street	la fecha de nacimiento	date of birth
casada	married (*feminine*)	femenino	feminine
casado	married (*masculine*)	el lugar de nacimiento	place of birth
la ciudad	city	el lugar donde trabaja	place of work
la dirección, el domicilio	address	masculino	masculine
divorciada	divorced (*feminine*)	la nacionalidad	nationality

[1] In Spanish, the name of the street is placed before the number.

el nombre	name	la ocupación	occupation[1]
norteamericana	North American (*feminine*)	separada	separated (*feminine*)
norteamericano	North American (*masculine*)	separado	separated (*masculine*)
el número	number	el sexo	sex
el número de la licencia para conducir	driver's license number	soltera	single (*feminine*)
		soltero	single (*masculine*)
el número de seguro social	social security number	el teléfono	telephone
		la viuda	widow
		el viudo	widower
		y	and

Exercise

Ask the person next to you the following questions:

1. ¿Nombre y apellido?
2. ¿Estado civil?
3. ¿Nacionalidad?
4. ¿Lugar de nacimiento?
5. ¿Ocupación?
6. ¿Dirección? (¿Domicilio?)
7. ¿Ciudad?

2. GREETINGS AND FAREWELLS

Buenos días, doctor Rivas.	*Good morning, Doctor Rivas.*
¿Cómo está usted?	*How are you?*
Muy bien, gracias. ¿Y usted?	*Very well, thank you. And you?*
Bien, gracias. Hasta luego. Adiós.	*Fine, thank you. See you later. Good-bye.*
Mucho gusto, profesor Vera.	*A pleasure to meet you, Professor Vera.*
El gusto es mío, señorita Reyes.	*The pleasure is mine, Miss Reyes.*

[1] For a list of occupations, see Appendix.

Buenas tardes, señora.	*Good afternoon, madam.*
Buenas tardes, señor.	*Good afternoon, sir.*
Pase y tome asiento, por favor.	*Come in and sit down, please.*
Gracias.	*Thank you.*
Buenas noches, señorita.	*Good evening, miss.*
¿Cómo está usted?	*How are you?*
No muy bien, doctor.	*Not very well, doctor.*
Lo siento. Hasta mañana.	*I'm sorry. I'll see you tomorrow.*
Muchas gracias, señora.	*Thank you very much, madam.*
De nada, señor. Adiós.	*You're welcome, sir. Good-bye.*

VOCABULARY

GREETINGS AND FAREWELLS

Adiós.	Good-bye.
Buenas noches.	Good evening. (Good night.)
Buenas tardes.	Good afternoon.
Buenos días.	Good morning. (Good day.)
¿Cómo está usted?	How are you?
El gusto es mío.	The pleasure is mine.
Hasta luego.	I'll see you later.
Hasta mañana.	I'll see you tomorrow.
Mucho gusto.	How do you do? (*lit.*, much pleasure)

FORMAL TITLES

doctor (*abbrev.* Dr.)	doctor
profesor	professor
señor (*abbrev.* Sr.)	Mr., sir, gentleman
señora (*abbrev.* Sra.)	Mrs., madam, lady
señorita (*abbrev.* Srta.)	Miss, young lady

USEFUL EXPRESSIONS

bien	well, fine
De nada.	You're welcome.
Lo siento.	I'm sorry.
Muchas gracias.	Thank you very much.
Muy bien, ¿y usted?	Very well, and you?
no	no, not
Pase.	Come in.
por favor	please
Tome asiento.	Sit down. *or* Take a seat.

Exercises

A. Memorize all the above dialogues, and act them out with another student.

B. What would you say in the following situations?

1. You meet Mr. García in the morning and ask him how he is.
2. You thank Miss Vera for a favor and tell her you will see her tomorrow.
3. You greet Mrs. Nieto (afternoon) and ask her to come in and sit down.
4. Professor Maria Rivas says *"mucho gusto"* to you.
5. Someone thanks you for a favor.
6. Mr. Ortiz says he is not feeling well.

3. DAYS OF THE WEEK

¿Qué día es hoy?	*What day is it today?*
Hoy es lunes.	*Today is Monday.*
Hoy es martes, ¿no?	*Today is Tuesday, isn't it?*
No, hoy es miércoles.	*No, today is Wednesday.*
¿Qué día es hoy?	*What day is it today?*
¿Jueves?	*Thursday?*
No, hoy es viernes.	*No, today is Friday.*
Hoy es . . . sábado . . . ¡no!	*Today is . . . Saturday*
domingo . . .	*. . . no! Sunday . . .*
Sí, hoy es domingo.	*Yes, today is Sunday.*

The days of the week are:

lunes	Monday	**viernes**	Friday
martes	Tuesday	**sábado**	Saturday
miércoles	Wednesday	**domingo**	Sunday
jueves	Thursday		

ATENCIÓN: The days of the week are not capitalized in Spanish.

Exercise

Respond, following the model:

Modelo: Hoy es lunes, ¿no?
          No, hoy es domingo.

1. Hoy es miércoles, ¿no?
2. Hoy es domingo, ¿no?
3. Hoy es viernes, ¿no?
4. Hoy es martes, ¿no?
5. Hoy es sábado, ¿no?
6. Hoy es jueves, ¿no?

4. CARDINAL NUMBERS (0–31)

0	cero	11	once
1	uno	12	doce
2	dos	13	trece
3	tres	14	catorce
4	cuatro	15	quince
5	cinco	16	diez y seis (dieciséis)
6	seis	17	diez y siete (diecisiete)
7	siete	18	diez y ocho (dieciocho)
8	ocho	19	diez y nueve (diecinueve)
9	nueve	20	veinte
10	diez	21	veinte y uno (veintiuno)

22	veinte y dos (veintidós)
23	veinte y tres (veintitrés)
24	veinte y cuatro (veinticuatro)
25	veinte y cinco (veinticinco)
26	veinte y seis (veintiséis)
27	veinte y siete (veintisiete)
28	veinte y ocho (veintiocho)
29	veinte y nueve (veintinueve)
30	treinta
31	treinta y uno

Exercise

Read the following numbers aloud:

0, 23, 18, 7, 9, 13, 30, 11, 5, 15, 4, 20, 12, 10, 14, 31, 16, 1, 8, 17, 25, 19, 3, 22, 6, 12, 29

5. MONTHS AND SEASONS OF THE YEAR

¿Qué fecha es hoy?	*What's the date today?*
Hoy es el quince de enero.	*Today is January the fifteenth.*
¿Qué fecha es hoy?	*What's the date today?*
Hoy es el primero de septiembre.	*Today is September the first.*

The months of the year are:

enero	January	**julio**	July
febrero	February	**agosto**	August
marzo	March	**septiembre**	September
abril	April	**octubre**	October
mayo	May	**noviembre**	November
junio	June	**diciembre**	December

ATENCIÓN: The names of the months are not capitalized in Spanish.

The seasons are:

primavera spring   **verano** summer
otoño fall   **invierno** winter

• To ask for the date, say:

¿**Qué fecha es hoy?** *What's the date today?*

• When telling the date, always begin with the expression **Hoy es el . . .:**

Hoy es el veinte de mayo.

• Start with the number followed by the preposition **de** (*of*), and then the month:

quince de mayo   *May 15th*
diez de septiembre *September 10th*
doce de octubre   *October 12th*

• The ordinal number **primero** (*first*) is used when referring to the first day of the month:

primero de febrero *February first*

Exercises

A. Give the Spanish equivalent of the following dates:

1. The 4th of July
2. The 31st of October
3. The 1st of January
4. May 5th
5. February 12th
6. December 25th

7. March 21st
8. April 1st
9. June 20th
10. September 9th
11. August 13th
12. November 11th

B. Say in which season the following months fall:

1. febrero
2. agosto
3. mayo
4. enero

5. octubre
6. julio
7. abril
8. noviembre

PERSONAL INFORMATION

Provide the information requested.

Apellido y nombres	Fecha de nacimiento		
	DÍA	MES[1]	AÑO

Dirección

....

Teléfono

....

Estado civil	Sexo	Edad
1. _____ soltero	Masculino _____	_____
2. _____ casado	Feminino _____	
3. _____ divorciado		
4. _____ viudo		
5. _____ separado		

Nacionalidad ....

Ocupación ....

Lugar donde trabaja ....

Número de seguro social ....

Número de la licencia para conducir ....

[1] **mes:** month

En el restaurante

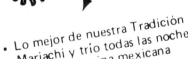
Lesson 1

1. SUBJECT PRONOUNS

	Singular		Plural
yo	*I*	{nosotros	*we (masculine)*
		{nosotras	*we (feminine)*
tú	*you (familiar)*}		
usted[1]	*you (formal)* }	ustedes[2]	*you*
él	*he*	ellos	*they (masculine)*
ella	*she*	ellas	*they (feminine)*

- The masculine plural form may refer to the masculine gender alone or to both genders together:

Juan y Roberto: **ellos**   *John and Robert: **they***
Juan y María: **ellos**   *John and Mary: **they***

ATENCIÓN: Use the **tú** form as the equivalent of *you* when addressing a close friend, a relative, or a child. Use the **usted** form in *all* other instances.

Exercise

Give the personal pronoun you would use for the following:

Modelo: You refer to Mr. Smith as . . .
I refer to Mr. Smith as *él*.

1. You point to yourself and say . . .
2. You refer to Mrs. Smith as . . .
3. You are talking to a little boy and you call him . . .
4. You are talking to a woman you just met and you call her . . .
5. Your mother refers to herself and her sister as . . .
6. Your father refers to himself and his sister as . . .
7. You are talking to a few people and you call them . . .
8. You refer to Mr. Smith and his daughter as . . .
9. You refer to Mrs. Smith and her daughter as . . .
10. You refer to Mr. and Mrs. Smith as . . .

---

[1] Abbreviated **Ud.**
[2] Abbreviated **Uds.** Appendix B, Pronouns, includes the less frequently used **vosotros** forms of the pronouns given in the text.

2. PRESENT INDICATIVE OF REGULAR -ar VERBS

Regular verbs ending in -ar are conjugated like **hablar.**

hablar *(to speak)*		
Singular		
	Stem Ending	
yo	habl- **o**	Yo **hablo** español.
tú	habl- **as**	Tú **hablas** español.
Ud.	habl- **a**	Ud. **habla** español.
él	habl- **a**	Juan **habla** español. Él **habla** español.
ella	habl- **a**	Ana **habla** español. Ella **habla** español.
Plural		
nosotros	habl- **amos**	Nosotros **hablamos** español.
Uds.	habl- **an**[1]	Uds. **hablan** español.
ellos	habl- **an**	Ellos **hablan** español.
ellas	habl- **an**	Ellas **hablan** español.

- The infinitive of all Spanish verbs consists of a stem (such as **habl-**) and an ending (such as **-ar**). When looking up a verb in the dictionary you will always find it listed under the infinitive. The infinitive endings for the three verb conjugations are **-ar, -er,** and **-ir.**

- The stem does not change. The endings change with the subjects.

- The Spanish present tense is equivalent to three English forms:

Yo **hablo** español.
$$\begin{cases} I \textbf{ speak } Spanish. \\ I \textbf{ do speak } Spanish. \\ I \textbf{ am speaking } Spanish. \end{cases}$$

- Since the verb endings indicate who the speaker is, the subject pronouns are frequently omitted:

Hablas inglés, ¿no?	*You speak English, don't you?*
Sí, **hablo** inglés.	*Yes, I speak English.*

However, they may be used for emphasis or clarification:

Uds. hablan inglés, ¿no?	*You speak English, don't you?*
Yo hablo inglés. **Él** habla español.	*I speak English. He speaks Spanish.*

[1] Appendix C, Verbs, includes the **vosotros** forms of the tenses studied in this text.

• Some other common verbs that follow the same pattern are: **trabajar**
  (*to work*), **necesitar** (*to need*), and **estudiar** (*to study*):

María y Juan **trabajan** en Los Ángeles, ¿no?	*María and Juan work in Los Angeles, don't they?*
Sí, ellos **trabajan** en Los Ángeles.	*Yes, they work in Los Angeles.*
Ud. **necesita** dinero, ¿no?	*You need money, don't you?*
Sí, **necesito** dinero.	*Yes, I need money.*
Uds. **estudian** español, ¿no?	*You study Spanish, don't you?*
Sí, **estudiamos** español.	*Yes, we study Spanish.*

Exercises

A. Item substitution: Conjugate the verbs according to the new subject:

   1. Yo **estudio** español. (nosotros, Ud., tú, ellos, él, Uds.)
   2. Ella **trabaja** en San Diego. (yo, nosotras, tú, Ud., ellos)
   3. Tú **necesitas** dinero. (ellos, nosotros, Ud., yo, ella)

B. Complete the following sentences with the present indicative of
   hablar, necesitar, trabajar, and **estudiar,** as needed. Use each verb
   twice.

   1. María y yo _____ en Los Ángeles.
   2. José _____ dinero.
   3. Tú _____ inglés, ¿no?
   4. Marta y Anita _____ dinero.
   5. Ud. _____ inglés, ¿no?
   6. Yo _____ en Harvard.
   7. María _____ en Buenos Aires.
   8. Uds. _____ en Chile, ¿no?

3. INTERROGATIVE SENTENCES

In Spanish there are several ways to ask a question to elicit a *yes/no*
answer:

   1. ¿**Ustedes** necesitan dinero?
   2. ¿Necesitan **ustedes** dinero?   Sí, nosotros necesitamos dinero.
   3. ¿Necesitan dinero **ustedes**?

These three questions ask for the same information and have the same
meaning. Example 1 is a declarative sentence that is made interrogative by a change in intonation:

   Ustedes necesitan dinero.   ¿Ustedes necesitan dinero?

Example 2 is an interrogative sentence formed by placing the subject (**ustedes**) after the verb. Example 3 is the most common interrogative form. The subject (**ustedes**) has been placed at the end of the sentence. Notice that Spanish uses two question marks, one at the end of the sentence and an inverted one at the beginning.

Exercise

Change the following sentences to interrogatives, according to the model:

Modelo: **Elena** trabaja en Buenos Aires.
  ¿Trabaja *Elena* en Buenos Aires?
  ¿Trabaja en Buenos Aires *Elena*?

1. Juan y María necesitan dinero.
2. Ella estudia inglés.
3. Uds. hablan español.
4. Pedro necesita estudiar.
5. Tú trabajas en California.

4. NEGATIVE SENTENCES

To make a sentence negative, simply place the word **no** in front of the verb:

Ella   habla inglés.   *She speaks English.*
Ella **no** habla inglés.   *She doesn't speak English.*

Yo   trabajo en California.   *I work in California.*
Yo **no** trabajo en California. *I don't work in California.*

If the answer to a question is negative, the word **no** will appear twice: at the beginning of the sentence, as in English, and in front of the verb:

¿Necesitas dinero?   *Do you need money?*
No, (yo) **no** necesito dinero.   *No, I don't need money.*

ATENCIÓN: The subject pronoun need not appear in the answer.

Exercise

Make the following sentences negative:

1. Pedro y yo hablamos inglés.
2. Tú necesitas dinero.
3. Nosotros necesitamos trabajar.
4. María trabaja en California.
5. Ud. estudia español.

5. GENDER

In Spanish all nouns, including those denoting nonliving things, are either masculine or feminine:

masculine	*feminine*
señor	señora
teléfono	banana

Some practical rules to determine gender of Spanish nouns:

1. Most words ending in **-a** are feminine; most words ending in **-o** are masculine:

masculine	*feminine*
teléfono	silla (*chair*)
dinero	casa (*house*)
libro (*book*)	mesa (*table*)

ATENCIÓN: There are exceptions to these rules. Two important exceptions are: día (*day*), which is masculine, and mano (*hand*), which is feminine.

2. Nouns ending in **-sión, -ción, -tad,** and **-dad** are feminine:

televi**sión**	ciu**dad**
lec**ción**	liber**tad**

ATENCIÓN: Although the following words end in **-a,** they are masculine:

sistema	programa
telegrama	problema
idioma	

3. The gender of other nouns must be learned. For example: **español** (*Spanish language*) is masculine, while **calle** (*street*) is feminine.

Exercise

Tell whether the following nouns are feminine or masculine:

1. número	5. día	9. libro
2. problema	6. dinero	10. mano
3. calle	7. nacionalidad	11. ciudad
4. dirección	8. silla	12. libertad

6. CARDINAL NUMBERS (31–200)

31	treinta y uno	80	ochenta
32	treinta y dos . . .	90	noventa
40	cuarenta	100	cien
50	cincuenta	101	ciento uno . . .
60	sesenta	150	ciento cincuenta . . .
70	setenta	200	doscientos

Exercise

Read the following numbers aloud:

33	48	57	69	74	80	91	100
123	200	197	136	115	175	169	185

STUDY OF COGNATES

Remember the following rules about cognates:[1]

1. Some words are exact cognates; only the pronunciation is different:

   singular *singular*   **plural** *plural*
   mineral *mineral*   **banana** *banana*

2. Some cognates are almost the same, except for a written accent mark, a final vowel, or a single consonant:

televisión	*television*	problema	*problem*
Roberto	*Robert*	telegrama	*telegram*
programa	*program*	profesor	*professor*
sexo	*sex*		

3. Most nouns ending in **-tion** in English end in **-ción** in Spanish:

   atención *attention*

4. English nouns ending in **-ty** end in **-tad** or **-dad** in Spanish:

   libertad *liberty*
   ciudad *city*

5. There are other easily recognizable cognates for which no rule can be given:

   lección *lesson*   **sistema** *system*   **teléfono** *telephone*

---

[1] Verbs will not be treated as cognates.

NEW VOCABULARY

NOUNS

la casa	house
el dinero	money
el español	Spanish (language)
el idioma	language
el inglés	English (language)
el libro	book
la mano	hand
la mesa	table
la silla	chair

VERBS

estudiar	to study
hablar	to speak
necesitar	to need
trabajar	to work

OTHER WORDS AND EXPRESSIONS

sí	yes
en	in

mejor técnica para
un mejor servicio...

PIDA INFORMACION
EN NUESTRAS OFICINAS
COMERCIALES

COMPAÑIA TELEFONICA

Una llamada telefónica

Lesson 2

1. PLURAL FORMS

Spanish nouns are made plural by adding an -s to words ending in a vowel and an -es to words ending in a consonant. Nouns ending in -z change the z to c and add -es:

teléfono	teléfonos
mesa	mesas
profesor	profesores
lápiz (*pencil*)	lápices

ATENCIÓN: When an accent mark falls on the *last* syllable of a word, it is omitted in the plural form:

lección	lecciones

Exercise

Give the plural of the following nouns:

1. silla
2. libro
3. lápiz
4. apellido
5. universidad
6. telegrama
7. ciudad
8. lección
9. ocupación
10. señor

2. THE DEFINITE ARTICLE

Spanish has four forms equivalent to the English definite article *the:*

	Singular	Plural
Masculine	el	los
Feminine	la	las

el profesor	la profesora
los profesores	las profesoras
el mineral	la banana
los minerales	las bananas

ATENCIÓN: Try to learn the accompanying definite article when you learn each noun. This will help you to remember its gender.

Exercise

Give the definite articles for the following nouns:

1. universidades
2. lápices
3. profesor
4. doctor
5. señora
6. señores
7. día
8. televisión
9. silla
10. profesoras
11. dinero
12. profesores
13. banana
14. telegrama

3. POSITION OF ADJECTIVES

A. In Spanish descriptive adjectives (such as adjectives of color, size, etc.) generally follow the noun:

el libro **rojo**   *the red book*
la casa **grande**   *the big house*

B. Adjectives denoting nationality always follow the noun:

el profesor **norteamericano**   *the North American professor*

C. Other kinds of adjectives (possessive, demonstrative, numerals, etc.) precede the noun, as in English:

cinco lápices   *five pencils*

Exercise

Give the Spanish equivalent:

1. the red pencil
2. the big city
3. the American doctor
4. fifteen chairs
5. the big table

4. FORMS OF ADJECTIVES

Adjectives whose masculine ends in **-o** have four forms, ending in **-o, -a, -os, -as.** Most other adjectives have only two forms, a singular and a plural. Like nouns, adjectives are made plural by adding **-s, -es,** or by changing **-z** to **c** and adding **-es.**

Singular		Plural	
Masculine	*Feminine*	*Masculine*	*Feminine*
negro (*black*)	negra	negros	negras
inteligente	inteligente	inteligentes	inteligentes
feliz (*happy*)	feliz	felices	felices
verde (*green*)	verde	verdes	verdes

Adjectives of nationality ending in a consonant are made feminine by adding -a to the masculine singular form:

español   española

5. AGREEMENT OF ARTICLES, ADJECTIVES, AND NOUNS

In Spanish the article, the noun, and the adjective agree in number and gender:

la silla blanca   *the white chair*
el libro blanco   *the white book*
las sillas blancas   *the white chairs*
los libros blancos   *the white books*

Exercise

Make the adjectives agree with the nouns in the list and add the corresponding definite article:

1.	_____	mesa	negra	3.	_____	profesor	inteligente
	_____	libro	_____		_____	profesores	_____
	_____	sillas	_____		_____	profesora	_____
	_____	lápices	_____		_____	profesoras	_____
2.	_____	señor	español	4.	_____	señorita	feliz
	_____	señores	_____		_____	señor	_____
	_____	señoras	_____		_____	señoritas	_____
	_____	señora	_____		_____	señores	_____

6. PRESENT INDICATIVE OF -er AND -ir VERBS

Regular verbs ending in -er are conjugated like **comer.**
Regular verbs ending in -ir are conjugated like **vivir.**

comer *(to eat)*		vivir *(to live)*	
yo	com- **o**	yo	viv- **o**
tú	com- **es**	tú	viv- **es**
Ud.⎤		Ud.⎤	
él ⎬	com- **e**	él ⎬	viv- **e**
ella⎦		ella⎦	
nosotros	com- **emos**	nosotros	viv- **imos**
Uds.⎤		Uds.⎤	
ellos⎬	com- **en**	ellos⎬	viv- **en**
ellas⎦		ellas⎦	

Some other common verbs that follow the same patterns are: **beber** (*to drink*), **aprender** (*to learn*), **leer** (*to read*), **comprender** (*to understand*), **escribir** (*to write*), **abrir** (*to open*), **recibir** (*to receive*), and **decidir** (*to decide*).

¿Tú **bebes** café o té?	*Do you drink coffee or tea?*
Bebo café.	*I drink coffee.*
¿**Comen** Uds. temprano?	*Do you eat early?*
No, **comemos** tarde.	*No, we eat late.*
¿Dónde **vive** Ud.?	*Where do you live?*
Vivo en la calle Unión.	*I live on Union Street.*
¿**Escribe** el profesor en español?	*Does the professor write in Spanish?*
Sí, **escribe** en español.	*Yes, he writes in Spanish.*

Exercises

A. Item substitution:

    1. Yo no **como** temprano. (nosotros, el profesor, tú, Uds., ella)
    2. Ud. no **comprende** la lección. (tú y yo, ellas, yo, Ana, Uds.)
    3. Eva **escribe** en español. (yo, José y Luis, nosotros, Ud., él)
    4. Tú **decides** estudiar inglés. (nosotras, Uds., él, yo, Juan)

B. Complete the following sentences with the present indicative form of **beber, leer, comprender, comer, escribir, vivir, abrir, recibir, decidir,** and **aprender,** as needed. Use each verb only once.

    1. Yo _____ té o café.
    2. Carmen y Elena no _____ la lección.
    3. Marta y yo _____ en la calle Universidad.
    4. ¿Dónde _____ tú? ¿En el restaurante?
    5. Uds. _____ en español.
    6. Ella _____ dinero.
    7. El profesor _____ los libros.
    8. Rosa _____ aprender español.
    9. Ud. _____ el libro.
    10. Yo no _____ inglés.

7. THE PERSONAL a

In Spanish, as in English, a verb has a subject and may have one or more objects. The function of the object is to complete the idea expressed by the verb.

In English, a direct object is one that cannot be separated from the verb by a preposition: *She killed the burglar. He sees the nurse.* In the preceding sentences, *the burglar* and *the nurse* are direct objects.

In Spanish, the preposition a must be used before a direct object referring to a definite person. This preposition is called the personal **a**. The personal **a** is *not* used when the direct object is not a person.

¿A quién espera Ud.?	*Whom are you waiting for?*
Espero **a** la profesora.	*I'm waiting for the professor.*
¿Qué esperas?	*What are you waiting for?*
Espero el ómnibus.	*I'm waiting for the bus.*
¿Visitan Uds. **a** Rafael?	*Do you visit Rafael?*
No, visitamos **a** Pedro.	*No, we visit Pedro.*
¿Visitan los estudiantes el museo o el teatro?	*Are the students visiting the museum or the theatre?*
Visitan el museo.	*They are visiting the museum.*

Exercise

Give the Spanish equivalent:

1. We are waiting for the professor. (*fem.*)
2. What are the students visiting? The theatre?
3. They are waiting for the bus.
4. Who visits Mary?
5. We are waiting for Carmen and Paco.

STUDY OF COGNATES

1. The following words are the same in Spanish and English, except for a written accent mark, final vowel, or single consonant:

el restaurante	restaurant
inteligente	intelligent

2. The following words are approximate cognates:

el museo	museum
el, la estudiante	student
el teatro	theater

NEW VOCABULARY

NOUNS

el café	coffee
el lápiz	pencil
el té	tea
el ómnibus	bus

VERBS

abrir	to open
aprender	to learn
beber	to drink
comer	to eat
comprender	to understand
decidir	to decide
escribir	to write
esperar	to wait for
leer	to read
recibir	to receive
visitar	to visit
vivir	to live

ADJECTIVES

blanco(a)	white
español(a)	Spanish
feliz	happy
grande	big
negro(a)	black
rojo(a)	red
verde	green

OTHER WORDS AND EXPRESSIONS

¿dónde?	where?
o	or
¿qué?	what?
¿quién?	who?
tarde	late
temprano	early

¡FELIZ CUMPLEAÑOS!

Tu amiga,
Yolanda

Una fiesta de cumpleaños

Lesson 3

1. POSSESSION WITH **de**

Possession is expressed in Spanish by the preposition **de** + *noun*. This is equivalent to the English construction *noun + apostrophe + s:*

El libro **de Ricardo**   *Richard's book*

Study the possessive constructions in the following examples:

¿Necesita Ud. el libro **de Ricardo?**   *Do you need **Richard's book?***

No, necesito el libro **de la profesora.**   *No, I need the **professor's book.***

ATENCIÓN: The apostrophe is never used in Spanish to express possession. There is no Spanish construction similar to *Richard's book.*

2. POSSESSIVE ADJECTIVES

Forms of the Possessive Adjectives		
Singular	*Plural*	
mi	mis	*my*
tu	tus	*your (familiar)*
su	sus	*his*
		her
		its
		your
		their
nuestro(a)	nuestros(as)	*our*

A. Possessive adjectives agree in number with the nouns they modify:

¿Necesita Ud. **mi libro?**   *Do you need **my book?***
No, no necesito **su libro.**   *No, I don't need **your book.***

¿Necesita Ud. **mis libros?**   *Do you need **my books?***
No, no necesito **sus libros.**   *No, I don't need **your books.***

B. **Nuestro** is the only possessive adjective that has the feminine endings **-a, -as**. The others use the same endings for both the masculine and feminine genders:

¿Con quién habla Ud.?   *With whom are you speaking?*
Hablo con nuestras amigas.   *I am speaking with our friends.*

ATENCIÓN: These forms of the possessive adjectives precede the nouns they introduce and are never stressed.

C. Since both **su** and **sus** may have different meanings, the form **de él** (**de ella, de ellos, de ellas, de Ud., de Uds.**) may be substituted to avoid confusion:

¿Con quién hablan Uds.?	*With whom are you talking?*
Hablamos con **su** amigo.	*We are talking with **his** (or: **her, your, their**) friend.*
Hablamos con el amigo **de Ud.**	*We are talking with **your** friend.*
¿Estudia con **mi** libro?	*Are you studying with **my** book?*
No, estudio con el libro **de ella.**	*No, I'm studying with **her** book.*

Exercise

Give the following possessive adjectives in Spanish:

1. (my) _____ amigos
2. (his) _____ libro / _____ libro _____ _____.
3. (our) _____ casa /
4. (her) _____ idioma / _____ idioma _____ _____.
5. (your—Ud.) _____ dinero / _____ dinero _____ _____.
6. (my) _____ mano
7. (our) _____ mesas
8. (your—tú) _____ silla
9. (your—Uds.) _____ lápices / _____ lápices _____ _____.
10. (their—fem.) _____ lección / _____ lecciones _____ _____.

3. THE INDEFINITE ARTICLE

The indefinite article is the Spanish equivalent of *a, an,* and *some.*

	Masculine	Feminine
Singular	un	una
Plural	unos	unas

¿Escribimos con **una** pluma o con **un** lápiz?	*Do we write with a pen or a pencil?*
Escribimos con **un** lápiz.	*We write with a pencil.*
¿Qué lee Ud. ahora?	*What are you reading now?*
Leo **unas** lecciones de español.	*I am reading some Spanish lessons.*

ATENCIÓN: Spanish uses the preposition **de** + *noun* as the equivalent of the English use of two nouns, when the first one functions as an adjective:

history   *lesson* = lección **de historia**
noun as adjective   noun

Exercise

Give the Spanish equivalent:

1. a pen
2. a friend (*masc.*)
3. some days
4. some chairs
5. a problem
6. a house

4. PRESENT INDICATIVE OF ser

yo	soy	*I am*
tú	eres	*you are (familiar)*
Ud.		*you are (formal)*
él	es	*he is*
ella		*she is*
nosotros	somos	*we are*
Uds.		*you are (formal)*
ellos	son	*they are (masculine)*
ellas		*they are (feminine)*

A. **Ser** is used to indicate characteristics of things and persons:

¿**Son altos** los hijos de Juan?
Sí, ellos **son altos.**

Are Juan's sons tall?
Yes, they are tall.

¿**Es difícil** tu lección de
    español?
No, mi lección no **es difícil.**

Is your Spanish lesson
*   difficult?*
No, my lesson is not difficult.

B. **Ser** is used with the preposition **de** to indicate origin and possession:

¿**De** dónde **es** Ud.?
Yo **soy de** Buenos Aires.

Where are you from?
I am from Buenos Aires.

¿**Son** tus copias?
No, **son** las copias **de** María.

Are they your copies?
No, they are Maria's copies.

Exercise

Complete the following sentences with the present indicative of **ser:**

1. María _____ alta.
2. Nosotros _____ los hijos de la señora Carreras.
3. Yo _____ de Buenos Aires.
4. Tú no _____ feliz.
5. ¿_____ Uds. de México?
6. La lección de historia _____ difícil.
7. Ud. _____ inteligente.
8. ¿_____ las copias de Ana?

5. THE IRREGULAR VERBS **ir, dar,** AND **estar**

	ir (*to go*)	**dar** (*to give*)	**estar** (*to be*)
yo	voy	doy	estoy
tú	vas	das	estás
Ud. él ella	va	da	está
nosotros	vamos	damos	estamos
Uds. ellos ellas	van	dan	están

¿A dónde **va** Ud.?	*Where are you going?*
Voy a la biblioteca.	*I'm going to the library.*
¿**Dan** Uds. dinero?	*Do you give money?*
Sí, **damos** dinero.	*Yes, we give money.*
¿Dónde **está** Elena?	*Where is Helen?*
Ella **está** en el hotel.	*She is at the hotel.*

Exercise

Complete the following sentences with the present indicative of **ir, dar,** and **estar,** as needed:

1. Él _____ su nombre y dirección.
2. Yo _____ a la biblioteca.
3. ¿Dónde _____ mis libros?
4. Ud. _____ a Los Ángeles con los hijos de él.
5. Ellos _____ dinero.

6. Uds. _____ en México.
7. Yo no _____ mi número de teléfono.
8. Nosotras _____ a la casa de María.
9. ¿_____ Ud. en el hotel?
10. Yo _____ en el hospital.

STUDY OF COGNATES

1. Exact cognates:

   el hospital   hospital
   el hotel   hotel

2. Spanish words ending in **-ia** or **-io,** instead of English *-y:*

   la copia   copy

3. Approximate cognates:

   Brasil   Brazil
   difícil   difficult

NEW VOCABULARY

NOUNS		ADJECTIVES	
el amigo	friend	**alto(a)**	tall
la biblioteca	library		
el hijo	son	OTHER WORDS AND EXPRESSIONS	
la pluma	pen	**a**	to
		¿con quién?	with whom?
VERBS		**de**	of
dar	to give	**lección de historia**	history lesson
estar	to be		
ir	to go		
ser	to be		

El vestíbulo del hotel

Lesson 4

1. THE VERBS ser AND estar (SUMMARY OF USES)

The verbs ser and estar (both meaning *to be*) are used to indicate the following:

ser	estar
1. Possession 2. Profession 3. Nationality 4. Origin 5. Basic characteristics 6. Marital status 7. Expressions of time and dates 8. Material that things are made of	1. Current condition 2. Location

El auto **es** de Pedro, ¿no?
No, **es** de Juan.

The auto is Peter's, isn't it?
No, it's John's.

¿Cuál **es** la profesión de José?
José **es** ingeniero.

What is Joseph's profession?
Joseph is an engineer.

Elena **es** muy inteligente.
Ella **es** de Argentina,
    ¿no?
Sí, **es** argentina.

Helen is very intelligent.
She's from Argentina, isn't she?
Yes, she's an Argentinian.

¿**Es** Ud. casada?
No, **soy** soltera.

Are you married?
No, I am single.

¿Qué día **es** hoy?
Hoy **es** martes.

What day is today?
Today is Tuesday.

¿**Es** la botella de plástico?
No, **es** de vidrio.

Is the bottle made of plastic?
No, it is made of glass.

¿Cómo **está** Ud.?
Estoy bien, gracias.

How are you?
I am fine, thanks.

¿Dónde **está** su hijo?
Está en el hospital. **Está**
    enfermo.

Where is your son?
He is in the hospital. He is sick.

Exercise

Complete the following sentences using the correct form of **ser** or **estar,** as needed:

1. ¿Dónde _____ los profesores?
2. ¿De qué color _____ los autos?
3. ¿Cómo _____ Ud.? ¿Bien?
4. Mi esposo _____ ingeniero y mis hijos _____ profesores.
5. Ella _____ en Lima.
6. El libro que _____ en la mesa _____ de Pedro.
7. Ellos _____ de Venezuela.
8. Ella _____ muy inteligente. ¿Cuál _____ su profesión?
9. ¿_____ Ud. enferma?
10. Hoy _____ jueves.
11. La botella no _____ de vidrio. _____ de plástico.
12. Yo _____ viudo.

2. CONTRACTIONS

There are only two contractions in Spanish:

The preposition **de** (*of, from*) plus the article **el** are contracted to form **del:**

Leen los libros **de** + **el** professor.   Leen los libros **del** profesor.

The preposition **a** (*to, toward*) plus the article **el** are contracted to form **al.**

Esperamos **a** + **el** profesor.   Esperamos **al** profesor.

ATENCIÓN: None of the other combinations of preposition and definite article (**de la, de los, de las, a la, a los, a las**) is contracted.

¿Esperan Uds. **al** profesor de español?	*Are you waiting for the Spanish professor?*
No, esperamos **a la** profesora de inglés.	*No, we are waiting for the English professor.*
¿A quién visitan Uds. cuando van a San Diego?	*Whom do you visit when you go to San Diego?*
Visitamos **al** señor García y a **los** señores Torres.	*We visit Mr. Garcia and Mr. and Mrs. Torres.*

El dinero es **del** profesor, ¿no?	*The money is the professor's, isn't it?*
No, el dinero es **de los** estudiantes.	*No, the money is the students'.*

Exercise

Complete the sentences using one of the following: **de la, de las, del, de los, a la, a las, al, a los:**

1. Necesito los libros _____ estudiantes.
2. Hablamos _____ doctor Gómez.
3. La casa es _____ señora Pérez.
4. Esperamos _____ señor García y _____ señorita Díaz.
5. ¿Cuándo vamos _____ hospital?
6. Recibimos dinero _____ universidad.
7. ¿Visitas _____ esposas _____ doctores?
8. El presidente recibe _____ profesores.

3. THE COMPARISON OF ADJECTIVES AND ADVERBS

A. In Spanish, the comparative of most adjectives and adverbs is formed by placing **más** (*more*) or **menos** (*less*) before the adjective or the adverb and **que** after:

más		adjective		
	+	*or*	+	**que**
menos		adverb		

In this construction, **que** is the equivalent of the English *than.*

Jorge es muy alto, ¿no?	*George is very tall, isn't he?*
Sí, pero yo soy **más alta que** él.	*Yes, but I am taller than he.*
¿Quién llega **más** tarde? ¿Tú o ella?	*Who arrives later? You or she?*
Ella llega **más** tarde **que** yo.	*She arrives later than I.*

B. In an equal comparison **tan . . . como** is used:

		adjective		
tan	+	*or*	+	**como**
		adverb		

Tan . . . como is the equivalent of the English *as . . . as:*

¿Está Ud. **tan** cansada **como** ellos?   *Are you as tired as they?*

No, yo estoy menos cansada que ellos.   *No, I am less tired than they.*

C. The superlative construction is similar to the comparative. It is formed by placing the definite article before the person or thing being compared:

definite article	+	[noun]	+	**más**	+	adjective

¿Quién es **la** chica **más** bonita **de** la clase?   *Who is the prettiest girl in the class?*

Elena es **la** chica **más** bonita **de** la clase.   *Helen is the prettiest girl in the class.*

ATENCIÓN: 1. The Spanish equivalent of the English *in* after a superlative is **de.**
2. In many instances, the noun may not be expressed in a superlative.

Elena es **la más** bonita **de** la clase.   *Helen is the prettiest (one) in the class.*

Exercise

Complete the following sentences with the Spanish equivalent of the words in parentheses:

1. Rosa es _____ (prettier than) Marcia.
2. Él llega _____ (as early as) ella.
3. Mis estudiantes son _____ (less intelligent than) Uds.
4. Mi hijo es _____ (as tall as) yo.
5. Él llega _____ (later than) Uds.
6. Es _____ (the most difficult lesson in the) libro.
7. José es _____ (the least intelligent boy in) la clase.
8. Ud. está _____ (less tired than) Rafael.

4. THE IRREGULAR COMPARISON OF ADJECTIVES AND ADVERBS

The following adjectives and adverbs have irregular comparative forms in Spanish:

Irregular Comparison of Adjectives and Adverbs				
				Comparative Forms
Adjectives	**mucho**	much (many)	**más**	more, most
	poco	little (few)	**menos**	less, fewer
	bueno	good	**mejor**	better, best
	malo	bad	**peor**	worse, worst
	grande	large	**mayor**	older, oldest
	pequeño	small	**menor**	younger, youngest
Adverbs	**mucho**	much	**más**	more, most
	poco	little	**menos**	less, least
	bien	well	**mejor**	better, best
	mal	badly	**peor**	worse, worst

ATENCIÓN: When the adjectives **grande** and **pequeño** refer to size, the regular form is used: **más grande** (*bigger*) and **más pequeño** (*smaller*).

¿Quién estudia **más?** ¿Ud. o Marta?
Yo estudio **mucho,** pero Marta estudia **más.**

Who studies more? You or Martha?
I study a great deal, but Martha studies more.

¿Quién es **mayor?** ¿Ud. o Elsa?
Yo soy **mayor** que Elsa.

Who is older? You or Elsa?
I am older than Elsa.

¿Quién habla **mejor** el español, Ud. o su esposo?
Yo hablo el español **mejor** que mi esposo.

Who speaks Spanish better, you or your husband?
I speak Spanish better than my husband.

La casa de Elena es **más grande** que la casa de José, ¿no?
Sí, la casa de Elena es **más grande** que la casa de José.

Helen's house is bigger than Joseph's house, isn't it?
Yes, Helen's house is bigger than Joseph's house.

Exercise

Give the Spanish equivalent:

1. I read many books, but he reads more.
2. Cuba is bigger than Puerto Rico.
3. My son is older than your daughter.
4. My professors are better than Robert's professors.
5. He speaks English worse than I.
6. My professor is younger than you.
7. My house is smaller than Mary's house.
8. I write well, but you write better.
9. You drink little coffee, but I drink less.
10. My book is bad, but your book is very good.

5. THE IRREGULAR VERBS **tener** AND **venir**

tener (*to have*)		venir (*to come*)	
yo	tengo	yo	vengo
tú	tienes	tú	vienes
Ud.		Ud.	
él }	tiene	él }	viene
ella		ella	
nosotros	tenemos	nosotros	venimos
Uds.		Uds.	
ellos }	tienen	ellos }	vienen
ellas		ellas	

¿Con quién **viene** Ud.? ¿Con su hijo?	*With whom are you coming? With your son?*
No, **vengo** sola.	*No, I am coming alone.*
¿Cuántos estudiantes **tiene** Ud.?	*How many students do you have?*
Tengo treinta estudiantes.	*I have thirty students.*

ATENCIÓN: The personal **a** is not used with the verb **tener**.

Exercise

Complete the following sentences with the present indicative of **tener** or **venir,** as needed:

1. Yo _____ tres hijos.
2. ¿Con quién _____ Uds. a la clase?

3. ¿_____ él tarde o temprano?
4. Ellos no _____ la dirección de Pedro, pero nosotros _____ su
número de teléfono.
5. ¿Cuándo _____ ellos?
6. ¿Cuántas botellas _____ tú?
7. Yo _____ sola, pero Marisa _____ con Carlos.
8. ¿Cuántos estudiantes _____ Ud. en la clase?
9. ¿Cuál es el mejor profesor que Uds. _____?
10. Él _____ una casa muy grande.

6. CARDINAL NUMBERS (200-1000)

200	doscientos	600	seiscientos
272	doscientos setenta y dos	700	setecientos
300	trescientos	800	ochocientos
400	cuatrocientos	900	novecientos
500	quinientos	1000	mil

Exercise

Read the following numbers aloud:

896	380	519	937	222	765
451	978	643	504	715	1000

STUDY OF COGNATES

1. Exact cognates:

   el auto   auto, automobile
   el color   color

2. The following words are the same in Spanish and English, except
   for a written accent mark, a final vowel, or a single consonant:

   el plástico   plastic
   el presidente president
   la clase   class
   la profesión   profession

3. Approximate cognates:

   el ingeniero   engineer

NEW VOCABULARY

Nouns

la botella	bottle
la chica	girl
el chico	boy
el vidrio	glass

Verbs

llegar	to arrive
tener	to have
venir	to come

Adjectives

bonito(a)	pretty
bueno(a)	good

cansado(a)	tired
enfermo(a)	sick
solo(a)	alone

Other words and expressions

¿a quién?	to whom?
con	with
¿cuál?	which?, what?
¿cuándo?	when?
¿cuántos(as)?	how many?
muy	very
pero	but

Una pensión en España

Lesson

5

1. EXPRESSIONS WITH **tener**

Many useful idiomatic expressions are formed with the verb **tener:**

tener frío	to be cold
tener hambre	to be hungry
tener sed	to be thirsty
tener calor	to be hot
tener sueño	to be sleepy
tener prisa	to be in a hurry
tener miedo	to be afraid
tener razón	to be right
tener . . . años (de edad)	to be . . . years old

ATENCIÓN: The equivalent of *I am very hungry,* for example, is **Tengo mucha hambre** (literally, *I have much hunger*).

¿Tienes hambre, Carlos?	*Are you hungry, Charles?*
No, pero **tengo** mucha **sed.**	*No, but I am very thirsty.*
¿Cuántos **años tiene** su hija?	*How old is your daughter?*
Mi hija **tiene** seis **años.**	*My daughter is six years old.*
Deseo hablar con el instructor, por favor.	*I wish to speak with the instructor, please.*
Ahora no. Lo siento. Él **tiene** mucha **prisa.**	*Not now. I'm sorry. He is in a big hurry.*
Tiene razón. Es tarde.	*You're right. It's late.*

Exercises

A. Answer the following questions, first in the affirmative and then in the negative:

1. ¿Tiene Ud. hambre?
2. ¿Tienen Uds. miedo?
3. ¿Tienes sueño?
4. ¿Tiene mucha sed el profesor (la profesora)?
5. ¿Tú tienes diez años?
6. ¿Tengo razón yo?
7. ¿Tienen Uds. prisa?
8. ¿Tiene calor?
9. ¿Tienen Uds. frío?

B. Give the Spanish equivalent:

1. Charles is not hungry, but he is very thirsty.
2. Are you sleepy, Madam?

3. My daughter is not afraid.
4. You are right, Miss Vera. The instructor is in a hurry.
5. I am twenty-seven years old.
6. I am not hot. I am cold.

2. TELLING TIME

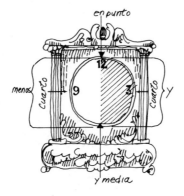

A. Remember the following points when telling time in Spanish:

1. Say the hour first, then the minutes:

Son las cuatro y diez.   *It is ten after four.*
(literally, *four and ten*)

2. The equivalent of *past* and *after* is **y**:

Son las doce **y** cinco.   *It's five after twelve.*

3. The equivalent of *to* and *till* is **menos**:

Son las ocho **menos** veinte.   *It's twenty to eight.*

4. The singular **es** is only used with **una** (*one*):

Es la una y media.   *It's one-thirty.*

5. The definite article is always used before the hour:

Son **las** nueve y cuarto.   *It's a quarter after nine.*

6. The equivalent of *at* + time is **a** + **la(s)** + time:

Mi clase es **a la una y media.**   *My class is at one-thirty.*
Su clase es **a las tres.**   *His class is at three.*

B. The difference between **de la** and **por la,** when used with time.

1. When a specific time is mentioned, **de la (mañana, tarde, noche)** should be used:

Mi clase de inglés es a las seis **de la** tarde. *My English class is at six in the evening.*

2. When a specific time is *not* mentioned, **por la (mañana, tarde, noche)** should be used:

> Nosotros trabajamos **por la** mañana. *We work in the morning.*

Exercises

A. ¿Qué hora es?

B. Give the Spanish equivalent:

1. We are coming at two-thirty in the afternoon.
2. He is going to the library in the morning.
3. They don't work in the evening.
4. It's three (o'clock) in the morning!
5. I am arriving at nine o'clock in the evening.

3. STEM-CHANGING VERBS (e > ie)

Certain verbs undergo a change in the stem in the present indicative. When the **e** is the last stem vowel and it is stressed, it changes to **ie.**

preferir (*to prefer*)	
yo pref**ie**ro	nosotros preferimos
tú pref**ie**res	
Ud. ⎤	Uds. ⎤
él ⎬ pref**ie**re	ellos ⎬ pref**ie**ren
ella ⎦	ellas ⎦

- Notice that the stem vowel is not stressed in the verb forms corresponding to **nosotros,** and therefore the **e** does not change to **ie.**
- Stem-changing verbs have regular endings like other **-ar, -er,** and **-ir** verbs.

ATENCIÓN: Some other verbs that undergo the same change are: **cerrar** (*to close*), **perder** (*to lose*), **comenzar** (*to begin*), **querer** (*to want*), **entender** (*to understand*), and **empezar** (*to start*).

¿Quieres ir al cine?	*Do you want to go to the movies?*
No, no **quiero** ir al cine. **Prefiero** ir al concierto.	*No, I don't want to go to the movies. I prefer going to the concert.*
¿A qué hora **cierran** Uds.? **Cerramos** a las nueve.	*What time do you close? We close at nine.*
¿Cuándo **comienzan** las clases? **Comienzan** en septiembre.	*When do classes start? They start in September.*
Pedro **entiende** el francés y el alemán, ¿no? **Entiende** el francés, pero no **entiende** el alemán.	*Pedro understands French and German, doesn't he? He understands French, but he doesn't understand German.*

Exercise

A. Practice the conjugations of each of the verbs used in the above example sentences.

B. Complete the following sentences with the present indicative of **preferir, cerrar, empezar, comenzar, querer, perder,** and **entender,** as needed. Use each verb once.

1. Nosotros no _____ estudiar alemán; _____ estudiar francés.
2. El concierto _____ a las ocho de la noche.
3. Yo no _____ la lección.
4. ¿Por qué _____ (tú) el libro?
5. Las clases _____ en marzo.
6. Roberto _____ su dinero en Las Vegas.

4. ir a + INFINITIVE

The construction **ir a** + *infinitive* is used to express future time. It is equivalent to the English expression *to be going to*. The formula is:

ir	+	**a**	+	infinitive	
Yo voy		a		**viajar**	**solo.**
I'm going		*to*		*travel*	*alone.*

¿Qué **vas a comprar?**	*What are you going to buy?*
Voy a comprar una camisa y una blusa.	*I'm going to buy a shirt and a blouse.*
¿Con quién **van a ir** Uds. a la reunión?	*With whom are you going (to go) to the meeting?*
Vamos a ir con la hermana de Enrique y el hermano de Juan.	*We are going (to go) with Henry's sister and John's brother.*
¿A qué hora **va a empezar** la clase?	*What time is the class going to start?*
Va a empezar a las siete.	*It's going to start at seven.*

Exercises

A. Item Substitution:

1. Tú **vas** a perder el dinero. (nosotros, mi hermana, yo, Ud., ellos)
2. El inspector **va** a hablar con ella. (yo, Uds., nosotras, tú)
3. Nosotros **vamos** a comenzar la lección. (ellas, Luis, yo, Uds.)

B. Answer the following questions, first in the affirmative, then in the negative:

1. ¿Va a cerrar Ud. el libro?
2. ¿Van a ir Uds. al cine solos?
3. ¿Vas a comprar una camisa?
4. ¿La reunión va a comenzar a las siete?
5. ¿Van a hablar en español los profesores?
6. ¿Su profesor va a dar su nombre y apellido?

5. THE USES OF hay

The form **hay** means *there is, there are.* It has no subject, and must not be confused with **es** (*it is*) and **son** (*they are*).

¿**Hay** pescado en el refrigerador?	*Is there (any) fish in the refrigerator?*
No, no **hay** pescado.	*No, there isn't (any) fish.*
¿**Hay** vuelos para Lima hoy?	*Are there flights to Lima today?*
Sí, **hay** un vuelo a las ocho de la noche.	*Yes, there is one flight at eight P.M.*

Exercise

Answer the following questions:

1. ¿Cuántos estudiantes hay en la clase?
2. ¿Hay pescado en su refrigerador?
3. Hay un vuelo para Bogotá esta noche. ¿Quiere ir?
4. Hoy es domingo. ¿Hay clase?
5. ¿Cuántos teatros hay en su ciudad?
6. ¿Hay niños en la clase?

STUDY OF COGNATES

1. Exact cognates:

el inspector	inspector
el instructor	instructor

2. Approximate cognates:

la blusa	blouse
el concierto	concert
el refrigerador	refrigerator

NEW VOCABULARY

Nouns

el alemán	German (language)
la camisa	shirt
el cine	movie (theater)
el francés	French (language)
la hermana	sister
el hermano	brother
la hija	daughter
la mañana	morning
la noche	(late) evening, night
el pescado	fish
la reunión	meeting
la tarde	afternoon
el vuelo	flight

Verbs

cerrar (e > ie)	to close
comenzar (e > ie)	to begin
comprar	to buy
desear	to wish
empezar (e > ie)	to begin
entender (e > ie)	to understand
perder (e > ie)	to lose
preferir (e > ie)	to prefer
querer (e > ie)	to want

Other words and expressions

para	to

Test Yourself: Lessons 1-5

A. Subject pronouns

Give the plural of the following:

1. yo (*masc.*)   4. ella
2. él   5. yo (*fem.*)
3. usted

B. Present indicative of **-ar** verbs

Item substitution. Make the necessary changes:

1. Yo hablo español.
2. Nosotros _____.
3. _____ inglés.
4. Tú _____.
5. _____ trabajas en Lima.
6. Ellos _____.
7. Ud. _____.
8. _____ estudia _____.
9. Yo _____.
10. _____ necesito dinero.
11. Él _____.
12. Nosotros _____.

C. Interrogative sentences / Negative sentences

Make the following sentences interrogative, then negative:

1. Elena trabaja en Buenos Aires.
2. Uds. hablan inglés.
3. Tú necesitas dinero.
4. Juan y María estudian español.
5. Usted trabaja en Los Ángeles.

D. Gender

Divide the following words into two columns: masculine and feminine:

programa, telegrama, televisión, señor, teléfono, señora, banana, libro, día, mano, silla, casa, sistema, mesa, dinero, problema, idioma, libertad, lección, ciudad, calle, número, nacionalidad, tema.

E. Cardinal numbers (0-200)

Give the answers to the following problems: (+: más; −: menos)

1. cuarenta + veinte y seis =
2. treinta − diez y siete =
3. doscientos − ciento nueve =
4. ochenta − siete =
5. catorce + cinco =
6. cincuenta + cien =

LESSON 2

A. Plural forms / Agreement of adjectives and nouns / Definite articles

Make the following plural:

1. la casa verde   4. la silla grande
2. el lápiz negro   5. el libro blanco
3. el profesor inteligente   6. la señorita feliz

B. Present indicative of -er and -ir verbs

Give the Spanish equivalent:

1. Where do you live, Mrs. Vera?
2. They drink coffee. I drink tea.
3. We read the lessons.
4. He decides to study English.
5. Do you (tú) understand?
6. You (Uds.) eat early.
7. She writes in Spanish.
8. We open the books.
9. I'm learning Spanish.
10. They don't receive the money.

C. The personal a

Read the following sentences. Use the personal a when needed:

1. ¿Esperan Uds. _____ el ómnibus?
2. Nosotros no visitamos _____ la señora Pérez.
3. Ellos visitan _____ los museos.
4. Rosa espera _____ Carlos.
5. Los estudiantes visitan _____ los profesores.

LESSON 3

A. Possession with **de**

Arrange the following in complete sentences, according to the model:

Modelo: Yo / necesitar / señorita Peña / libro
Yo necesito el libro de la señorita Peña.

1. Nosotros / recibir / Carlos / dinero
2. Ella / leer / la profesora / lección
3. Los / estudiantes / visitar / Enrique / esposa
4. ¿Tú / esperar / Teresa / profesora?
5. Ud. / no necesitar / María / silla

B. Possessive adjectives

Use the possessive adjective that corresponds to each subject. Follow the model:

Modelo: **Yo** necesito _____ libro.
Yo necesito mi libro.
1. **Tú** necesitas _____ mesa.
2. **Ella** necesita _____ lápices. (Los lápices _____ _____)
3. **Nosotros** necesitamos _____ dinero.
4. **Ud.** necesita _____ pluma. (La pluma _____ _____)
5. **Yo** necesito _____ sillas.
6. **Tú** necesitas a _____ amigos.
7. **Nosotros** necesitamos _____ casas.
8. **Él** necesita _____ teléfono. (El teléfono _____ _____)

C. The indefinite article

Give the indefinite article for each of the following nouns:

1. sistema   5. calle   8. telegrama
2. mano   6. lápices   9. día
3. señoritas   7. lecciones   10. ciudad
4. señor

D. Present indicative of **ser**

Answer the following questions in the affirmative:

1. ¿Es Ud. alto(a)?   4. ¿Soy yo el (la) profesor(a)?
2. ¿Eres de California?   5. ¿Es difícil tu lección de español?
3. ¿Son Uds. felices?   6. ¿Son ellos de México?

E. The irregular verbs **ir, dar,** and **estar**

Item substitution. Change the verbs according to each new subject.
Make all other necessary changes.

1. Yo **doy mi** número de teléfono. (ellos, nosotros, tú, Uds., ella)
2. Ud. **está** en **su** casa. (yo, ellos, nosotros, ella, tú, Uds.)
3. Ella **va** a **sus** clases. (nosotros, Ud., tú, yo, ellos)

LESSON 4

A. The verbs **ser** and **estar**

Write sentences using the following pairs of items and **ser** or **estar,**
as needed. Follow the model:

Modelo: Mi esposo / profesor
   Mi esposo es profesor.

1. La botella / plástico
2. La señorita López / enferma
3. Las casas / de Jorge
4. Los estudiantes / mexicanos
5. El profesor / en el hospital
6. Yo / de Arizona
7. Nosotros / bien
8. María / alta
9. Gustavo y yo / casados
10. Mañana / sábado
11. Yo / en la calle Universidad
12. El hijo de la señora Nieto / ingeniero

B. Contractions

Give the Spanish equivalent:

1. We are waiting for Mr. Peña.
2. She is visiting Mr. Linares and Mrs. Viera.
3. The money is Mr. Diaz's.
4. He goes to the hospital.
5. We need Dr. Mena's phone number.

C. The comparative of adjectives and adverbs

Answer the following questions in the negative:

1. ¿Es Ud. tan alto(a) como el profesor (la profesora)?
2. ¿Llega el profesor más tarde que los estudiantes?
3. ¿Es Ud. el (la) estudiante menos inteligente de la clase?

4. ¿Es Ud. la persona más feliz de la clase?
5. ¿Es Ud. el (la) peor estudiante?
6. ¿Son Uds. mayores que sus amigos?
7. ¿Soy yo el (la) mejor de la clase?
8. ¿La casa de su amigo es más grande que su casa?

D. The irregular verbs **tener** and **venir**

Item substitution. Change the verb according to each new subject. Make all other necessary changes.

1. **Yo** vengo con **mi** hijo. (nosotros, tú, ellos, Ud., Uds., él)
2. **Nosotros** tenemos **nuestros** libros. (yo, ella, tú, Uds., Ud.)

E. Cardinal numbers (200-1000)

Give the answers to the following problems:

1. setecientos − doscientos =
2. cien + novecientos =
3. trescientos + doscientos cincuenta =
4. mil − ochocientos =
5. cuatrocientos + quinientos =
6. seiscientos − ciento cincuenta =

LESSON 5

A. Expressions with **tener**

Tell what is happening in each of the pictures. Follow the model:

Modelo:

Ella . . . .
Ella tiene hambre.

1. Carlos . . . .

2. Él . . . .

3. Yo . . . .

4. Ellas . . . .

5. ¿Ud. . . .?

6. Tú . . . .

7. Nélida . . . .

B. Telling time

Answer the following questions:

1. ¿A qué hora es su clase de español?
2. ¿A qué hora comen Uds.?
3. ¿A qué hora va Ud. a la universidad?
4. ¿Estudia Ud. por la mañana, por la tarde o por la noche?
5. ¿A qué hora llega el profesor a clase?

C. Stem-changing verbs (**e > ie**)

Answer the following questions:

1. ¿Prefieren Uds. estudiar francés o alemán?
2. ¿Quieres ir al cine hoy?
3. ¿A qué hora empieza la clase de español?
4. ¿Entienden Uds. las lecciones?
5. ¿Pierden Uds. mucho dinero en Las Vegas?
6. ¿A qué hora cierran la biblioteca?
7. ¿A qué hora comienza su programa de televisión favorito?

D. **Ir a** plus infinitive

Complete the following sentences using **ir a** plus the infinitive of the verb given in parentheses. Follow the model:

Modelo: Yo _____ por la tarde. (*study*)
   Yo voy a estudiar por la tarde.

1. Nosotros _____ pescado hoy. (*eat*)
2. Él _____ una camisa. (*buy*)
3. ¿A qué hora _____ la reunión? (*start*)
4. Tú no _____ a tu hermano. (*visit*)
5. Mi hija _____ en el vuelo de las ocho de la noche. (*arrive*)
6. Yo _____ sola. (*come*)
7. Nosotros _____ mucho dinero. (*need*)
8. ¿_____ Uds. a casa de Roberto? (*go*)

E. The uses of **hay**

Give the Spanish equivalent:

1. How many students are there?
2. There is not (any) money.
3. There are two flights to Lima.
4. There is a meeting today.
5. How many chairs are there?

Los vuelos internacionales

Lesson 6

1. SOME USES OF THE DEFINITE ARTICLE

A. The definite article is used in Spanish with expressions of time, the seasons, and the days of the week:

¿Cuándo es su clase de español?	*When is your Spanish class?*
Tengo clase de español **los**[1] lunes, miércoles y viernes.	*I have Spanish class on Mondays, Wednesdays, and Fridays.*

ATENCIÓN: It is omitted with the seasons and days of the week when used after the verb **ser:**

¿Es primavera ahora en Chile?	*Is it spring in Chile now?*
Sí, es primavera.	*Yes, it is spring.*
¿Qué día de la semana es hoy?	*What day of the week is today?*
Hoy es domingo.	*Today is Sunday.*

B. The definite article is included with nouns used in a general sense:

¿Qué quieren **las** mujeres y **los** hombres de hoy?	*What do today's women and men want?*
Quieren igualdad.	*They want equality.*

C. The definite article is used with abstract nouns:

¿Es importante **la** libertad?	*Is freedom important?*
Sí, **la** libertad es importante.	*Yes, freedom is important.*

D. The definite article is used before **próximo** (*next*) and **pasado** (*last*) with expressions of time:

¿Cuándo comienzan las clases?	*When do classes begin?*
Comienzan **la** semana **próxima.**	*They begin next week.*

Exercise

Complete the following sentences with the appropriate definite article, if one is needed:

1. Hoy es _____ jueves.
2. Vamos al hospital _____ domingos.
3. Prefiero _____ verano a _____ primavera.
4. Tengo clase de español _____ miércoles.
5. ¿Qué _____ fecha es hoy?

[1] Notice that the definite article is used here as the equivalent of *on*.

6. _____ libertad es importante.
7. Empiezo mis clases _____ próximo lunes.
8. Ahora es _____ invierno en Canadá.
9. _____ hombres y _____ mujeres quieren _____ igualdad.
10. La reunión es _____ semana próxima.

2. STEM-CHANGING VERBS (o > ue)

A. As you learned in Lesson 5, certain verbs undergo a change in the stem in the present indicative. When **o** is the last vowel of the stem and it is stressed, it changes to **ue**.

volver (*to come back*)	
vuelvo	volvemos
vuelves	
vuelve	**vuel**ven

- Notice that the stem vowel is not stressed in the verb form corresponding to **nosotros,** and therefore the **o** does not change to **ue**.

¿Cuándo **vuelven** Uds.?   *When are you coming back?*
Volvemos a las siete.   *We are coming back at seven.*

- Some other common verbs that follow the same change in the stem are: the **-ar** verbs **recordar** (*to remember*) and **volar** (*to fly*), the **-er** verb **poder** (*to be able*), and the **-ir** verb **dormir** (*to sleep*).

¿**Puede** Ud. trabajar   *Are you able to work*
  mañana?   *tomorrow?*
Sí. ¡Ah! No, porque ahora   *Yes. Oh! No, because now I*
  recuerdo que voy a   *remember that I'm going to*
  estudiar.   *study.*

¿Cuándo **vuela** Ud.?   *When are you flying?*
Vuelo la próxima semana.   *I'm flying next week.*

¿Cuándo **pueden** Uds. ir al   *When can you go to the*
  hospital?   *hospital?*
Podemos ir mañana.   *We can go tomorrow.*

¿Cuántas horas **duerme**   *How many hours does he*
  él?   *sleep?*
Él **duerme** diez horas.   *He sleeps ten hours.*

Exercise

Complete the following sentences with the correct form of the verb given in parentheses:

1. ¿Cuándo _____ (volver) Ud. de México?
2. Yo nunca _____ (recordar) su número de teléfono.
3. Nosotras _____ (volar) la semana que viene.
4. Ellos no _____ (poder) ir con sus hijos ahora.
5. Tú no _____ (volver) en el verano porque no _____ (poder).
6. Uds. _____ (volar) en mayo.
7. Yo _____ (poder) venir mañana.
8. ¿_____ (recordar) Ud. a la hija de Juan?
9. Nosotros _____ (dormir) mucho pero él _____ (dormir) más.
10. Nosotras no _____ (poder) estudiar hoy.

3. AFFIRMATIVE AND NEGATIVE EXPRESSIONS

A. Study the expressions in the following table:

Affirmative		Negative	
algo	something	**nada**	nothing
alguien	someone, anyone	**nadie**	nobody, no one
alguno(a) **algún** **algunos(as)**	any, some	**ninguno(a)** **ningún**	none, not any
siempre	always	**nunca** **jamás**	never
también	also, too	**tampoco**	neither
o . . . o	either . . . or	**ni . . . ni**	neither . . . nor

¿Hay **algo** en la mesa? No. No hay **nada.**	*Is there anything on the table? No. There is nothing.*
¿Hay **alguien** con el director? No, no hay **nadie.**	*Is there anyone with the director? No, there is nobody.*
¿Van Uds. **siempre** a Los Ángeles? No, no vamos **nunca.**	*Do you always go to Los Angeles? No, we never go.*
¿Quieren venir Uds. **también?** No, Juan no quiere ir **ni** yo tampoco.	*Do you want to come too? No, John doesn't want to go and neither do I.*
¿Qué quiere Ud.? ¿El piano **o** la radio?	*What do you want? The piano or the radio?*

No quiero **ni** el piano **ni** la radio.

I want neither the piano nor the radio.

- **Alguno** and **ninguno** drop the **-o** before a masculine singular noun; but **alguna** and **ninguna** keep the final **-a**.

¿Hay **algún** libro o **alguna** pluma en la mesa?

Is there any book or pen on the table?

No, no hay **ningún** libro ni **ninguna** pluma.

No, there isn't any book or pen.

- **Alguno(a)** may be used in the plural form, but **ninguno(a)** is used in the singular form.

¿Desea comprar **algunos** regalos?

Do you want to buy any presents?

No, no deseo comprar **ningún** regalo.

No, I don't want to buy any presents.

B. Spanish frequently uses a double negative. In this construction, the adverb **no** is placed before the verb. The second negative word either follows the verb or appears at the end of the sentence. However, if the negative word precedes the verb, **no** is never used:

¿Habla Ud. español **siempre?**
No, yo **no** hablo español **nunca.** ⎫
Yo **nunca** hablo español. ⎭

Do you always speak Spanish?

No, I never speak Spanish.

¿Compra Ud. **algo** aquí?
No, **no** compro **nada nunca.** ⎫
Nunca compro **nada.** ⎭

Do you buy anything here?

No, I never buy anything.

Exercise

Answer the following questions in the negative:

1. ¿Necesita Ud. algo?
2. ¿Hay alguien aquí?
3. ¿Estudia Ud. siempre por la noche?
4. ¿Quieres un piano o una radio?
5. ¿Va a traer Ud. algunos regalos?
6. Juan no va a la reunión. ¿Vas tú?

4. ORDINAL NUMBERS AND THEIR USES

primero(a)	*first*	sexto(a)	*sixth*
segundo(a)	*second*	séptimo(a)	*seventh*
tercero(a)	*third*	octavo(a)	*eighth*
cuarto(a)	*fourth*	noveno(a)	*ninth*
quinto(a)	*fifth*	décimo(a)	*tenth*

- The ordinal numbers **primero** and **tercero** drop the final -o before masculine singular nouns:

¿Qué día llegan Uds.?	*What day are you arriving?*
Llegamos el **primer** día del mes.	*We are arriving the first day of the month.*

- Ordinal numbers agree in gender and number with the nouns they modify:

¿Qué oficina prefiere?	*Which office do you prefer?*
Prefiero **la** quinta.	*I prefer the fifth (one).*

- Ordinal numbers are seldom used after *the tenth:*

¿En qué piso viven Uds.?	*On which floor do you live?*
Vivimos en el piso **doce.**	*We live on the twelfth floor.*

- Spanish uses cardinal numbers for dates except for *the first:*

¿Qué día es hoy?	*What day is it today?*
Hoy es el **treinta** de abril. Mañana es el **primero** de mayo.	*Today is April 30th. Tomorrow is the first day of May.*

Exercise

Complete the following sentences with the correct ordinal number:

1. Él es el _____ (*first*) estudiante.
2. Yo vivo en el _____ (*fifth*) piso.
3. Ella prefiere la _____ (*second*) mesa.
4. La oficina de mi esposo está en el _____ (*third*) piso.
5. Llegamos el _____ (*first*) de mayo.
6. Vuelven en los _____ (*first*) días del mes.
7. Yo quiero la _____ (*fourth*), la _____ (*sixth*), y la _____ (*seventh*) sillas.
8. No tenemos clases ni la _____ (*ninth*) ni la _____ (*tenth*) semana.

5. USES OF **tener que** AND **hay que**

A. The Spanish equivalent of *to have to* is **tener que:**

¿Qué **tiene que** hacer hoy?	*What do you have to do today?*
Tengo que trabajar.	*I have to work.*

B. The Spanish equivalent of *one must* is **hay que:**

¿Qué **hay que** hacer para tener éxito?	*What must one do to succeed?*
Hay que trabajar.	*One must work.*

Exercise

Complete the following sentences with **hay que** or the correct forms of **tener que,** as needed:

1. Para tener éxito, _____ trabajar.
2. Yo _____ estudiar mucho.
3. Nosotros _____ trabajar mañana.
4. _____ llegar temprano.
5. Ud. _____ volver a las diez de la noche.
6. _____ comenzar más tarde.

STUDY OF COGNATES

1. Exact cognates:

   el director   director
   el piano   piano
   la radio   radio

2. The following words are the same in Spanish and in English, except for a written accent mark or a final vowel:

   Canadá   Canada
   importante   important

3. Approximate cognates:

   la igualdad equality   **la oficina** office

NEW VOCABULARY

NOUNS

el hombre	man
el mes	month
la mujer	woman
el piso	floor (story)
el regalo	present, gift
la semana	week

VERBS

dormir (o > ue)	to sleep
poder (o > ue)	to be able
recordar (o > ue)	to remember
volar (o > ue)	to fly
volver (o > ue)	to come back, return

ADJECTIVES

pasado(a)	last
próximo(a)	next

OTHER WORDS AND EXPRESSIONS

ahora	now
aquí	here
mañana	tomorrow
porque	because
tener éxito	to succeed

Los pasajeros suben al avión

Lesson 7

1. STEM-CHANGING VERBS (e > i)

A. Certain **-ir** verbs undergo a special change in the stem. When **e** is the last stem vowel and it is stressed, the **e** changes to **i** in the present indicative.

servir *(to serve)*	**pedir** {to ask for, to request, to order	**seguir** {to follow, to continue
sirvo servimos	pido pedimos	sigo seguimos
sirves	pides	sigues
sirve sirven	pide piden	sigue siguen

- Notice that the stem vowel is not stressed in the verb form corresponding to **nosotros**. Therefore, the **e** does not change to **i**.

- Verbs like **seguir** drop the **u** before an **a** or an **o: yo sigo.** For example, **conseguir** *(to obtain)*: **yo consigo; perseguir** *(to pursue, to persecute)*: **yo persigo.**

- The verb **decir** *(to say, to tell)* undergoes the same change, but in addition it is irregular in the first person singular: **yo digo.**

¿Qué **sirven** en la cafetería de la universidad?	*What do they serve in the college cafeteria?*
Sirven sopa, ensalada, carne y postre.	*They serve soup, salad, meat, and dessert.*
¿Qué **pide** Enrique?	*What is Henry ordering?*
Pide un refresco.	*He's ordering a soda.*
¿A quién **siguen** ustedes?	*Whom are you following?*
Seguimos a nuestra maestra.	*We are following our teacher.*
¿**Dice** Ud. la verdad siempre?	*Do you always tell the truth?*
Sí, yo siempre **digo** la verdad.	*Yes, I always tell the truth.*

Exercise

Complete the following sentences with the correct form of the verb given in parentheses:

1. Yo _____ (conseguir) el dinero.
2. Ud. _____ (servir) sopa y ensalada.
3. Ella _____ (pedir) un refresco.
4. Nosotros _____ (seguir) al maestro.
5. Uds. _____ (decir) la verdad.
6. Ud. _____ (perseguir) a los estudiantes.

7. Yo _____ (decir) la verdad siempre.
8. Uds. siempre _____ (pedir) postre.
9. Ellos no _____ (servir) carne en la cafetería.
10. ¿_____ (seguir) Ud. en la clase?

2. MORE ABOUT IRREGULAR VERBS

Some common verbs are irregular only in the first person singular of the present indicative. The other persons are regular:

salir (to go out):	yo **salgo**	traducir (to	
hacer (to do, to		translate):	yo **traduzco**
make):	yo **hago**	conocer (to	
poner (to put,		know, to be	
to place):	yo **pongo**	acquainted	
caer (to fall):	yo **caigo**	with):	yo **conozco**
traer (to bring):	yo **traigo**	caber (to fit):	yo **quepo**
conducir (to		ver (to see):	yo **veo**
conduct, to		saber (to know	
drive):	yo **conduzco**	how, to know	
		a fact):	yo **sé**

¿**Sale** Ud. a menudo?	*Do you go out often?*
Sí, yo **salgo** a menudo.	*Yes, I go out often.*
¿Dónde **pone** Ud. la información?	*Where do you put the information?*
Yo **pongo** la información en el fichero.	*I put the information in the file.*
¿**Sabe** Ud. conducir?	*Do you know how to drive?*
Sí, yo **sé** conducir. **Conduzco** muy bien.	*Yes, I know how to drive. I drive very well.*
¿**Conoce** Ud. a mi hermano?	*Do you know my brother?*
Sí, yo **conozco** a su hermano.	*Yes, I know your brother.*

Exercise

Answer the following questions, first in the affirmative, then in the negative:

1. ¿Sabe Ud. español?
2. ¿Hace Ud. algo los domingos?
3. ¿Conduce Ud. bien?
4. ¿Pone Ud. la información en el fichero?
5. ¿Sale Ud. a menudo?
6. ¿Cabe Ud. en el coche?

7. ¿Conoce Ud. la ciudad de Nueva York?
8. ¿Traduce Ud. del español al inglés?
9. ¿Trae Ud. sus libros a clase?
10. ¿Ve Ud. a sus amigos los sábados?

3. THE IMPERSONAL se

A. Spanish uses the reflexive object se before the third person of the verb (either singular or plural, depending on the subject) as the equivalent of the passive voice in English:

The library is opened at eight.
La biblioteca **se abre** a las ocho.

The offices are closed at five.
Las oficinas **se cierran** a las cinco.

Notice the use of se in the following impersonal constructions, announcements, and general directions:

¿A qué hora **se abre** la biblioteca?	*What time does the library open?*
Se abre a las ocho.	*It opens at eight.*
¿A qué hora **se cierran** las oficinas?	*What time do the offices close?*
Las oficinas **se cierran** a las cinco de la tarde.	*The offices close at 5 P.M.*
¿Aquí **se habla** inglés?	*Is English spoken here?*
No, **se habla** sólo español.	*No, only Spanish is spoken (here).*

B. Se is also used as the equivalent of **one, they,** or **people,** when the subject of the verb is not definite:

No se puede hacer eso.	*One can't do that.*
¿Cómo **se dice** *always* en español?	*How does one say "always" in Spanish?*
Se dice «siempre».	*One says siempre.*

Exercise

Answer the following questions:

1. ¿A qué hora se abre la biblioteca?
2. ¿Se habla inglés en los Estados Unidos?
3. ¿Cómo se dice *address* en español?
4. ¿A qué hora se cierran los restaurantes en esta ciudad?

5. ¿Se abren las oficinas de la universidad los domingos?
6. ¿A qué hora se cierra el museo?
7. ¿Se habla español o inglés en Chile?
8. ¿Cómo se escribe su apellido?

4. DIRECT OBJECT PRONOUNS

The forms of the direct object pronouns are as follows:

Subject	Direct Object	
yo	**me** (me)	Ella **me** visita.
tú	**te** (you, *familiar*)	Yo **te** sigo.
Ud.	{**lo** (you, *masc., formal*)	Yo **lo** conozco. (a Ud.)
	{**la** (you, *fem., formal*)	Yo **la** conozco. (a Ud.)
él	**lo** (him, it)	Él **lo** ve.
ella	**la** (her, it)	Él **la** ve.
nosotros} nosotras}	**nos** (us, *masc. and fem.*)	Tú **nos** comprendes.
Uds.	{ **los** (you, *masc., pl., formal*)	Nosotros **los** visitamos. (a Uds.)
	{ **las** (you, *fem., pl., formal*)	Nosotros **las** visitamos. (a Uds.)
ellos	**los**	Él **los** ve.
ellas	**las**	Él **las** ve.

A. The direct object pronoun is placed *before* a conjugated verb:

Yo conozco al <u>señor Lima</u>.
Yo   **lo**   conozco.

Ella escribe <u>la carta</u>.
Ella   **la**   escribe.

Nosotros vemos a <u>nuestros amigos</u>.
Nosotros   **los**   vemos.

B. In a negative sentence the **no** must precede the object pronoun:

Yo traduzco las lecciones.
Yo   **las**   traduzco.
Yo   **no**   **las**   traduzco.

C. Whenever two verbs are used in the same clause, the pronoun is either added to the infinitive or placed before the conjugated verb:

Te quiero ver. ⎱
OR: Quiero ver**te**. ⎰ *I want to see you.*

¿**Me** ves ahora?	*Do you see me now?*
Sí, ahora **te** veo.	*Yes, now I see you.*
¿Conduce Ud. el coche?	*Do you drive the car?*
Sí, yo **lo** conduzco.	*Yes, I drive it.*
¿Pone Ud. la información en la mesa?	*Do you put the information on the table?*
Sí, yo **la** pongo en la mesa.	*Yes, I put it on the table.*
¿Pides las cartas?	*Are you asking for the letters?*
Sí, **las** pido.	*Yes, I am asking for them.*

Exercises

A. Replace the object in italics with the appropriate pronoun. Follow the model:

Modelo: Sirvo *el café*.
  Lo sirvo.

1. Pedimos *los refrescos*.
2. Digo *la verdad*.
3. Ud. sirve *los postres*.
4. Él ve a *Juan*.
5. Yo conozco a *Pedro y a Enrique*.
6. Ana conduce *el coche*.
7. Ud. da *la información*.
8. Ellos ven a *Ana y a Pilar*.
9. Ud. pide *las mesas*.
10. Ellos dicen *la verdad*.

B. Answer the questions, following the model:

Modelo: ¿Quieres escribir las cartas?
  No, no quiero escribirlas.
  OR: **No, no las quiero escribir.**

1. ¿Vas a ver a tus amigos?
2. ¿Quieren Uds. poner la información en el fichero?
3. ¿Va a traer Marta las mesas y las sillas?
4. ¿Quiere Ud. conocer al señor Aranda?
5. ¿Va Ud. a traducir la lección al inglés?
6. ¿Quieren Uds. conducir el coche?

7. ¿Vas a traerme a la universidad?
8. ¿Voy a llevarte al cine?

C. Give the Spanish equivalent:

1. Do you know him?
2. Does he want to see her? (*both ways*)
3. The books? I am going to bring them. (*both ways*)
4. She doesn't know us.
5. Now I see you, my son.
6. You don't know me, Mr. Lima.

5. saber VS. conocer

Spanish has two verbs that mean *to know:* **saber** and **conocer.**

A. **Saber** means to know something by heart, to know how to do something, or to know a fact:

¿**Sabe** Ud. ya la lección de hoy?	*Do you already know today's lesson?*
Sí, ya la **sé.**	*Yes, I already know it.*
¿**Saben** ellos nadar?	*Do they know how to swim?*
Sí, ellos **saben** nadar.	*Yes, they know how to swim.*
¿**Sabes** que el embajador llega hoy?	*Do you know that the ambassador arrives today?*
Sí, ya lo **sé.**	*Yes, I (already) know (it).*

B. **Conocer** means to be familiar or acquainted with a person, a thing, or a place:

¿**Conoce** a la hija del vecino?	*Do you know the neighbor's daughter?*
Sí, la **conozco.**	*Yes, I know her.*
¿**Conocen** Uds. las novelas de Cervantes?	*Do you know Cervantes' novels?*
Sí, las **conocemos.**	*Yes, we know them.*
¿**Conocen** ellos Puerto Rico?	*Do they know Puerto Rico?*
No, ellos no lo **conocen.**	*No, they don't know it.*

Exercise

Complete the following sentences with the present indicative of **saber** and **conocer,** as needed:

1. Ellos _____ California.
2. Ud. no _____ a mi vecino.
3. ¿Tú _____ la lección de hoy?
4. Él ya _____ al embajador.
5. Yo no _____ nadar.
6. Uds. _____ las novelas de Cervantes.
7. ¿_____ Uds. qué día es hoy?
8. Yo no _____ la ciudad de Madrid.
9. Nosotras _____ inglés y español.
10. Ellas _____ a la esposa del profesor.

6. FORMATION OF ADVERBS

A. Most Spanish adverbs are formed by adding **-mente** (the equivalent of English *-ly*) to the adjective:

especial   *special*   especial**mente**   *specially, especially*
reciente   *recent*   reciente**mente**   *recently*

B. If the adjective ends in **-o,** change the ending to **-a** before adding **-mente:**

lento   *slow*   lent**amente**   *slowly*
rápido   *rapid*   rápid**amente** *rapidly*

C. If two or more adverbs are used together, only the last one ends in *-mente:*

lenta y cuidadosa**mente**   *slowly and carefully*

D. If the adjective has a written accent mark, the adverb retains it:

fácil   fácil**mente**

Study the use of the adverbs in the following sentence:

Traigo estos libros   *I'm bringing these books*
   especialmente para Ud.   *especially for you.*
Un millón de gracias.   *Thanks a million.*

El niño escribe la carta **lenta** y   *The child writes the letter*
   cuidadosamente.   *slowly and carefully.*
¡Pero la escribe muy bien!   *But he writes it very well!*

Exercise

Give the Spanish equivalent:

1. She reads slowly.
2. I need to do it carefully.
3. The chair is especially for you, sir.
4. She is going to do it rapidly but carefully.
5. Recently?
6. The lesson? We can translate it easily.

STUDY OF COGNATES

1. The following words are the same in Spanish and English, except for a written accent mark or a final vowel:

la cafetería	cafeteria
la novela	novel

2. Spanish words ending in -ción, instead of -tion in English:

la información	information

3. Approximate cognates:

especial	special
reciente	recent

NEW VOCABULARY

Nouns		Verbs	
la carne	meat	conseguir (e > i)	to obtain
la carta	letter	nadar	to swim
el coche	car	pedir (e > i)	to request,
el embajador	ambassador		to ask for,
la ensalada	salad		to order
el fichero (archivo)	file	perseguir (e > i)	to pursue, to persecute
la maestra ⎫ el maestro ⎭	teacher (elementary school)	seguir (e > i)	to follow, to continue
el postre	dessert	servir (e > i)	to serve
el refresco	soda, beverage	**Adjectives**	
la sopa	soup	cuidadoso(a)	careful
el vecino	neighbor	fácil	easy
la verdad	truth	lento(a)	slow
		rápido(a)	fast

OTHER WORDS AND EXPRESSIONS

a menudo	often
siempre	always
un millón de gracias	thanks a million
ya	already

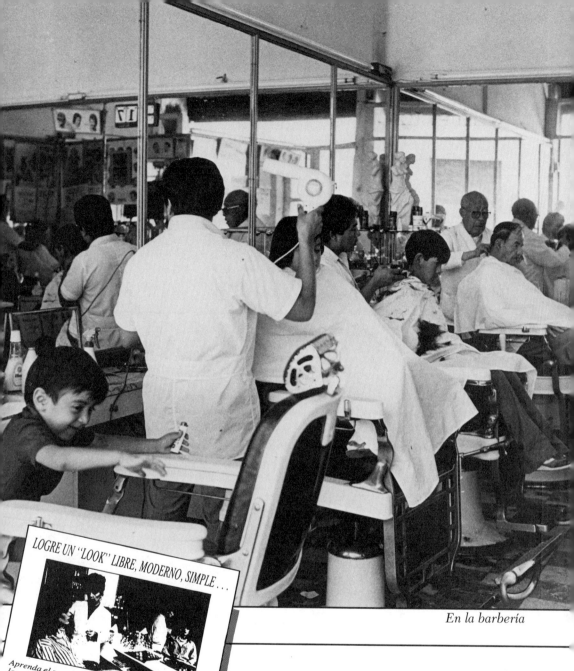

En la barbería

Lesson 8

1. DEMONSTRATIVE ADJECTIVES

Demonstrative adjectives point out persons or things. They agree in gender and number with the nouns they modify or point out.

The forms of the demonstrative adjectives are as follows:

	Masculine		Feminine	
	Singular	Plural	Singular	Plural
this, these	este	estos	esta	estas
that, those	ese	esos	esa	esas
that, those (at a distance)	aquel	aquellos	aquella	aquellas

¿Para quién son **estas** revistas?
Estas revistas son para Marta y **esos** cuadernos son para Jorge.

Who are these magazines for?
These magazines are for Martha, and those notebooks are for George.

¿Podemos comer hoy en **este** restaurante?
No, vamos a comer en **aquella** cafetería que está allá.

Can we eat in this restaurant today?
No, we are going to eat in that cafeteria (which is) over there.

Exercise

Change the demonstrative adjectives according to the new nouns:

1. Este cuaderno, _____ casa, _____ revistas, _____ programas.
2. Esas ciudades, _____ biblioteca, _____ lápices, _____ idioma.
3. Aquella cafetería, _____ sillas, _____ museo, _____ números.

2. DEMONSTRATIVE PRONOUNS

The demonstrative pronouns are the same as the demonstrative adjectives, except that the pronouns take a written accent.

The forms of the demonstrative pronouns are as follows:

	Masculine		Feminine		Neuter
	Singular	Plural	Singular	Plural	
this (one), these	éste	éstos	ésta	éstas	esto
that (one), those	ése	ésos	ésa	ésas	eso
that (one), those (at a distance)	aquél	aquéllos	aquélla	aquéllas	aquello

● Each demonstrative pronoun has a neuter form. The neuter pronoun has no accent, because there are no corresponding demonstrative adjectives.

¿Qué corbata quiere Ud.?
  ¿**Ésta** o **aquélla?**
Quiero **aquélla.**

Which tie do you want? This one or that one over there?
I want that one over there.

¿Necesitan Uds. estos periódicos o **ésos?**
No, necesitamos **aquél** que está en la mesa.

Do you need these newspapers or those ones?
No, we need that one (which is) on the table.

¿Qué crees de **esto?**
Creo que **esto** es un problema para el presidente.

What do you think about this?
I think this is a problem for the president.

Exercise

Complete the following sentences with the Spanish equivalent of the pronouns in parentheses:

1. Quiero este libro y _____ (that one).
2. Necesitamos esa pluma y _____ (that one over there).
3. Compramos esos lápices y _____ (these ones).
4. Recibimos este periódico y _____ (those ones).
5. ¿Estudia Ud. esta lección o _____ (that one)?
6. ¿Comienza Ud. con este programa o con _____ (that one over there)?
7. ¿Prefieren ellos estas mesas o _____ (those ones over there)?
8. ¿Va Ud. a leer este libro o _____ (those ones)?
9. Deseo aquellas botellas y _____ (these ones).
10. ¿Van Uds. a comprar esa corbata o _____ (this one)?

3. PRESENT PROGRESSIVE

A. The present progressive describes an action that is in progress at the moment we are talking. It is formed with the present of **estar** and the gerund (equivalent to the English *-ing* form) of the conjugated verb.

Gerund Endings		
hablar	**comer**	**vivir**
habl- **ando**	com- **iendo**	viv- **iendo**

B. Some irregular gerunds:

pedir	**pidiendo**	servir	**sirviendo**
decir	**diciendo**	leer	**leyendo**[1]
venir	**viniendo**	ir	**yendo**

¿Qué **estás estudiando?**	*What are you studying?*
Estoy estudiando mi lección de historia.	*I am studying my history lesson.*
¿Dónde **están viviendo** Uds. ahora?	*Where are you living now?*
Estamos viviendo en la avenida Unión.	*We are living on Union Avenue.*
¿Qué lección **está leyendo** Ud.?	*Which lesson are you reading?*
Estoy leyendo la lección de química.	*I am reading the chemistry lesson.*

Exercise

Change the verbs into the progressive form. Follow the model:

Modelo: Yo tomo café.
   Yo estoy tomando café.

1. Tú lees la lección de historia.
2. Ellos piden dinero.
3. Nosotros decimos la verdad.
4. ¿Come Ud. ahora en este restaurante?
5. José sirve el café.
6. ¿A quién esperas?
7. Ella habla con el presidente.

---

[1] Notice that the **-i** of **-iendo** becomes **y** between vowels.

8. Tú trabajas mucho.
9. Yo vivo en la avenida Washington.
10. Ellos estudian química.

4. INDIRECT OBJECT PRONOUNS

The forms of the indirect object pronouns are as follows:

Subject	Indirect Object	
yo	**me** (to)(me)	Él **me** da las revistas.
tú	**te** (to)(you, *familiar*)	Yo **te** doy el cuaderno.
Ud.	**le** (to)(you, *formal, masc.* and *fem.*)	Ella **le** compra una corbata.
él ⎱ ella ⎰	**le** (to)(him, her)	Yo **le** hablo en inglés.
nosotros ⎱ nosotras ⎰	**nos** (to)(us, *masc.* and *fem.*)	Ella **nos** da la lección.
Uds.	**les** (to)(you, *formal pl., masc.* and *fem.*)	Yo **les** digo la verdad.
ellos ⎱ ellas ⎰	**les** (to)(them, *masc.* and *fem.*)	El presidente **les** da el dinero.

A. The indirect object pronouns are the same as the direct object pronouns, except in the third person. Indirect object pronouns are usually placed *in front* of the verb:

¿Quién **les** compra a Uds. los pasajes?
Who is buying you the tickets?

Mi hermano **nos** compra los pasajes.
My brother is buying us the tickets.

¿Qué **le** pregunta Ud.?
What are you asking him?

Le pregunto su dirección.
I'm asking him his address.

EXCEPTIONS:

1. When an infinitive follows the conjugated verb, the indirect object pronoun is placed in front of the conjugated verb or after the infinitive:

¿Qué vas a comprar**me**?
What are you going to buy me?

Voy a comprar**te** un abrigo.
I'm going to buy you a coat.

OR:

¿Qué **me** vas a comprar?
Te voy a comprar un abrigo.

2. With present participles, the indirect object pronouns can be used both ways also:

¿A quién está Ud. escribiéndo**le**? — *To whom are you writing?*

Estoy escribiéndo**le** a mi esposo. — *I'm writing to my husband.*

OR:

¿A quién **le** está Ud. escribiendo?

Le estoy escribiendo a mi esposo.

3. With affirmative commands, they are always placed after the verb. The affirmative formal commands (**Ud.** and **Uds.**) are discussed in Lesson 9.

· · ·

B. With the indirect objects **le** and **les**, clarification is necessary when the sentence or the context of the conversation does not specify the gender of the person to which the pronoun refers. Spanish uses the preposition **a** + *the personal pronouns* for this purpose:

Le doy la información. (*to whom?*)

Le doy la información **a él.** (*to him*)
Le doy la información **a ella.** (*to her*)
Le doy la información **a Ud.** (*to you, formal*)

Exercises

A. Complete the following sentences with the correct indirect object pronouns and clarify when necessary:

1. Yo _____ compro el abrigo _____, señor Vera. (*for you*)
2. _____ da un refresco. (*to me*)
3. _____ pido los cuadernos _____. (*to her*)
4. _____ está escribiendo una carta. (*to us*) (*two forms*)
5. _____ pregunto su número de teléfono _____. (*to you, form. pl.*)
6. _____ doy los pasajes, mi hija. (*to you*)
7. _____ voy a decir la verdad _____. (*to him*)
8. _____ estamos hablando en inglés _____. (*to them, fem.*) (*two forms*)

B. Give the Spanish equivalent:

1. I am giving you the tickets, Mr. Smith.
2. Are you writing to him? (*two forms*)
3. She always tells me the truth.
4. Are you going to buy us a magazine? (*two forms*)
5. I speak to them (*fem.*) in English.

5. DIRECT AND INDIRECT OBJECT PRONOUNS USED TOGETHER

A. When an indirect object pronoun and a direct object pronoun are used in the same sentence, the indirect object always appears first.

¿Cuándo me pagas el dinero?	*When are you paying me the money?*
Te lo pago¹ mañana.	*I'll pay (it to) you tomorrow.*

B. With an infinitive, the pronouns can be placed either before or after:

Necesito el diccionario. ¿Puedes prestár**melo?**	*I need the dictionary. Can you lend it to me?*
Sí, puedo prestár**telo.**	*Yes, I can lend it to you.*

OR:

¿**Me lo** puedes prestar?
Sí, **te lo** puedo prestar.

C. If both pronouns start with **l,** the indirect object pronoun (**le** or **les**) is changed to **se.** For clarification it is sometimes necessary to add: **a él, a ella, a Ud., a Uds., a ellos, a ellas:**

¿**Le** sirves la comida **a él** o **a ella?**	*Do you serve dinner to him or to her?*
Se la sirvo **a él.**	*I serve it to him.*
¿**Les** dan Uds. la medicina a **ellas** o **a ellos?**	*Are you giving the medicine to them(fem.) or to them(masc.)?*
Se la damos **a ellos.**	*We are giving it to them (masc.).*

¹ The present indicative is frequently used in Spanish to express future.

Exercises

A. Change the following sentences, according to the model:

Modelo: Voy a comprártelo.
   Te lo voy a comprar.

1. Quiere dárselo.
2. No va a creérmelo.
3. Va a preguntártelo.
4. Ella va a traérnoslas mañana.
5. No quiere prestármela.
6. Estoy leyéndoselos.
7. No voy a pagársela.
8. ¿Puedes traérmelas?
9. Va a dárselos.
10. Estamos diciéndoselo ahora.

B. Complete the following sentences with the appropriate direct and indirect object pronouns:

1. Yo ____ ____ traigo. (*to you, fam. / them, fem.*)
2. Ud. ____ ____ dice. (*to me / it, masc.*)
3. Vamos a traer ____ ____. (*to him / it, fem.*)
4. Uds. ____ ____ pagan. (*to us / them, masc.*)
5. Estamos leyendo ____ ____. (*to them / it, masc.*)

C. Answer the following questions, first in the affirmative, then in the negative. Substitute pronouns for the italicized nouns, according to the model:

Modelo: ¿Me compra Ud. *el abrigo?*
   Sí, se lo compro.
   No, no se lo compro.

1. ¿Va a servirme Ud. *la comida?*
2. ¿Le presta Ud. *los cuadernos* a Paco?
3. ¿Me compra Ud. *la corbata?*
4. ¿Les paga Ud. *los pasajes* a ellos?
5. ¿Está Ud. leyéndole *el periódico* a Inés?

6. pedir VS. preguntar

A. **Pedir** means *to ask for* in the sense of *to request:*

¿Qué te **piden** los muchachos?	*What do the boys ask you for?*
Me **piden** la medicina para su madre.	*They ask me for the medicine for their mother.*

¿Vas a **pedir**le dinero a tu tío?	*Are you going to ask your uncle for money?*
No, voy a **pedír**selo a mi tía. Ella es más generosa.	*No, I'm going to ask my aunt (for it). She's more generous.*

B. **Preguntar** means *to ask (a question)*:

¿Qué vas a **preguntar**le a René?	*What are you going to ask René?*
Voy a **preguntar**le si conoce a mi primo.	*I'm going to ask him if he knows my cousin.*
¿Qué le vas a **preguntar** a Ana?	*What are you going to ask Ana?*
Le voy a **preguntar** qué hora es.	*I'm going to ask her what time it is.*

Exercise

Complete the following sentences with the present indicative of **pedir** and **preguntar**, as needed:

1. Ellos me _____ dinero.
2. Yo le _____ qué quiere.
3. Ella le va a _____ si es el tío de Jorge.
4. Yo nunca le _____ nada. Ella no es muy generosa.
5. Le voy a _____ a Margarita si quiere ir allá.
6. ¿Qué le vas a _____ tú a Santa Claus?[1]
7. ¿Qué te _____ Carlos? ¿Dinero?
8. Yo nunca les _____ nada a mis primos, porque ellos no saben nada.

STUDY OF COGNATES

1. Spanish words ending in **-a** or **-o** instead of *-e* in English:

   la medicina   medicine

2. Spanish words ending in **-ia** or **-io** instead of *-y* in English:

   la historia   history

3. Spanish adjectives ending in **-oso(a)** instead of *-ous* in English:

   generoso(a)   generous

4. Approximate cognates:

   la avenida   avenue
   el diccionario dictionary

---

[1] In most Latin American countries and in Spain, it is the custom to expect presents from the Three Wise Men on January 6.

NEW VOCABULARY

NOUNS

el **abrigo**	coat
la **comida**	dinner, meal
la **corbata**	tie
el **cuaderno**	notebook
la **madre**	mother
el **muchacho**	boy, young man
el **pasaje**	ticket
el **periódico**	newspaper
la **prima** ⎱ el **primo** ⎰	cousin
la **química**	chemistry

la **revista**	magazine
la **tía**	aunt
el **tío**	uncle

VERBS

creer	to believe
pagar	to pay
preguntar	to ask (a question)
prestar	to lend

OTHER WORDS AND EXPRESSIONS

allá	over there
¿**para quién?**	for whom?

Ropa para damas

Blusas
Faldas
Pantalones

WADD'S
ropa joven

Lesson 9

1. POSSESSIVE PRONOUNS

Singular		Plural		
Masculine	Feminine	Masculine	Feminine	
el mío	la mía	los míos	las mías	mine
el tuyo	la tuya	los tuyos	las tuyas	yours (*familiar*)
el suyo	la suya	los suyos	las suyas	⎧his ⎨hers ⎩yours (*formal*)
el nuestro	la nuestra	los nuestros	las nuestras	ours
el suyo	la suya	los suyos	las suyas	⎧theirs ⎩yours (*formal*)

A. The possessive pronouns in Spanish agree in gender and number with the thing possessed. They are generally used with the definite article:

Aquí están los zapatos de ellos.
  ¿Dónde están **los nuestros?**
Los nuestros están en el dormitorio.

Here are their shoes. Where are ours?
Ours are in the bedroom.

Tus pantalones están aquí.
  ¿Dónde están **los míos?**
Los tuyos están en la tintorería.

Your trousers are here. Where are mine?
Yours are at the cleaners.

Mi vestido está allá.
  ¿Dónde está el suyo?
El mío está en la cama.

My dress is over there. Where is yours?
Mine is on the bed.

EXCEPTION: After the verb **ser,** the article is omitted when mere expression of ownership is indicated.

¿Es **tuya** esta maleta?
Sí, esta maleta es **mía,** pero aquéllas son **tuyas.**

Is this suitcase yours?
Yes, this suitcase is mine, but those are yours.

¿Este talonario de cheques es **suyo,** señor Muñoz?
Sí, es **mío.** Gracias.

Is this checkbook yours, Mr. Muñoz?
Yes, it's mine. Thank you.

B. Since the third-person forms of the possessive pronouns (**el suyo, la suya, los suyos, las suyas**) could be ambiguous, they may be replaced for clarification by the following:

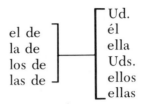

el de
la de
los de
las de

Ud.
él
ella
Uds.
ellos
ellas

Estos muebles son de Marta y Arturo, ¿no?	*These (pieces of) furniture are Martha's and Arthur's, aren't they?*
Bueno, el sofá es **de ella,** pero la cama y el escritorio son **de él.**	*Well, the sofa is hers, but the bed and the desk are his.*

Exercises

A. Supply the correct possessive pronouns and read aloud. Follow the models:

Modelos: Yo tengo una cama. Es _____.
Yo tengo una cama. Es mía.

Juan tiene un libro. Es _____. Es _____.
Juan tiene un libro. Es suyo. Es de él.

1. Tú tienes un talonario de cheques. Es _____.
2. Juan tiene un escritorio. Es _____. Es _____.
3. Nosotras tenemos una maleta. Es _____.
4. Ud. tiene unos muebles. Son _____. Son _____.
5. Yo tengo un sofá. Es _____.
6. Uds. tienen dos lápices. Son _____. Son _____.
7. Yo tengo unos pantalones. Son _____.
8. Ud. tiene tres hijos. Son _____. Son _____.

B. Give the Spanish equivalent:

1. This desk is mine. Where is yours, Mr. Britos?
2. These shoes aren't ours.
3. My pants are at the cleaners. Where are yours?
4. The books are hers, but the pens are theirs.
5. My bed is here, Mrs. Ortiz. Yours is in the bedroom.

2. REFLEXIVE CONSTRUCTIONS

A reflexive verb is one in which the verb acts upon the subject. Most Spanish verbs can be made reflexive. The reflexive consists of the reflexive pronoun and the verb:

Reflexive Pronouns	
me	myself, to (for) myself
te	yourself, to (for) yourself (**tú** form)
nos	ourselves, to (for) ourselves
se	yourself, to (for) yourself (**Ud.** form)
	yourselves, to (for) yourselves (**Uds.** form)
	himself, to (for) himself
	herself, to (for) herself
	itself, to (for) itself
	themselves, to (for) themselves

ATENCIÓN: Notice that except for **se**, the reflexive pronouns are the same as the direct and indirect object pronouns.

vestirse (to dress oneself)	
Yo me visto	I dress myself
Tú te vistes	You dress yourself
Ud. se viste	You dress yourself
Él se viste	He dresses himself
Ella se viste	She dresses herself
Nosotros nos vestimos	We dress ourselves
Uds. se visten	You dress yourselves
Ellos se visten	They (*masc.*) dress themselves
Ellas se visten	They (*fem.*) dress themselves

ATENCIÓN: Both the reflexive pronouns and the verb agree with the subject. The rules governing the position of the reflexive pronouns are the same as for other subject pronouns.

A. The following common verbs are frequently used in the reflexive:

despertarse (e > ie)	*to wake up*
levantarse	*to get up*
vestirse (e > i)	*to get dressed*
desvestirse (e > i)	*to get undressed*
afeitarse	*to shave*
bañarse	*to bathe*

sentarse (e > ie)   *to sit*
acostarse (o > ue)   *to go to bed*
preocuparse   *to worry*

B. Some verbs are *always* used with reflexive pronouns in Spanish:

acordarse (o > ue) (de)   *to remember*
quejarse (de)   *to complain*
suicidarse   *to commit suicide*

Notice that the use of a reflexive pronoun does not necessarily imply a reflexive action.

C. Some verbs change their meaning when they are used with reflexive pronouns:

acostar (o > ue)	*to put to bed*	acostarse	*to go to bed*
dormir (o > ue)	*to sleep*	dormirse	*to fall asleep*
levantar	*to lift, to raise*	levantarse	*to get up*
probar (o > ue)	*to try, to taste*	probarse	*to try on*
poner	*to put*	ponerse	*to put on*

Notice the use of the reflexive in the following sentences:

¿A qué hora **se levanta** Ud., señorita López?

What time do you get up, Miss Lopez?

Generalmente **me levanto** a las ocho, pero no **me acuesto** hasta la medianoche.

I generally get up at eight o'clock, but I don't go to bed until midnight.

¿**Se acuerda** Ud. de Rosita?
Sí, **me acuerdo** de ella.

Do you remember Rosita?
Yes, I remember her.

¿Por qué no **te acuestas**, querido?

Why don't you go to bed, dear?

Primero voy a **acostar** a los niños.

First I'm going to put the children to bed.

Exercises

A. Complete the following sentences, using the present indicative of the verbs in parentheses:

1. Elena _____ (probarse) los zapatos.
2. Él _____ (acostarse) y Ud. _____ (acostar) a los niños.
3. Juan _____ (bañarse) y Luis _____ (vestirse).
4. Tú siempre _____ (dormirse) en la clase de historia.
5. Nosotros no _____ (preocuparse) por eso.
6. Los muchachos _____ (levantarse) a las siete.
7. Debes _____ (desvestirse) antes de _____ (bañarse).
8. ¿No vas a _____ (ponerse) el abrigo, querida?

B. Answer the following questions:

1. ¿A qué hora se levanta Ud. generalmente?
2. ¿Siempre te despiertas temprano?
3. ¿Se acuerda Ud. de sus amigos?
4. ¿A qué hora se acuestan Uds.? ¿A la medianoche?
5. ¿Se queja el profesor de los estudiantes?
6. ¿Se van a poner Uds. los zapatos para salir?
7. ¿Cuántas horas duerme Ud.?
8. ¿Siempre pruebas la comida?

3. THE COMMAND FORMS (Ud. and Uds.)

To form the command for **Ud.** and **Uds.**,[1] add the following endings to the stem of the first person singular of the present indicative, after dropping the **-o:**

-ar verbs: **-e** (Ud.) and **-en** (Uds.)
-er verbs: **-a** (Ud.) and **-an** (Uds.)
-ir verbs: **-a** (Ud.) and **-an** (Uds.)

ATENCIÓN: Notice that the endings for the **-er** and **-ir** verbs are the same.

Infinitive	First Person Present Ind.	Stem	Commands Ud.	Uds.
hablar	Yo hablo	habl-	hable	hablen
comer	Yo como	com-	coma	coman
abrir	Yo abro	abr-	abra	abran
cerrar	Yo cierro	cierr-	cierre	cierren
volver	Yo vuelvo	vuelv-	vuelva	vuelvan
pedir	Yo pido	pid-	pida	pidan
decir	Yo digo	dig-	diga	digan

¿Con quién debo hablar?   *With whom must I speak?*
Hable con la secretaria.   *Speak with the secretary.*

¿Vengo por la mañana o por la   *Shall I come in the morning or*
  tarde?   *in the afternoon?*
Venga por la mañana y **traiga**   *Come in the morning and*
  sus documentos.   *bring your documents.*

¿Cierro la puerta?   *Shall I close the door?*
No, **cierre** la ventana, por favor. *No, close the window, please.*

[1] The **tú** form will be studied in lesson 18.

| ¿Sigo derecho o doblo a la derecha? | *Shall I continue straight ahead or shall I turn right?* |
| **Doble** a la izquierda. | *Turn left.* |

B. The command forms of the following verbs are irregular:

	dar	estar	ser	ir
Ud.	dé	esté	sea	vaya
Uds.	den	estén	sean	vayan

| ¿Podemos ir solas? | *Can we go alone?* |
| No, no **vayan** solas. **Vayan** con sus padres. | *No, don't go alone. Go with your parents.* |

| ¡Le digo que quiero ver a mis hijos! | *I'm telling you I want to see my children!* |
| Un momento, señora. ¡No **sea** tan impaciente! | *One moment, madam. Don't be so impatient.* |

Exercise

A. Answer the following questions, according to the models:

Modelos: ¿Hablo con el secretario? (director)
   No, hable con el director.

   ¿Hablamos con el secretario? (director)
   No, hablen con el director.

1. ¿Hago la lección número uno? (la lección número dos)
2. ¿Cerramos las ventanas? (las puertas)
3. ¿Compramos plumas? (lápices)
4. ¿Damos nuestra dirección? (mi dirección)
5. ¿Duermo aquí? (en el dormitorio)
6. ¿Estudiamos la lección cuatro? (la lección tres)
7. ¿Trabajamos hoy? (mañana)
8. ¿Vuelvo el lunes? (el martes)
9. ¿Sirvo café? (té)
10. ¿Pedimos refrescos? (sopa y postre)
11. ¿Doblo a la derecha? (a la izquierda)
12. ¿Digo que sí? (que no)
13. ¿Salimos por la tarde? (por la noche)
14. ¿Traducimos la lección ocho? (la lección seis)
15. ¿Traigo la carne? (la ensalada)
16. ¿Vamos al cine? (al teatro)

B. Give the Spanish equivalent:

1. You mustn't continue straight ahead. Turn left.
2. Don't be so impatient, ladies.
3. Wait one moment, Mr. Peña.
4. Go with the secretary.
5. Bring your documents, Miss Ruiz.

4. USES OF OBJECT PRONOUNS WITH THE COMMAND FORMS

A. In all direct *affirmative* commands, the object pronouns are placed *after* the verb and attached to it, thus forming only one word:

¿Dónde pongo las maletas?	*Where shall I put the suitcases?*
Póngalas en la cama.	*Put them on the bed.*
¿Dónde sirvo el café?	*Where shall I serve (the) coffee?*
Sírvalo en la terraza.	*Serve it on the terrace.*
¿Qué le digo?	*What shall I tell him?*
Dígale que sí.	*Tell him yes.*
¿Qué les doy a las niñas?	*What shall I give the girls?*
Déles el postre.	*Give them dessert.*
¿Abrimos la puerta?	*Shall we open the door?*
Sí, **ábranla**.	*Yes, open it.*
¿Se lo digo a Ana?	*Shall I tell (it to) Ana?*
Sí, **dígaselo** a Ana.	*Yes, tell (it to) Ana.*

Exercise

Answer the following questions, according to the models:

Modelos: ¿Traigo las sillas?
Sí, tráigalas, por favor.

¿Traemos las sillas?
Sí, tráiganlas, por favor.

¿Le traigo el dinero?
Sí, tráigamelo, por favor.

¿Le traemos el dinero?
Sí, tráiganmelo, por favor.

1. ¿Traduzco la lección?
2. ¿Abrimos la puerta de la terraza?

3. ¿Cerramos las ventanas?
4. ¿Te servimos la sopa?
5. ¿Le decimos que sí?
6. ¿Hago el café?
7. ¿Le escribo la carta a Luis?
8. ¿Te traemos el vestido?
9. ¿Me baño?
10. ¿Nos acostamos ahora?
11. ¿Me visto?
12. ¿Nos desvestimos?
13. ¿Te traigo el té?
14. ¿Le doy el dinero a Marta?
15. ¿Le decimos tu número de teléfono a Pedro?

B. In all *negative* commands, the object pronouns are placed *in front* of the verb:

¿Nos levantamos ahora?
No, **no se levanten** todavía.

Shall we get up now?
No, don't get up yet.

Quiero traerle una corbata a Luis.
No, **no le traiga** una corbata. Tráigale una camisa.

I want to bring Luis a tie.
No, don't bring him a tie. Bring him a shirt.

Voy a traducir la lección al francés.
No, **no la traduzca** al francés. Tradúzcala al español.

I'm going to translate the lesson into French.
No, don't translate it into French. Translate it into Spanish.

¿Te traemos los vestidos?
No, **no me traigan** los vestidos. Tráiganme los abrigos.

Shall we bring you the dresses?
No, don't bring me the dresses. Bring me the coats.

¿Sirvo los refrescos?
No, **no los sirva** todavía.

Shall I serve the sodas?
No, don't serve them yet.

¿Te traemos las maletas?
No, **no me las** traigan.

Shall we bring you the suitcases?
No, don't bring them to me.

Exercise

Respond, following the models:

Modelos: Voy a traer el escritorio.
No, no lo traiga todavía.

Vamos a traer el escritorio.
No, no lo traigan todavía.

Le voy a traer el escritorio.
No, no se lo traiga todavía.

1. Voy a comprar ese vestido.
2. Vamos a traerle la camisa a Raúl.
3. Le voy a dar un cheque.
4. Voy a acostarme.
5. Voy a desvestirme.
6. Voy a cerrar las ventanas.
7. Vamos a quejarnos.
8. Voy a levantarme.
9. Vamos a afeitarnos.
10. Le voy a dar las plumas a María.
11. Vamos a traerte el té.
12. Le voy a decir mi edad al director.
13. Le vamos a hablar.
14. Voy a ponerme los zapatos.
15. Vamos a traerte la botella.

STUDY OF COGNATES

1. These words are the same in Spanish and English, except for written accent mark or final vowel:

   el sofá   sofa
   el documento   document
   el momento   moment

2. Spanish adverbs ending in **-mente** instead of English -*ly:*

   generalmente   generally

3. Spanish words ending in **-ia** or **-io** instead of English *y:*

   la secretaria⎫
   el secretario⎭ secretary

4. Approximate cognates:

   impaciente   impatient
   la terraza   terrace

NEW VOCABULARY

NOUNS

la cama	bed
el dormitorio	bedroom
el escritorio	desk
la maleta	suitcase
la medianoche	midnight
los muebles (m.)	furniture (pieces of)
los pantalones	trousers, pants
la puerta	door
el talonario de cheques	checkbook
la tintorería	cleaner
la ventana	window
el vestido	dress
los zapatos (m.)	shoes

VERBS

deber	must, to have to
doblar	to turn
vestir(se) (e > i)	to dress, to get dressed

ADJECTIVES

querido(a)

OTHER WORDS AND EXPRESSIONS

a la derecha	to the right
a la izquierda	to the left
antes de	before
seguir (e > i) derecho	to continue straight ahead
tan	so
todavía	yet

Los UNIVERSITARIOS HOY

La Universidad
de Puerto Rico

Lesson 10

1. PRETERIT OF REGULAR VERBS

The preterit tense is used to refer to past actions that were completed in past time.[1] The preterit of regular verbs is formed as follows:

entrar (to enter)	comer (to eat)	escribir (to write)
entré	comí	escribí
entraste	comiste	escribiste
entró	comió	escribió
entramos	comimos	escribimos
entraron	comieron	escribieron

• Notice that the endings for the -er and -ir verbs are the same.

ATENCIÓN: Spanish has no equivalent for the English *did* used as an auxiliary verb in questions and negative sentences.

¿Quién te **prestó** esa bicicleta?   *Who lent you that bicycle?*
Me la **prestó** Carlos   *Charles lent it to me*
  ayer.   *yesterday.*

¿A qué hora **comió** Ud.   *At what time did you eat last*
  anoche?   *night?*
Comí a las ocho.   *I ate at eight o'clock.*

¿**Abrió** Ud. las ventanas?   *Did you open the windows?*
No, no las **abrí**.   *No, I didn't open them.*

Exercise

Complete the sentences with the preterit of the following verbs: **esperar, estudiar, recibir, aprender, abrir, comprar, decidir, preguntar, entender, beber.** Use each verb only once.

1. ¿Dónde _____ Ud. a hablar español?
2. ¿Qué _____ Uds.? ¿Ir al hospital?
3. Yo no _____ su carta.
4. ¿Dónde _____ tú esa bicicleta?
5. Lidia y Gerardo no _____ la lección.
6. ¿_____ Ud. las puertas?
7. ¿Qué _____ Uds. acerca del examen?
8. El profesor no me _____ nada ayer.
9. Carmen y yo _____ té.
10. ¿Cuántas horas lo _____ Ud.?

---

[1] Spanish has two past tenses, the preterit and the imperfect. The imperfect will be studied in Lesson 11.

2. PRETERIT OF **ser, ir,** AND **dar**

The preterits of **ser, ir,** and **dar** are irregular. Note that **ser** and **ir** have the same preterit forms:

ser (to be)	ir (to go)	dar (to give)
fui	fui	di
fuiste	fuiste	diste
fue	fue	dio
fuimos	fuimos	dimos
fueron	fueron	dieron

Ud. **fue** profesora en la universidad de Arizona, ¿no?	*You were a professor at the University of Arizona, weren't you?*
Sí, yo **fui** profesora de Economía.	*Yes, I was a professor of Economics.*
¿Con quién **fue** Ud. a la tienda ayer?	*With whom did you go to the store yesterday?*
Fui con mis padres.	*I went with my parents.*
¿Quién le **dio** la medicina al niño?	*Who gave the medicine to the boy?*
Se la **dio** la enfermera.	*The nurse gave it to him.*

Exercise

Complete the following sentences with the preterit of the verbs **ir, ser,** or **dar,** as needed:

1. Yo _____ con mis padres al hospital.
2. Ella _____ mi profesora de Economía el año pasado.
3. Nosotros no le _____ el dinero anoche.
4. ¿Le _____ a Ud. la medicina el dentista?
5. El doctor _____ al laboratorio.
6. Yo no tè _____ el cuaderno.
7. Nosotros no _____ sus estudiantes.
8. ¿Le _____ Ud. la maleta a la enfermera?
9. ¿Quién _____ el primer presidente de los Estados Unidos?
10. ¿A dónde _____ tú ayer? ¿A la tienda?
11. Carlos y Roberto _____ al laboratorio anoche.
12. ¿Le _____ tú el paraguas a tu prima?
13. María y yo _____ a Santiago el año pasado.
14. Yo les _____ a mis hermanos esos zapatos.

3. THE EXPRESSION acabar de

Acabar de means *to have just*. While English uses the present perfect tense plus the word *just*, Spanish uses this formula:

subject	+	acabar (present tense)	+	de	+	infinitive
Pedro		acaba		de		llegar

¿Tiene Elena un puesto?   *Does Helen have a job?*
Sí, **acaba de encontrar** uno.   *Yes, she has just found one.*

¿Quieres un poco de sopa?   *Do you want some soup?*
No, gracias. **Acabo de comer.**   *No, thanks. I have just eaten.*

• Notice that the conjugation of **acabar** is completely regular.

Exercise

Complete the following sentences with the correct form of **acabar de** + *infinitive:*

1. Juan (*has just arrived*) _____ a esta ciudad.
2. Yo (*have just bought*) _____ esta casa.
3. Ellas (*have just found*) _____ un puesto.
4. Él (*has just eaten*) _____ un poco de carne.
5. Elena (*has just got dressed*) _____.
6. Uds. (*have just gone*) _____ a la oficina.
7. Elena (*has just written*) _____ la carta.
8. Tú (*have just read*) _____ la revista.
9. Yo (*have just bathed*) _____.
10. Ellos (*have just lent me*) _____ el periódico.
11. Nosotros (*have just found*) _____ las maletas.
12. Marta y Ana (*have just gotten dressed*) _____ .

4. THE ABSOLUTE SUPERLATIVE

Sometimes a high degree of a given quality is expressed without comparing it to the same quality of another person or thing. Spanish has two ways of expressing this:

A. By modifying the adjective with an adverb (**muy, sumamente**):

¿Cómo es tu novia?   *What is your girlfriend like?*
Es **muy** inteligente y   *She is very intelligent and*
    sumamente buena.   *extremely kind.*

B. By adding the suffix -ísimo (-a, -os, -as) to the adjective. If the word ends in a vowel, the vowel is dropped before adding the suffix. Notice that the í of the suffix always has a written accent:

alto	alt-	ísimo	altísimo
ocupada	ocupad-	ísima	ocupadísima
lentos	lent-	ísimos	lentísimos
buenas	buen-	ísimas	buenísimas
difícil	dificil-	ísimo	dificilísimo

¿Fuiste a Madrid el verano pasado?	*Did you go to Madrid last summer?*
Sí, es una cíudad **bellísima,** pero es **dificilísimo** conducir allí.	*Yes, it is a very beautiful city, but it is extremely difficult to drive there.*
¿Pueden ir a la tienda con nosotros?	*Can you go to the store with us?*
No, estamos **ocupadísimas.**	*No, we are extremely busy.*

Exercise

Change the following sentences, using the absolute superlative:

1. Mis padres son muy inteligentes.
2. Mi novio es sumamente alto.
3. Ellos están muy ocupados.
4. Es muy fácil conducir en esta ciudad.
5. Ellas son muy buenas.
6. La enfermera está sumamente ocupada.
7. Ellos son muy lentos.
8. La lección es sumamente difícil.

5. WEATHER EXPRESSIONS

In the following expressions, Spanish uses the verb **hacer** *(to make)* followed by a noun, whereas English uses the verb *to be* followed by an adjective:

Hace (mucho) frío. *It is (very) cold.*
Hace (mucho) calor. *It is (very) hot.*
Hace (mucho) viento. *It is (very) windy.*
Hace sol. *It is sunny.*

The following weather expressions do not combine with **hacer:**

llover (o > ue) *(to rain):* **llueve**
nevar (e > ie) *(to snow):* **nieva**

As in English, Spanish uses the impersonal verbs in the infinitive, present or past participle, and third person singular forms only.

¿Hace viento hoy?	*Is it windy today?*
Sí y también **está lloviendo** mucho.	*Yes and it is raining a lot also.*
¿Qué tiempo hace hoy, Marta?	*How's the weather today, Martha?*
Hace mucho **frío** y **está nevando.**	*It is very cold and it is snowing.*

Exercises

A. Study these words and then complete the following sentences:

el paraguas   umbrella
el impermeable   raincoat
el suéter   sweater

1. ¿Necesitas un paraguas? — Sí, porque _____.
2. ¿No necesitas un abrigo? — No, porque _____.
3. ¿Quieres un impermeable? — No, no está _____.
4. ¿Necesitas un suéter? — No, hoy _____.
5. Está nevando. Lleve el _____.

B. Give the Spanish equivalent:

1. It is very windy today.
2. It is very cold and it is also snowing.
3. It is very hot in Cuba.
4. How is the weather today?
5. Is it sunny?

STUDY OF COGNATES

1. These words are the same in Spanish and English, except for a final vowel:

   el dentista   dentist

2. Spanish words ending in **-ia** or **-io** instead of English *y:*

   el laboratorio   laboratory

3. Approximate cognates:

   la bicicleta   bicycle
   la economía   economics
   el suéter   sweater

NEW VOCABULARY

NOUNS

la enfermera el enfermero	nurse
el impermeable	raincoat
la novia	girl friend
el novio	boy friend
los padres	parents
el paraguas	umbrella
el puesto	job, position
la tienda	store

VERBS

encontrar (o > ue)	to find
llover (o > ue)	to rain
nevar (e > ie)	to snow

ADJECTIVES

bello(a)	pretty
bueno(a)	kind
ocupado(a)	busy

OTHER WORDS AND EXPRESSIONS

anoche	last night
ayer	yesterday
¿Qué tiempo hace hoy?	How's the weather today?
sumamente	extremely
un poco de	some

Test Yourself: Lessons 6-10

LESSON 6

A. Some uses of the definite article

Give the Spanish equivalent:

1. Today is Wednesday.
2. Women want equality with men.
3. Freedom is important.
4. We're going to study next week.
5. I don't have classes on Fridays.

B. Stem-changing verbs (o > ue)

Answer the following questions:

1. ¿A qué hora vuelve Ud. a su casa?
2. Cuando Uds. van a México, ¿vuelan o van en coche?
3. ¿Recuerdan Uds. los verbos irregulares?
4. ¿Cuántas horas duermes tú?
5. ¿Pueden Uds. ir al cine hoy?

C. Affirmative and negative expressions

Change the following sentences to the affirmative:

1. Ellos no recuerdan nada.
2. No hay nadie en el cine.
3. Yo no quiero volar tampoco.
4. No recibimos ningún regalo.
5. Nunca tiene éxito.

D. Ordinal numbers

For each of the following cardinal numbers, give the corresponding ordinal number:

cinco	tres	seis
ocho	nueve	cuatro
diez	dos	siete
uno		

E. Uses of **tener que** and **hay que**

Give the Spanish equivalent:

1. To succeed, one must work.
2. You have to come back next week, Mr. Vega.

3. She has to work tomorrow.
4. One must start early.
5. Do we have to begin at eight?

LESSON 7

A. Stem-changing verbs (**e** > **i**)

Answer the following questions:

1. ¿Qué sirven Uds., sopa o ensalada?
2. ¿Qué pide Ud. para beber cuando va a un restaurante?
3. ¿Dice Ud. su edad?
4. ¿Sigue Ud. en la clase de español?
5. ¿Uds. siempre piden postre?

B. More about irregular verbs

Complete the sentences with the present indicative of the verbs in the following list. Use each verb once:

traer   traducir   conducir
caber   poner   saber
conocer   hacer   ver
salir

1. Yo _____ mi coche.
2. Yo siempre _____ con ella.
3. Yo _____ los documentos en el fichero.
4. Yo _____ del inglés al español.
5. Yo no _____ al maestro de mi hijo.
6. Yo no _____ aquí. Soy muy grande.
7. Yo _____ el postre.
8. Yo no _____ el regalo. ¿Dónde está?
9. Yo no _____ nadar.
10. Yo _____ la carne.

C. **Saber** vs. **Conocer**

Give the Spanish equivalent:

1. I know your son.
2. He doesn't know French.
3. Can you (do you know how to) swim, Miss Vera?
4. Do you know the ambassador?
5. Do the students know Cervantes' novels?

D. Direct object pronouns

Complete the following sentences with the Spanish equivalent of the direct object pronouns in parentheses. Follow the models:

Modelos: Yo veo   (*him*)
        Yo lo veo.

        Yo quiero ver   (*him*)
        Yo quiero verlo.

1. Yo conozco   (*them, fem.*)
2. Uds. van a comprar   (*it, masc.*)
3. **Nosotros no** queremos ver   (*you, familiar*)
4. Ella sirve   (*it, fem.*)
5. ¿Ud. no conoce . . . ?   (*me*)
6. Él escribe   (*them, masc.*)
7. Carlos va a traer   (*us*)
8. Nosotros no vemos   (*you, formal, sing., masc.*)

E. Formation of adverbs

Write the adverbs corresponding to the following adjectives:

1. feliz   4. fácil
2. especial   5. lento y cuidadoso
3. rápido

LESSON 8

A. Demonstrative adjectives / Demonstrative pronouns

Give the Spanish equivalent:

1. I need these magazines and those ones (over there).
2. Do you want this notebook or that one?
3. I prefer these newspapers, not those ones (over there).
4. Do you want to buy this tie or that one?
5. I don't want to eat at this restaurant. I prefer that one (over there).
6. I don't understand that. (*neuter form*)

B. Present progressive

Complete the following sentences with the present progressive of **leer, decir, estudiar, comprar,** or **comer,** as needed:

1. Él _____ la lección.
2. Ella _____ en la cafetería.
3. Nosotros _____ el periódico.

   4. Tú no _____ la verdad.
   5. Yo _____ un abrigo.

C. Indirect object pronouns

   Answer the following questions, according to the model:

   Modelo: ¿Qué me vas a traer de México? (un abrigo)
   Te voy a traer un abrigo.

   1. ¿Qué te va a comprar Carlos? (los pasajes)
   2. ¿Qué le das tú a Luis? (las revistas)
   3. ¿En qué idioma les habla a Uds. el profesor? (en español)
   4. ¿Qué va a decirles Ud. a los niños? (la verdad)
   5. ¿Qué nos pregunta Ud.? (la dirección de la oficina)
   6. ¿A quién están escribiéndole Uds.? (a nuestro profesor)
   7. ¿Cuándo le escribe Ud. a su esposo? (los lunes)
   8. ¿A quién le da Ud. la información? (al señor Vera)
   9. ¿En qué idioma me hablas tú? (en inglés)
   10. ¿Qué te compran tus hijos? (nada)

D. Direct and indirect object pronouns used together

   Give the Spanish equivalent:

   1. The money? I'm giving it to you tomorrow, Mr. Peña.
   2. I know you need the dictionary, Anita, but I can't lend it to you.
   3. I need my coat. Can you bring it to me, Miss López?
   4. The pens? She is bringing them to us.
   5. When I need new shoes, my mother buys them for me.

E. **Pedir** vs. **Preguntar**

   Give the Spanish equivalent:

   1. I'm going to ask her where she lives.
   2. I always ask my husband for money.
   3. She always asks how you are, Mrs. Nieto.
   4. They are going to ask me for the chemistry books.
   5. We aren't going to ask you any (questions), sir.

LESSON 9

A. Possessive pronouns

   Answer the following questions in the negative, according to the
   model:

   Modelo: ¿Estos pantalones son *de Juan?*
   No, no son de él.

1. ¿Son *tuyas* estas maletas?
2. ¿Estos zapatos son *de Julia?*
3. ¿El vestido que está en la tintorería es *suyo,* señora?
4. ¿Es *de Uds.* esta cama?
5. ¿Este talonario de cheques es *de Eva y Gustavo?*
6. ¿Son *tuyos* estos muebles?
7. ¿Es *de Uds.* este sofá?
8. ¿Es *nuestro* este escritorio?

B. Reflexive constructions

Give the Spanish equivalent:

1. I get up at seven, I bathe, I get dressed, and leave at seven-thirty.
2. What time do the children wake up?
3. She doesn't want to sit down.
4. You always worry about your son, Mrs. Cruz.
5. Do you remember your teachers, Carlitos?
6. They are always complaining.
7. First she puts the children to bed. She goes to bed at ten.
8. Do you want to try on this coat, miss?
9. Where are you putting the money, ladies?
10. The students always fall asleep in this class.

C. The command forms: **Ud.** and **Uds.**

Complete the sentences with the command forms of the verbs in the following list, as needed, and read each sentence aloud. Use each verb once:

escribir	venir	dar	hablar	doblar
servir	cerrar	volver	seguir	ser
estar	poner	ir	abrir	traer

1. _____ la puerta, señor Benítez.
2. _____ español, señores.
3. _____ sus documentos, señorita.
4. _____ mañana por la mañana, señoras.
5. No _____ la ventana, señorita. Hace calor.
6. _____ a la izquierda, señores.
7. _____ derecho, señorita.
8. _____ su nombre y dirección, señores.
9. _____ en la oficina mañana por la tarde, señores.
10. ¡No _____ tan impacientes, señoritas!
11. _____ a la casa del director, señor Vega.

12. _____ el martes, señora. El doctor no está.
13. _____ el café en la terraza, señorita.
14. _____ las maletas aquí, señores.
15. _____ las cartas mañana, señoras.

D. Uses of object pronouns and reflexive pronouns with the command forms

Give the Spanish equivalent:

1. Tell them yes, Mr. Mena.
2. The dessert? Don't bring it to me now, Miss Ruiz.
3. Don't tell (it to) Ana, please.
4. Bring the chairs, gentlemen. Bring them to the terrace.
5. Don't get up, Mrs. Miño.
6. The tea? Bring it to her at four o'clock in the afternoon, Mr. Vargas.

LESSON 10

A. Preterit of regular verbs / Preterit of **ser, ir,** and **dar**

Rewrite the following sentences according to the new beginnings. Follow the model:

Modelo: Voy al cine. (Ayer . . .)
        Ayer fui al cine.

1. Ella entra en la cafetería y come una ensalada. (Ayer . . .)
2. María le escribe a Pedro. (Ayer . . .)
3. Ella me presta su bicicleta. (Anoche . . .)
4. Ellos son los mejores estudiantes. (El año pasado . . .)
5. Ellos te esperan cerca[1] del cine. (El sábado pasado . . .)
6. Mis hermanos van a Buenos Aires. (El verano pasado . . .)
7. Le doy dinero. (Ayer . . .)
8. Nosotros decidimos comprar la bicicleta. (El lunes pasado . . .)
9. Le pregunto la hora. (Anoche . . .)
10. Tú no entiendes la lección. (Ayer . . .)
11. Somos los primeros. (El jueves pasado . . .)
12. Me dan muchos problemas. (Ayer . . .)
13. Marta no bebe café. (Anoche . . .)
14. Yo no voy a la clase. (El miércoles pasado . . .)
15. Te damos té. (Ayer por la mañana . . .)

[1] **cerca (de)** near

B. The expression **acabar de**

Answer the following questions, according to the model:

Modelo: ¿Ya llegó Juan? **Sí, acaba de llegar.**

1. ¿Ya comieron Uds.?
2. ¿Ya se levantó Pedro?
3. ¿Ya hablaste con Susana?
4. ¿Ya compraron ellos la casa?
5. ¿Ya te bañaste?
6. ¿Ya llegaron los estudiantes?

C. The absolute superlative

Answer the following questions, according to the model:

Modelo: ¿Es inteligente el hijo de Yolanda?
    ¡Ah, sí! Es inteligentísimo.

1. ¿Es alto Roberto?
2. ¿Están Uds. ocupadas?
3. ¿Son lentos los niños?
4. ¿Es buena la profesora?
5. ¿Es difícil esta lección?
6. ¿Es bella la ciudad donde viven Uds.?
7. ¿Es fácil el español?
8. ¿Estás ocupado?

D. Weather expressions

Look at the following pictures and say what kind of weather they show:

De compras en Madrid

Lesson 11

1. TIME EXPRESSIONS WITH **hacer** AND **llevar**

A. English uses the present perfect tense to express how long something has been going on:

*I **have lived** in this city for fifteen years.*

Spanish follows this formula:

Hace +	length of time +	**que** +	*verb* (in the present tense)
Hace	**quince años**	**que**	**vivo en esta ciudad.**

¿Cuánto tiempo **hace que** trabaja Ud. para el gobierno?	*How long have you been working for the government?*
Hace tres años **que** trabajo para el gobierno.	*I have worked for the government for three years.*
¿Cuánto tiempo **hace que** Uds. viven aquí?	*How long have you lived here?*
Hace un mes **que** vivimos aquí.	*We have lived here for one month.*

B. English uses *has (have) been* + *gerund* to describe an action that started in the past and is still going on in the present:

*I **have been studying** for three hours.*

Spanish uses the verb **llevar** followed by a period of time and a gerund, as shown below:

Llevar +	length of time +	*gerund*
Llevo	**tres horas**	**estudiando.**

¿Cuánto tiempo **llevas escribiendo?**	*How long have you been writing?*
Llevo media hora **escribiendo.**	*I've been writing for half an hour.*
¿Cuánto tiempo **llevan** Uds. **estudiando** español?	*How long have you been studying Spanish?*
Llevamos dos años **estudiando** español.	*We've been studying Spanish for two years.*

Exercise

Answer the following questions, according to the model:

Modelo: ¿Cuánto tiempo llevan Uds. trabajando? (dos horas)
Llevamos dos horas trabajando.

1. ¿Cuánto tiempo hace que Ud. estudia español? (tres meses)
2. ¿Cuánto tiempo lleva Ud. trabajando en este puesto? (un año)
3. ¿Cuánto tiempo hace que Ud. no come? (media hora)
4. ¿Cuánto tiempo llevan Uds. viviendo en esta ciudad? (un mes)
5. ¿Cuánto tiempo hace que no llueve aquí? (cuatro meses)
6. ¿Cuánto tiempo llevan ellos trabajando para el gobierno? (un mes)
7. ¿Cuánto tiempo hace que el presidente vive en Washington? (un año)
8. ¿Cuánto tiempo hace que Uds. no van a clase? (cinco días)

2. IRREGULAR PRETERITS

The following Spanish verbs are irregular in the preterit:

tener:	tuve, tuviste, tuvo, tuvimos, tuvieron
estar:	estuve, estuviste, estuvo, estuvimos, estuvieron
poder:	pude, pudiste, pudo, pudimos, pudieron
poner:	puse, pusiste, puso, pusimos, pusieron
hacer:	hice, hiciste, hizo, hicimos, hicieron
venir:	vine, viniste, vino, vinimos, vinieron
querer:	quise, quisiste, quiso, quisimos, quisieron
decir:	dije, dijiste, dijo, dijimos, dijeron
traer:	traje, trajiste, trajo, trajimos, trajeron
conducir:	conduje, condujiste, condujo, condujimos, condujeron

ATENCIÓN: Notice that the third person singular of the verb **hacer** changes the **c** to **z** in order to maintain the soft sound of the **c** in the infinitive.

● All verbs ending in **-ducir** follow the same pattern as the verb **conducir: traducir,** *to translate;* **producir,** *to produce.*

¿Llamaste por teléfono a Juan?	*Did you phone John?*
No, porque él **vino** a mi casa.	*No, because he came to my house.*
¿Qué **hiciste** ayer?	*What did you do yesterday?*
Caminé por la ciudad.	*I walked around the city.*

¿Dónde **pusieron** Uds. el dinero?	*Where did you put the money?*
Lo **pusimos** en el banco.	*We put it in the bank.*

Exercise

Complete the following paragraph with the preterit of the verbs in parentheses:

Isabel le escribe una carta a Teresa:

Toledo, 15 de julio de 19..

Querida Teresa:

Ayer yo _____ (estar) en Madrid, pero no _____ (poder) ir a verte. Salí de Toledo por la mañana y _____ (conducir) por tres horas hasta llegar a Madrid. Allí _____ (tener) que ir al hospital para ver a Gustavo. Caminé por la ciudad y _____ (querer) llamarte por teléfono, pero no _____ (poder) encontrar uno. Como siempre, ayer _____ (hacer) mucho calor. _____ (Venir) de Madrid muy cansada. Esta mañana hablé por teléfono con Ramón. Él me _____ (decir) muchas cosas interesantes. ¡Ah . . . ! Me _____ (poner) el vestido que compré en Madrid y salí con Jorge. El sábado vuelvo a Madrid para verte.

Tu amiga,

Isabel

3. ¿De quién . . . ? FOR "WHOSE?"

¿**De quién** . . . ? is the interrogative form that Spanish uses to express the English *whose*. It can be singular or plural.

¿**De quién** es esta máquina de escribir?	*Whose typewriter is this?*
Es del contador.	*It's the accountant's.*
¿**De quiénes** son estos televisores?	*Whose TV sets are these?*
Éste es de Pedro y ése es mío.	*This one is Peter's and that one is mine.*

Exercise

Give the Spanish equivalent:

1. Whose typewriter is that?
2. Whose books are these? The accountant's?
3. Whose revolver is this?
4. Whose raincoat is this?
5. Whose umbrellas are these?

4. THE IMPERFECT TENSE

A. There are two simple past tenses in Spanish: the preterit, which you studied in lessons 10 and 11, and the imperfect. The imperfect is a descriptive tense: it does not express a completed action. It expresses a continued, habitual or repeated action in the past.

To form the imperfect tense, add the following endings to the stem:

-ar *Verbs*	-er *and* -ir *Verbs*	
hablar	comer	vivir
habl- **aba**	com- **ía**	viv- **ía**
habl- **abas**	com- **ías**	viv- **ías**
habl- **aba**	com- **ía**	viv- **ía**
habl- **ábamos**	com- **íamos**	viv- **íamos**
habl- **aban**	com- **ían**	viv- **ían**

● Notice that the endings of the **-er** and **-ir** verbs are the same. Notice also that there is a written accent mark on the final í of the **-er** and **-ir** verbs.
● The Spanish imperfect tense is equivalent to three English forms:

Yo **vivía** en Chicago.
$\begin{cases} \textit{I used to live in Chicago.} \\ \textit{I was living in Chicago.} \\ \textit{I lived in Chicago.} \end{cases}$

¿De qué te **hablaba** Pedro?	*What was Peter talking to you about?*
Me **hablaba** de la inflación.	*He was talking to me about inflation.*
¿Qué **comían** ellos?	*What were they eating?*
Comían arroz con pollo.	*They were eating chicken and rice.*
¿Dónde **vivía** Ud. en esa época?	*Where did you live in those days?*
Yo **vivía** en La Habana.	*I lived in Havana.*
Yo siempre **depositaba** todo mi dinero en el banco.	*I always used to deposit all my money in the bank.*
Yo también **ahorraba** mi dinero, pero ahora lo gasto.	*I used to save my money too, but now I spend it.*

Exercise

Complete the following sentences with the imperfect tense of the verbs in this list. Use each verb once:

acostarse	creer	dormir
gastar	dar	ahorrar
poder	servir	hablar
comenzar	tener	depositar
preferir		

1. Ellos no _____ ir a la universidad porque las clases _____ a las ocho de la mañana.
2. Mamá siempre me _____ dinero para comprar café.
3. En esa época yo _____ en Santa Claus.
4. ¿Tú _____ todo tu dinero en el banco o lo _____?
5. ¿Qué _____ Uds.? ¿Arroz con pollo o sopa?
6. Yo no _____ muy bien por la noche.
7. Papá siempre _____ su dinero.
8. En esa época nosotros _____ muy temprano porque _____ que ir a trabajar.
9. Yo siempre _____ la sopa.
10. Nosotros siempre _____ de la inflación en esa época.

B. There are only three verbs that are irregular in the imperfect tense: **ser, ir,** and **ver.**

ser	ir	ver
era	iba	veía
eras	ibas	veías
era	iba	veía
éramos	íbamos	veíamos
eran	iban	veían

¿Dónde **vivías** tú cuando **eras** chico?

Where did you live when you were little?

Yo **vivía** en Arizona cuando **era** chico.

I lived in Arizona when I was little.

Los vi esta mañana en la calle Quinta. ¿Adónde **iban** Uds.?

I saw you this morning on Fifth Street. Where were you going?

Íbamos a la escuela.

We were going to school.

Cecilia siempre **veía** a sus abuelos, ¿no?

Cecilia always used to see her grandparents, didn't she?

Veía a su abuela a veces, pero casi nunca **veía** a su abuelo.	*She used to see her grandmother sometimes, but she hardly ever saw her grandfather.*

Exercise

Item Substitution. Change the verbs according to the new subjects. Make any additional change needed:

1. Cuando yo **era** chica vivía con mis abuelos. (nosotros / tú / Gustavo / ellos / Uds.)
2. Ellos casi nunca **iban** a la escuela. (Yo / María / Nosotros / Tú / Uds.)
3. Nosotros **veíamos** que venía la inflación. (Ud. / Ellos / Yo / Tú / El presidente)

STUDY OF COGNATES

1. Spanish word ending in **-ción** instead of English *-tion:*

   la inflación   inflation

2. Approximate cognates:

el banco	bank
la escuela	school
La Habana	Havana

NEW VOCABULARY

NOUNS		VERBS	
la abuela	grandmother	**ahorrar**	to save (money)
el abuelo	grandfather		
los abuelos	grandparents	**caminar**	to walk
el arroz	rice	**depositar**	to deposit
el contador	accountant	**gastar**	to spend (money)
el gobierno	government		
la máquina de escribir	typewriter	**llamar**	to call
el pollo	chicken	**ADJECTIVE**	
el televisor	TV set	**chico(a)**	little

OTHER WORDS AND EXPRESSIONS

arroz con pollo	chicken and rice	**en esa época**	in those days
a veces	sometimes	**llamar por teléfono**	to phone
casi nunca	hardly ever	**media hora**	half an hour
¿de quién?	whose?	**por**	around

MIRE ANTES DE CRUZAR

CORREOS

ESPAÑA

Una policía de tránsito

Lesson 12

1. THE PAST PROGRESSIVE

To stress the idea of action in progress in the past, Spanish uses the imperfect tense of the verb **estar** and the gerund of the conjugated verb.

¿En qué **estabas pensando** tú cuando tu coche chocó con el ómnibus?	*What were you thinking about when your car collided with the bus?*
Estaba pensando en todas las cuentas que tengo que pagar.	*I was thinking about all the bills (that) I have to pay.*
¿Qué **estaba haciendo** la secretaria cuando Ud. la llamó?	*What was the secretary doing when you called her?*
Estaba escribiendo a máquina.	*She was typing.*
¿Qué **estaban haciendo** Uds. cuando llegó el policía?	*What were you doing when the policeman arrived?*
Estábamos leyendo el periódico.	*We were reading the paper.*
¿A quién **estaban esperando** los niños?	*Who were the children waiting for?*
Estaban esperando al señor García.	*They were waiting for Mr. García.*

Exercise

Answer the following questions:

1. ¿Qué estaban haciendo Uds. cuando llegó el policía?
2. ¿Qué estabas haciendo tú con esa pluma?
3. ¿En qué estaba Ud. pensando cuando yo le hablé?
4. ¿Estaba Ud. escribiendo a máquina cuando yo vine?
5. ¿Con quién estaba hablando Ud. por teléfono cuando yo lo (la) vi?
6. ¿Qué estaban leyendo Uds.?
7. Esta mañana mi auto chocó con un ómnibus. ¿En qué cree Ud. que yo estaba pensando?
8. ¿Estaban Uds. hablando de la inflación o de las cuentas que tienen que pagar?

2. PRETERIT VS. IMPERFECT

Spanish has two simple past tenses: the imperfect and the preterit. The difference between the two can be visualized this way:

The continuous moving line of the imperfect represents an action or state as it was taking place in the past. We don't know when the action started or ended. The vertical line represents the event as a completed unit in the past, and the preterit records such action.

The following table summarizes the uses of the preterit and the imperfect:

Preterit	Imperfect
1. Records, narrates, and reports an independent act or event as a completed and undivided whole, regardless of its duration. 2. Sums up a condition or state viewed as a whole.	1. Describes an action in progress at a certain time in the past. 2. Indicates a continuous and habitual action: *"used to . . ."* 3. Describes a physical, mental, or emotional state or condition in the past. 4. Expresses time in the past. 5. Is used in indirect discourse.

THE PRETERIT:

¿A qué hora **se acostó** Ud. anoche?

What time did you go to bed last night?

Anoche **me acosté** a las once y media.

Last night I went to bed at eleven-thirty.

Ayer **estuve** enferma.
Yo también.

Yesterday I was sick.
Me too.

THE IMPERFECT:

Cuando **íbamos** al cine vimos a María Ortiz.

When we were going to the movies we saw Maria Ortiz.

¿Sí? Ella y yo **estudiábamos** inglés juntas.

Yeah? She and I used to study English together.

Me fui porque no **me sentía** muy bien.	*I left because I wasn't feeling very well.*
¡Pero **eran** las ocho de la noche!	*But it was eight o'clock in the evening!*
¿Qué dijo Eduardo?	*What did Edward say?*
Dijo que **quería** salir con María.	*He said he wanted to go out with Maria.*

Exercise

Complete the following sentences with the preterit or the imperfect of the verbs in parentheses, as needed:

1. Anoche él y yo _____ (ir) al cine juntos.
2. Cuando nosotros _____ (ser) chicos, _____ (ir) a casa de nuestros abuelos.
3. _____ (ser) las cuatro de la tarde cuando él _____ (llegar).
4. Anoche Roberto me _____ (decir) que _____ (necesitar) el coche.
5. La semana pasada yo _____ (estar) muy enfermo también.
6. Yo _____ (venir) por la calle Octava cuando _____ (ver) a los niños que _____ (ir) al cine.
7. Ellos _____ (irse) porque no _____ (sentirse) bien.
8. Yo siempre los _____ (ver) cuando ellos _____ (ir) al teatro.
9. Ellos no _____ (estar) en casa anoche.
10. ¿Qué hora _____ (ser) cuando Uds. lo _____ (ver)?

3. **en** AND **a** FOR "AT"

A. **En** is used in Spanish to indicate a certain place or location:

¿Dónde están los chicos? ¿No están **en** casa?	*Where are the boys? Aren't they (at) home?*
No, están **en** la estación de policía.	*No, they are at the police station.*
¿Qué hacen allí?	*What are they doing there?*
Tuvieron un accidente **en** la esquina de Domínguez y Figueroa.	*They had an accident at the corner of Dominguez and Figueroa.*

B. **A** is used in Spanish:

1. To refer to a specific moment in time:

¿Cuándo tuvieron el accidente?	*When did they have the accident?*
Esta mañana **a** las once.	*This morning at eleven.*

2. After the verb **llegar** to indicate direction towards a point:

¿Cuándo llegaron **al**   *When did they arrive at the*
  aeropuerto?   *airport?*
Llegaron **al** aeropuerto ayer.   *They arrived at the airport*
                                    yesterday.

Exercise

Complete the following sentences using **a** or **en:**

1. Ellos están _____ la universidad.
2. Hoy no voy a estar _____ casa.
3. Mamá llegó _____ aeropuerto _____ las diez y media.
4. Llegó _____ la estación de policía.
5. Estoy _____ la esquina de Montevideo y Séptima.
6. El accidente fue _____ las ocho.
7. ¿Están _____ el aeropuerto?
8. Tuvimos un accidente cuando llegamos _____ la esquina.

4. CHANGES IN MEANING WITH IMPERFECT AND PRETERIT OF conocer, saber, querer, AND poder

In Spanish, a few verbs change their meaning when used in the preterit or the imperfect:

Preterit		Imperfect	
conocer		**conocer**	
conocí	*I met*	conocía	*I knew, I was acquainted with*
saber		**saber**	
supe	*I found out*	sabía	*I knew (a fact, how to)*
querer		**querer**	
quise	*I tried*	quería	*I wanted*
no quise	*I refused*	no quería	*I didn't want to*
poder		**poder**	
pude	*I succeeded, I was able*	podía	*I had the ability or chance*

Mario, ¿**conocías** a los suegros de Luisa?	*Mario, did you know Louise's parents-in-law?*
No, los **conocí** ayer.	*No, I met them yesterday.*
Rita, ¿**sabías** que teníamos examen hoy?	*Rita, did you know that we had an exam today?*
No, lo **supe** esta mañana.	*No, I found out this morning.*
¿Por qué no fuiste el domingo a la fiesta?	*Why didn't you go to the party on Sunday?*
Yo **quería** ir, pero Carlos **no quiso** llevarme.	*I wanted to go, but Charles refused to take me.*
Ramón, ayer me dijiste que **podías** ayudarme con la tarea y no viniste.	*Raymond, yesterday you told me you could help me with the homework and you didn't come.*
No **pude** salir porque mamá estaba enferma.	*I wasn't able to go out because mother was sick.*

Exercise

Give the Spanish equivalent:

1. We met Julia's father yesterday.
2. She said she couldn't help you with the homework.
3. My father-in-law wasn't able to take his wife to the party.
4. They found out that they had an exam.
5. I didn't know your mother-in-law.
6. He refused to help me.
7. Did you know my address and my telephone number?
8. They wanted to go but weren't able to.

STUDY OF COGNATES

1. This word is the same in Spanish and English, except for a final vowel:

   el accidente   accident

2. Approximate cognates:

el aeropuerto	airport
la estación	station
el examen	exam
el policía	policeman
la policía	police (organization)

NEW VOCABULARY

NOUNS

la cuenta	bill	**llevar**	to take (some-
la esquina	corner		one or
la fiesta	party		something
la suegra	mother-in-law		somewhere)
el suegro	father-in-law	**pensar**	to think
la tarea	homework	**(e > ie)**	
		sentirse	to feel
VERBS		**(e > ie)**	
ayudar	to help		
chocar	to collide, to	OTHER WORDS AND EXPRESSIONS	
	run into	**en casa**	at home
escribir a	to type	**juntos(as)**	together
máquina		**también**	also, too
irse	to leave, to		
	go away		

En la estación de servicio

AL
CONDUCIR
OLVIDE
EL MACHISMO

DGSPvSS

DISTRIBUIDORA
ELECTRO MORELOS, S. A.

Lesson **13**

1. MORE ABOUT IRREGULAR PRETERITS

Stem-changing verbs of the -**ir** conjugation change **e** to **i** or **o** to **u** in the third person singular and plural of the preterit:

sentir (*to feel*)		**dormir** (*to sleep*)	
sentí	sentimos	dormí	dormimos
sentiste		dormiste	
sintió	sintieron	durmió	durmieron

Other verbs that follow the same pattern:

pedir	servir	conseguir
reir(se) (*to laugh*)	repetir	morir (*to die*)
mentir (*to lie*)	seguir	despedirse (*to say good-bye*)

Sra. López, ¿**sintió** Ud. dolor cuando le sacaron la muela?	*Mrs. López, did you feel (any) pain when they took out your tooth?*
No, no sentí nada.	*No, I didn't feel anything.*
¿Cuántas horas **durmió** Ud. anoche?	*How many hours did you sleep last night?*
Yo dormí seis horas, pero Ana y Luis sólo **durmieron** tres.	*I slept six hours, but Anna and Louis slept only three.*
¿A quién le **pidieron** Uds. los documentos?	*Whom did you ask for the documents?*
Se los **pedimos** al director.	*We asked the director (for them).*

Exercise

Complete the sentences with the preterit of the following verbs, as needed. Use each verb only once: **sentir, dormir, pedir, mentir, servir, repetir, seguir, conseguir, morir, reir:**

1. Ellos no me _____ la información.
2. Ayer yo no _____ dolor cuando me sacaron la muela.
3. Ella no me _____. Me dijo la verdad.
4. ¿_____ ellos los refrescos o los _____ tú?
5. El hijo de Carmen no _____ el puesto.
6. Pedro _____ en el accidente de anoche.
7. ¿Dónde _____ Uds. anoche? Yo _____ en el sofá.
8. ¿A quién le _____ Ud. la maleta?
9. Los niños _____ a la maestra.
10. Las niñas se _____ mucho.

2. USES OF **por** AND **para**

A. The preposition **por** is used to indicate:

1. Motion (*through, along, by*):

¿**Por** dónde entró el ladrón?	*How (through where) did the burglar get in?*
Entró **por** la ventana.	*He got in through the window.*
¿A qué hora pasaste **por** mi casa ayer?	*At what time did you go by my house yesterday?*
Pasé **por** tu casa a las tres.	*I went by your house at three o'clock.*

2. Cause or motive of an action (*because of, on account of, in behalf of*):

¿Por qué no vinieron anoche?	*Why didn't you come last night?*
No pudimos venir **por** la lluvia.	*We weren't able to come on account of the rain.*

3. Agency, means, manner, unit of measure (*by, for, per*):

¿Vas a San Francisco **por** avión?	*Are you going to San Francisco by plane?*
No, llevo el coche.	*No, I'm taking the car.*
¿Cuál es el límite de velocidad en California?	*What's the speed limit in California?*
Cincuenta y cinco millas **por** hora.	*Fifty-five miles per hour.*

4. *In exchange for:*

¿Cuánto pagaste **por** ese abrigo?	*How much did you pay for that coat?*
Pagué[1] cien dólares **por** él.	*I paid one hundred dollars for it.*

B. The preposition **para** is used to indicate:

1. Destination in space:

¿A qué hora hay vuelos **para** México?	*What time are there flights to Mexico?*
A las diez y a las doce de la noche.	*At ten and twelve P.M.*

[1] Verbs ending in **-gar** change **g** to **gu** before **e** in the first person of the preterit. (See Verb paradigms in Appendix.)

2. Direction in time (*by, for*); a certain date in the future:

¿Cuándo necesita Ud. las cartas?   *When do you need the letters?*

Las necesito **para** mañana.   *I need them for tomorrow.*

3. Direction toward a recipient:

¿**Para** quién es ese vestido?   *Who is that dress for?*

Es **para** mi suegra.   *It's for my mother-in-law.*

4. *In order to:*

¿**Para** qué necesita Ud. el dinero?   *What do you need the money for?*

Lo necesito **para** pagar la cuenta del hospital.   *I need it (in order) to pay the hospital bill.*

Exercise

Complete the following sentences using **para** or **por,** as needed:

1. Salimos _____ México mañana. Vamos _____ avión.
2. Necesito los exámenes _____ mañana.
3. Anoche Juan pasó _____ mi casa _____ verme.
4. Hoy no hay vuelos _____ Madrid.
5. El ladrón no entró _____ la ventana.
6. ¿Cuánto pagaste _____ esos zapatos?
7. El abrigo no es _____ mi suegra.
8. Conduzco mi coche a 55 millas _____ hora. Ése es el límite de velocidad.
9. No puedo conducir a mucha velocidad _____ la lluvia.
10. Pagué diez dólares _____ este libro.

3. SPECIAL CONSTRUCTION WITH **gustar, doler,** AND **hacer falta**

A. The English verb *to like* is translated in Spanish by the verb **gustar,** which means *to be pleasing:*

English: **I**   *like* **your suit.**
           Subj.   D.O.

Spanish: **Me gusta tu traje.**
           I.O.   Subject

Literally: *Your suit is pleasing to me.*

Notice that the subject of the English sentence (*I*) becomes the indirect object (**me**) of the Spanish sentence. The direct object of the English sentence (*your suit*) becomes the subject of the Spanish sentence (**tu traje**).

ATENCIÓN:

1. When the Spanish subject is plural, the verb is also plural:

Me gust**an esos trajes**   *I like those suits.*
            Subj.

¿**Le gustan** estos edificios?   *Do you like these buildings?*
No, no **me gustan**.   *No, I don't like them.*

2. This construction may also be followed by an infinitive:

¿**Te gusta** caminar?   *Do you like to walk?*
Sí, **me gusta** mucho.   *Yes, I like it very much.*

3. **Más** is the equivalent of *better*. It is placed directly after **gustar:**

¿**Les gusta** a Uds. este modelo?   *Do you like this model?*
Sí, pero **nos gusta más** el otro.   *Yes, but we like the other (one)*
                                             better.

B. The verbs **doler** (*to hurt, to ache*) and **hacer falta** (*to need*) are
   constructed in the same way as **gustar:**

¿Por qué estás tomando   *Why are you taking aspirins?*
   aspirinas?
Porque **me duele** la cabeza.   *Because my head hurts.*

¿Qué **les hace falta**, señoras?   *What do you need, ladies?*
Nos hacen falta toallas y jabón.   *We need towels and soap.*

Exercises

A. Give the Spanish equivalent:

   1. They like those buildings.
   2. I need a suit.
   3. I like this model.
   4. We don't like to take aspirins.
   5. Does your head hurt, madam?
   6. Do you need towels or soap?

B. Answer the following questions:

   1. ¿Qué le duele?
   2. ¿Qué le hace falta a Ud.?
   3. ¿Qué te gusta más, el piano o la radio?
   4. ¿Les hacen falta a Uds. más toallas?
   5. ¿Le duele a Ud. la cabeza?
   6. ¿Te gusta caminar?
   7. ¿Cuándo toman Uds. aspirinas?
   8. ¿Les gusta a Uds. el español?

4. PRONOUNS AS OBJECT OF A PREPOSITION

mí	*me*		nosotros	*us*	
ti	*you*	*(familiar)*			
Ud.	*you*	*(formal)*	Uds.	*you*	*(formal, plural)*
él	*him*		ellos	*them*	*(masc.)*
ella	*her*		ellas	*them*	*(fem.)*

- Notice that the first and second persons singular have special forms. The other persons use the subject pronouns.
- When used with the preposition **con,** the first and second person singular forms become **conmigo** and **contigo:**

¿Viene Ud. a la conferencia **conmigo?**	*Are you coming to the lecture with me?*
No. Voy **con ellos.**	*No. I'm going with them.*
¿Quieres darle las toallas **a ella?**	*Do you want to give the towels to her?*
No. Te las doy **a ti.**	*No. I'm giving them to you.*
¿Es **para nosotros** el regalo?	*Is the gift for us?*
Sí, el regalo es **para Uds.**	*Yes, the gift is for you.*

Exercise

Complete the following sentences with the correct forms of the pronouns:

1. Ella va a la conferencia con _____ (*us*).
2. Le doy el regalo a _____ (*him*).
3. Yo les traigo el jabón a _____ (*you, pl.*)
4. El regalo es para _____ (*her*).
5. Nosotros venimos con _____ (*you, fam. sing.*).
6. Juan se los da a _____ (*them, masc.*).
7. Yo se lo pregunto a _____ (*you, form. sing.*).
8. A _____ (*them, fem.*) les duele la cabeza.
9. La botella de plástico es para _____ (*you, form. sing.*).
10. Ud. viene a clase con _____ (*me*).

STUDY OF COGNATES

1. These words are the same in Spanish and English, except for a final vowel or a single consonant:

   la aspirina aspirin
   el límite limit
   el modelo model

2. Approximate cognates:

   el dólar dollar
   la milla mile

NEW VOCABULARY

Nouns

el avión plane
la cabeza head
la conferencia lecture
el dolor pain
el edificio building
el jabón soap
el ladrón burglar
la lluvia rain
la muela tooth (molar)
el regalo present, gift

la toalla towel
el traje suit
la velocidad speed
el vuelo flight

Verbs

doler (o > ue) to hurt, to ache
entrar to enter
pasar to go by
sacar to take out
tomar to take

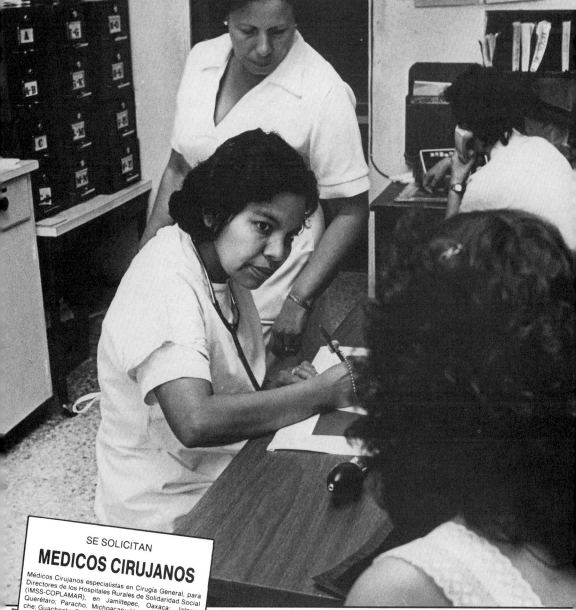

Con la doctora

Lesson 14

1. ¿qué? AND ¿cuál? FOR "WHAT?"

A. When asking for a definition, opinion, or explanation, use ¿qué? to translate *what:*

¿**Qué** es un termómetro?	*What is a thermometer?*
Un termómetro es un instrumento que usamos para medir la temperatura.	*A thermometer is an instrument we use to measure temperature.*
¿**Qué** piensa Ud. de ese perfume?	*What do you think about that perfume?*
Me gusta mucho. Es mi perfume favorito.	*I like it very much. It is my favorite perfume.*
¿**Qué** haces aquí?	*What are you doing here?*
Estoy esperando a un amigo.	*I'm waiting for a friend.*

B. When asking for a choice, use ¿**cuál?** to translate *what.* ¿**Cuál?** carries the idea of selection from among many objects or ideas:

¿**Cuál** es su número de seguro social?	*What is your social security number?*
Mi número de seguro social es 243-50-8139.	*My social security number is 243-50-8139.*
¿**Cuáles** son sus ideas sobre la economía?	*What are your ideas about the economy?*
Está muy mal.	*It is very bad.*

Exercise

Use **qué** or **cuál** to complete the following questions:

1. ¿_____ piensan ellos de la economía?
2. ¿_____ es su número de seguro social?
3. ¿_____ es un termómetro? ¿Un instrumento?
4. ¿_____ hacen ellos aquí?
5. ¿_____ son sus ideas sobre la economía?
6. ¿_____ usamos para medir la temperatura?
7. ¿_____ es su estado civil?
8. ¿_____ es tu perfume favorito?
9. ¿_____ hace el profesor en clase?
10. ¿_____ es tu libro?

2. **hace** MEANING "AGO"

With sentences in the preterit, **hace** + period of time is equivalent to *ago*. When **hace** is placed at the beginning of the sentence, the construction is **hace** + period of time + **que**.

---

　　　　　　hace + *period of time*
La conocí **hace   un año.**

　　　　　　　　　　　　　　　　　　　　　　I met her one year ago.

Hace + *period of time* + **que**
Hace   un año   que la conocí.

¿Cuánto tiempo **hace que** conoció al profesor?　　　*How long ago did you meet the professor?*

Hace un año que lo conocí.　　　*I met him a year ago.*

¿Cuánto tiempo **hace que** llegó?　　　*How long ago did you arrive?*

Llegué **hace dos horas.**　　　*I arrived two hours ago.*

Exercise

Answer the following questions in complete sentences:

1. ¿Cuánto tiempo hace que comenzó la clase?
2. ¿Cuánto tiempo hace que Ud. comió?
3. ¿Cuánto tiempo hace que Uds. empezaron a estudiar español?
4. ¿Cuánto tiempo hace que Uds. terminaron la lección trece?
5. ¿Cuánto tiempo hace que Ud. vino a esta ciudad?

3. USES OF **hacía . . . que**

Hacía . . . que is used:

1. To describe a situation that had been going on for a period of time and was still going on at a given moment in the past:

¿Cuánto tiempo **hacía que** Ud. vivía allí?　　　*How long had you been living there?*

Hacía diez años que vivía allí.　　　*I had been living there for ten years.*

2. To tell of something that was going on in the past when something else happened:

¿Cuánto tiempo **hacía que** esperabas cuando él llegó?	*How long had you been waiting when he arrived?*
Hacía dos horas y media que esperaba cuando él llegó.	*I had been waiting for two and a half hours when he arrived.*

ATENCIÓN: Notice that in the **hacía . . . que** construction, the verb that follows it is always in the imperfect tense:

¿Cuánto tiempo **hacía que estudiabas?**	*How long had you been studying?*
Hacía tres años **que estudiaba.**	*I had been studying for three years.*

Exercise

Give the Spanish equivalent:

1. She had been living there for two months when she met him.
2. How long had you been living there?
3. They had been studying for four years.
4. I had been working for two weeks when she arrived.
5. How long had you known him?

4. MORE USES OF THE DEFINITE ARTICLE

Spanish uses the definite article in the following cases:

1. With parts of the body or with articles of clothing in place of the possessive adjectives:

¿Dónde le duele?	*Where does it hurt?*
Me duele **el** estómago.	*My stomach hurts.*
Lávese **las** manos, por favor.	*Wash your hands, please.*
¿Por qué te quitas **el** abrigo?	*Why are you taking your coat off?*
Porque tengo calor.	*Because I'm hot.*

2. With the nouns **cárcel, iglesia,** and **escuela** when they are preceded by a preposition:

¿Por qué está Jorge en **la** cárcel?	*Why is George in jail?*
Porque mató a un hombre.	*Because he killed a man.*
¿A dónde va esa mujer todos los domingos?	*Where does that woman go every Sunday?*
Va a **la** iglesia.	*She goes to church.*
¿Dónde está Felipe?	*Where is Philip?*
Está en **la** escuela.	*He is at school.*

3. Before titles such as **señor, señora, doctor, profesora,** etc., when talking about the person and not directly to him or her:

Buenos días, señor García.	*Good morning, Mr. Garcia.*
¿Cómo está **el** doctor Orta?	*How is Doctor Orta?*
Está bien, gracias.	*He is well, thank you.*

Exercise

Give the Spanish equivalent:

1. I want to see Mrs. Mata.
2. Does your stomach hurt?
3. I washed my hands and put on my dress.
4. Good afternoon, doctor Morales.
5. The man is in jail because he killed a woman.
6. They are not in school. They went to church.

5. PAST PARTICIPLES

A. Regular past participles are formed by adding the following endings to the stem of the verb:

Part Participle Endings		
-ar Verbs	*-er Verbs*	*-ir Verbs*
habl- **ado**	ten- **ido**	ven- **ido**

B. The following verbs have irregular past participles in Spanish:

abrir	**abierto**	morir	**muerto**
cubrir	**cubierto**	poner	**puesto**
decir	**dicho**	ver	**visto**
escribir	**escrito**	volver	**vuelto**
hacer	**hecho**	romper	**roto**

● The past participle is used with the auxiliary verb **haber** (*to have*)[1] to form the compound tenses. These will be discussed in Lesson 15.

Exercise

Give the past participles of the following verbs:

1. dormir	6. cubrir	11. caminar	16. abrir
2. romper	7. recibir	12. pedir	17. ver
3. estar	8. hacer	13. decir	18. volver
4. comer	9. cerrar	14. comprar	19. aprender
5. poner	10. ser	15. morir	20. escribir

[1] Note that *to have* has two equivalents in Spanish: **haber** (used only as an auxiliary verb) and **tener.**

STUDY OF COGNATES

1. Exact cognates:

   la idea   idea
   el perfume   perfume

2. This word is the same in Spanish and English, except for a final vowel:

   el instrumento   instrument

3. Approximate cognates:

   favorito   favorite
   la temperatura temperature
   el termómetro   thermometer

NEW VOCABULARY

NOUNS

la cárcel   jail
el estómago stomach
la iglesia   church

VERBS
cubrir   to cover
lavar(se) to wash
               (oneself)

matar   to kill
medir (e > i) to measure
quitar(se)   to take off
romper   to break
usar   to use

OTHER WORDS AND EXPRESSIONS

sobre   about
todos   every, all

En el tren para Sevilla

RENFE

BILLETE

AZ 261943

23 JUL 1976
Sello dependencia expendedora
SALAMANCA

5

EXPEDICION ELECTRONICA

NUM. DE TREN	FECHA	CLASE	NUM. DE COCHE	ASIENTO	HORA DE SALIDA	TARIFA	PRECIO	PTS.
						01291168.		

0164122907304017000023000011C1291168.
TER 29.07 1 G.1 S R C8.27 1C 667
3411C1041C1C0C304

NUM. DE CONTROL

Lesson 15

1. THE PRESENT PERFECT TENSE

A. The present indicative of the auxiliary verb **haber** is as follows:

yo	he	nosotros	hemos
tú	has		
Ud. ⎱		Uds. ⎱	
él ⎬ ha		ellos ⎬ han	
ella ⎰		ellas ⎰	

B. The present perfect tense is formed by using the present tense of the auxiliary verb **haber** and the past participle of the verb to be conjugated:

Present Perfect Tense

hablar		tener		venir	
he	hablado	**he**	tenido	**he**	venido
has	hablado	**has**	tenido	**has**	venido
ha	hablado	**ha**	tenido	**ha**	venido
hemos	hablado	**hemos**	tenido	**hemos**	venido
han	hablado	**han**	tenido	**han**	venido

¿**Ha terminado** Ud. su lección de matemáticas?
No, no la **he terminado** todavía.

Have you finished your math lesson?
No, I haven't finished it yet.

¿Cuántas veces **ha venido** ella a este lugar?
Ella **ha venido** muchas veces.

How many times has she come to this place?
She has come many times.

¿De qué **han hablado** Uds.?
Hemos hablado de negocios.

What have you talked about?
We have talked about business.

¿Qué les **ha dicho** el gerente?
El gerente nos **ha dicho** que tenemos que terminar el trabajo para mañana.

What has the manager said to you?
The manager has told us that we have to finish the work for tomorrow.

ATENCIÓN: Note that when the past participle is part of a perfect tense, it is invariable and cannot be separated from the auxiliary verb **haber**:

¿Qué **ha hecho** Ud. hoy?
Hoy, no **he hecho** nada.

*What **have you done** today?*
Today, I haven't done anything.

Exercise

Item Substitution:

1. El gerente **ha hablado** de negocios. (Yo, Ud., Nosotras, Ella, Tú)
2. Ellos ya **han terminado** el trabajo. (Ud., Nosotros, Tú, Él, Yo)
3. Yo **he escrito** la carta. (Nosotros, Uds., Ella, Yo, Tú)
4. Ud. **ha abierto** la puerta. (Yo, Él, Uds., Nosotras, Ellas)
5. Uds. **han venido** a este lugar. (Tú, Ellos, Yo, Él, Nosotros)

2. THE PAST PERFECT TENSE (PLUPERFECT)

The pluperfect tense is formed by using the imperfect tense of the auxiliary verb **haber** and the past participle of the verb to be conjugated:

Past Perfect Tense					
hablar		**tener**		**venir**	
había	hab**lado**	**había**	ten**ido**	**había**	ven**ido**
habías	hab**lado**	**habías**	ten**ido**	**habías**	ven**ido**
había	hab**lado**	**había**	ten**ido**	**había**	ven**ido**
habíamos	hab**lado**	**habíamos**	ten**ido**	**habíamos**	ven**ido**
habían	hab**lado**	**habían**	ten**ido**	**habían**	ven**ido**

¿No trajiste las sábanas?
Ya las **había traido** Ernesto.

Didn't you bring the sheets?
Ernest had already brought them.

¿De qué **había hablado** el doctor Peña?
El Dr. Peña **había hablado** de sus experimentos con plantas tropicales.

What had Dr. Peña talked about?
Dr. Peña had talked about his experiments with tropical plants.

¿Para qué **habían venido** ellos?
Habían venido para ver al administrador.

What had they come for?
They had come to see the administrator.

Exercise

Change the following sentences to the past perfect:

1. Ella está enferma.
2. Vinieron a ver al administrador.
3. Ud. cubrió los instrumentos.
4. Yo hablo de mis experimentos con plantas tropicales.
5. Nosotros vimos las sábanas.

6. Uds. rompieron la puerta.
7. Yo salí a las cinco.
8. Ellas ya estudiaron la lección de matemáticas.
9. Tú puedes hacerlo.
10. Ud. durmió hasta muy tarde.

3. PAST PARTICIPLES USED AS ADJECTIVES

In Spanish most past participles may be used as adjectives. As such, they agree in number and gender with the nouns they modify:

¿Ha tenido Ud. un accidente?	*Have you had an accident?*
Sí, y tengo **la pierna rota.**	*Yes, and I have a broken leg.*
¿Y el brazo?	*And your arm?*
No, **el brazo** no está **roto.**	*No, my arm is not broken.*
Entonces, ¿no ha terminado los artículos?	*Then, haven't you finished the articles?*
Sí, **los artículos** ya están **escritos.**	*Yes, the articles are already written.*

Exercise

Complete the following sentences with the past participle of the verbs in parentheses. Read the completed sentences aloud:

1. Los niños están _____ (morir).
2. Pedro y yo estamos _____ (cansar).
3. Juan tiene las piernas _____ (romper).
4. El libro _____ (abrir) es del administrador.
5. Entonces la lección está _____ (terminar).
6. Los instrumentos están _____ (cubrir).
7. Las puertas no están _____ (abrir).
8. El brazo del niño no está _____ (romper).
9. Las ventanas estaban _____ (cerrar).
10. Todos los artículos están _____ (escribir).

4. DIMINUTIVE SUFFIXES

To express the idea of size, and also to denote affection, Spanish uses different suffixes. The most common suffixes are **-ito(a)** and **-cito(a).** There are no set rules for forming the diminutive, but usually if the word ends in **-a** or **-o,** these vowels are dropped and **-ito(a)** is added:

niño	niñ + **ito** =	**niñito** (*little boy*)
niña	niñ + **ita** =	**niñita** (*little girl*)
abuelo	abuel + **ito** =	**abuelito** (*grandpa*)
Ana	An + **ita** =	**Anita**

If the word ends in a consonant other than **-n** or **-r**, the suffix **ito(a)** is added:

árbol + **ito** =	**arbolito** (*little tree*)
Luis + **ito** =	**Luisito**

If the word ends in **-e, -n** or **-r**, the suffix **-cito(a)** is added:

coche + **cito** =	**cochecito** (*little car*)
mujer + **cita** =	**mujercita** (*little woman*)
Carmen + **cita** =	**Carmencita**

Hola, **abuelo.** ¿Me trajiste el **arbolito** de Navidad?   *Hello, grandpa. Did you bring me the little Christmas tree?*
Sí, **Tomasito.**   *Yes, Tommy.*

Me gusta tu **cochecito.**   *I like your little car.*
Gracias, **Carmencita.**   *Thanks, Carmen.*

Exercise

Give the diminutive corresponding to each of the following:

1. primo
2. escuela
3. árbol
4. Raúl
5. coche
6. hermana
7. favor
8. Juan
9. Adela
10. mamá

STUDY OF COGNATES

1. Exact cognate:

   tropical   tropical

2. These words are the same in Spanish and English, except for a final vowel:

   la planta   plant
   el experimento   experiment

3. Approximate cognates:

   el administrador   administrator
   el artículo   article
   las matemáticas   mathematics

NEW VOCABULARY

NOUNS		VERB	
el árbol	tree	terminar	to finish
el brazo	arm		
el gerente	manager	OTHER WORDS AND EXPRESSIONS	
el lugar	place	¿cuántas veces?	how many times?
los negocios	business		
la Navidad	Christmas	entonces	then
la niña	girl, child	muchas veces	many times, often
el niño	boy, child		
la pierna	leg		
la sábana	sheet		
el trabajo	work		

Test Yourself: Lessons 11-15

LESSON 11

A. Time expressions with **hacer** and **llevar**

Give two Spanish equivalents for each of the sentences. Follow the models:

Modelos: How long have you lived in California?
a) **¿Cuánto tiempo hace que vive en California?**
b) **¿Cuánto tiempo lleva viviendo en California?**

I have been living in California for two months.
a) **Hace dos meses que vivo en California.**
b) **Llevo dos meses viviendo en California.**

1. How long have you worked in Lima?
2. We have worked in Lima for five years.
3. How long have they waited?
4. They have waited for three hours.
5. How long has she studied Spanish?
6. She has studied Spanish for two years.

B. Irregular preterits

Rewrite the sentences, according to the new beginnings. Follow the model:

Modelo: Tenemos que salir. (Ayer)
Ayer tuvimos que salir.

1. María está muy ocupada. (Ayer)
2. No pueden venir. (Anoche)
3. Pongo el dinero en el banco. (La semana pasada)
4. No haces nada. (El domingo pasado)
5. Ella viene con Juan. (Ayer)
6. No queremos venir a clase. (La semana pasada)
7. Yo no digo nada. (Anoche)
8. Traemos la máquina de escribir. (Ayer)
9. Yo conduzco mi coche. (Anoche)
10. Ellos traducen las lecciones. (Ayer)

C. **¿De quién . . . ?** for "Whose?"

Ask who these items belong to. Follow the model:

Modelo: esta máquina de escribir
¿De quién es esta máquina de escribir?

1. ese paraguas
2. esos revólveres
3. estos zapatos
4. este dinero
5. aquella silla

D. The imperfect tense

Answer the following questions, according to the model:

Modelo: ¿Qué querían ellos? (arroz con pollo)
Querían arroz con pollo.

1. ¿Dónde vivían Uds. cuando eran chicos? (en Alaska)
2. ¿Qué idioma hablabas tú cuando eras chico(a)? (inglés)
3. ¿A quién veías siempre cuando eras chico(a)? (a mi abuela)
4. ¿En qué banco depositaban Uds. el dinero? (en el Banco de América)
5. ¿A qué hora se acostaban los niños? (a las nueve)
6. ¿A dónde iba Rosa? (al cine)
7. ¿Qué compraba Ud.? (café)
8. ¿En qué gastaban Uds. su dinero? (en libros)

LESSON 12

A. The past progressive

Complete the sentences with the past progressive of the following verbs, as needed. Use each verb once: **hacer, hablar, estudiar, comer, pensar, leer, trabajar, escribir**

1. Nosotros _____ arroz con pollo cuando llegó Elsa.
2. ¿Qué _____ Uds. cuando yo llamé?
3. Elena _____ a máquina cuando llegó el doctor Vargas.
4. Yo _____ por teléfono con mi hijo.
5. ¿En qué _____ tú cuando yo te hablé?
6. Ud. _____ el periódico cuando yo vine.
7. Los niños _____ la lección.
8. Roberto _____ en el garaje cuando yo lo vi.

B. Preterit vs. imperfect

Give the Spanish equivalent:

1. We went to bed at eleven last night.
2. She was very busy when I saw her.
3. We used to go to Buenos Aires.
4. It was ten-thirty when I called him.
5. She said she wanted to read.

C. **En** and **a** for "at"

Write sentences, using these items. Follow the model:

Modelo: Yo / estar / universidad / anoche
     Yo estuve en la universidad anoche.

1. Nosotros / llegar / aeropuerto / seis y media
2. Mi hermana / estar / casa
3. Ellos / estar / esquina de Unión y Figueroa
4. El accidente / ser / las doce
5. Yo / estar / la estación de policía / ayer

D. Changes in meaning with imperfect and preterit of **conocer, saber, querer,** and **poder**

Complete the sentences with the preterit or the imperfect of the verbs **conocer, saber, querer,** and **poder,** as needed:

1. Yo no _____ a los abuelos de María. Los _____ ayer.
2. Nosotros no _____ que ella era casada. Lo _____ anoche.
3. Pedro dijo que no _____ venir, pero vino a eso de las dos.
4. Ellos no _____ llamarte por teléfono porque estaban trabajando. Por eso no te llamaron.
5. Mamá no vino a la reunión porque no _____ venir.
6. Yo no _____ ir a la fiesta, pero cuando _____ que Carlos iba a ir, decidí ir también.

LESSON 13

A. More about irregular preterits

Rewrite the sentences, according to the new beginnings. Follow the model:

Modelo: Él no pide dinero. (Ayer)
     Ayer él no pidió dinero.

1. Él siente mucho dolor. (Ayer)
2. Marta no duerme bien. (Anoche)
3. No le pido nada. (Ayer)
4. Ella te miente. (La semana pasada)
5. Ellos sirven los refrescos. (El sábado pasado)
6. No lo repito. (Ayer)
7. Ella sigue estudiando. (Anoche)
8. Tú no consigues nada. (El lunes pasado)

B. Uses of **por** and **para**

Give the Spanish equivalent:

1. The thief went in through the window.
2. She went by my house.
3. She wasn't able to come on account of the rain.
4. There are flights to Mexico on Saturdays.
5. We are going by plane.
6. He needs the shirt for tomorrow.
7. He was going at ninety miles per hour.
8. Who is the newspaper for?
9. I need the money to pay the bill.
10. She paid two hundred dollars for that dress.

C. Special construction with **gustar, doler,** and **hacer falta**

Complete the sentences with the appropriate forms of **gustar, doler,** and **hacer falta,** as needed:

1. No _____ esos edificios. Prefiero aquéllos.
2. ¿Qué _____ señora? ¿Jabón?
3. A Marta _____ la cabeza. ¿Tienes aspirinas?
4. A nosotros no _____ dinero. No necesitamos comprar nada.
5. ¿_____ a Ud. este modelo, o prefiere el otro?
6. _____ toallas. ¿Puede traérmelas, por favor?
7. _____ la muela. Tengo que ir al dentista.
8. ¿No _____ caminar? ¡Podemos ir en coche!

D. Pronouns as object of a preposition

Give the Spanish equivalent:

1. Can you come with me?
2. Are you going to work with them?
3. To whom did she give the towels? To you?
4. The gift is not for me. It is for her.
5. No, Charlie. I can't go with you.

LESSON 14

A. **¿Qué?** and **¿cuál?** for "what?"

Give the Spanish equivalent:

1. What is freedom?
2. What are you doing here?

3. What does the teacher think about him?
4. What is your telephone number?
5. What are his ideas about this?

B. **Hace** meaning "ago"

Write two sentences for each set of items. Follow the model:

Modelo: Un año / yo / conocer / él
Hace un año que yo lo conocí.
Yo lo conocí hace un año.

1. tres meses / nosotros / llegar / a California
2. doce horas / Ud. / comer
3. dos días / ellos / terminar / el trabajo
4. veinte años / ella / ver / él
5. quince días / tú / venir / a esta ciudad

C. Uses of **hacía . . . que**

Answer the following questions, according to the model:

Modelo: ¿Cuánto tiempo hacía que Ud. vivía allí? (tres años)
Hacía tres años que yo vivía allí.

1. ¿Cuánto tiempo hacía que Ud. no comía? (diez horas)
2. ¿Cuánto tiempo hacía que Uds. lo esperaban cuando él llegó? (media hora)
3. ¿Cuánto tiempo hacía que estudiabas español cuando fuiste a Madrid? (dos meses)
4. ¿Cuánto tiempo hacía que él vivía en Quito? (cuatro años)
5. ¿Cuánto tiempo hacía que Uds. trabajaban para el gobierno? (quince años)

D. More uses of the definite article

Write sentences using these items. Follow the model:

Modelo: A mí / doler / estómago
Me duele el estómago.

1. Ana / estar / escuela
2. Ella / lavarse / manos
3. Tú / quitarse / abrigo
4. Mamá / ir / iglesia / domingos
5. Felipe / estar / cárcel
6. Nosotros / visitar / señorita García

E. Past participles

Complete the following chart:

Infinitive	Past Participle
1. trabajar	1. trabajado
2. recibir	2. _____
3. _____	3. vuelto
4. hablar	4. _____
5. escribir	5. _____
6. _____	6. ido
7. aprender	7. _____
8. _____	8. abierto
9. cubrir	9. _____
10. comer	10. _____
11. _____	11. visto
12. hacer	12. _____
13. ser	13. _____
14. _____	14. dicho
15. cerrar	15. _____
16. _____	16. muerto
17. _____	17. roto
18. dormir	18. _____
19. estar	19. _____
20. _____	20. puesto

LESSON 15

A. The present perfect tense

Complete the sentences with the present perfect of the following verbs. Use each verb once: **hablar, hacer, abrir, venir, decir, terminar, escribir, tener, poner.**

1. Yo _____ muchas veces a este lugar.
2. ¿_____ Uds. la lección de matemáticas?
3. Nosotros todavía no _____ de negocios con el gerente del hotel.
4. Ellos me _____ que tengo que venir el sábado y el domingo.
5. ¿No _____ (tú) las cartas todavía?
6. Hoy nosotros no _____ nada, porque no _____ tiempo.
7. ¿Quién _____ las puertas?
8. ¿Dónde _____ Ud. las sillas?

B. The past perfect tense

Give the Spanish equivalent:

1. I had already brought the sheets.
2. We had written to him about our experiments with tropical plants.
3. They had broken the pencils.
4. He had already seen the administrator.
5. Had you covered the tables, Miss Peña?

C. Past participles used as adjectives

Give the Spanish equivalent:

1. The article is written.
2. These are the broken chairs.
3. The door is open.
4. Are the books closed?
5. The work is finished.

D. Diminutive suffixes

Complete the following sentences with the Spanish equivalent of the words in parentheses:

1. Yo ya compré el _____ (*little tree*) de Navidad.
2. Mi _____ (*little sister*) se llama _____ (*little Theresa*).
3. Puedes hacerme un _____ (*little dress*) para mi _____ (*little daughter*)
4. Fuimos a Disneylandia con _____ (*little John*).
5. Tenemos un _____ (*little car*) muy bueno.

Joyas en la vidriera

COMPOSTURAS DE RELOJES
CON APARATOS ELECTRONICOS
COMPOSTURAS DE ALHAJAS
GARANTIZADAS

562-7001-22-51

La Joya Suiza
en
Relojes

ORIS

Lesson **16**

1. THE FUTURE TENSE

A. Most Spanish verbs are regular in the future. The infinitive serves as the stem of almost all verbs. The endings are the same for all three conjugations. The English equivalent is *will* plus *verb*.

The Future Tense			
Infinitive		*Stems*	*Endings*
trabajar	yo	trabajar-	é
aprender	tú	aprender-	ás
escribir	Ud.	escribir-	á
hablar	él	hablar-	á
decidir	ella	decidir-	á
entender	nosotros	entender-	**emos**
caminar	Uds.	caminar-	án
perder	ellos	perder-	án
recibir	ellas	recibir-	án

ATENCIÓN: Notice that all the endings, except the one for the **nosotros** form, have written accent marks.

¿**Irán** ustedes a la conferencia sobre la civilización y la cultura de México?	*Will you go to the lecture on the civilization and the culture of Mexico?*
Sí, **iremos** todos, sin falta.	*Yes, we'll all go without fail.*
¿Ud. cree que el paciente **mejorará** pronto?	*Do you think the patient will improve soon?*
Yo creo que sí.	*I think so.*
¿Cuándo **estarán** listos los análisis?	*When will the tests be ready?*
Estarán listos mañana por la tarde.	*They will be ready tomorrow afternoon.*

Exercise

Change the following sentences to the future tense:

1. Nosotros somos los primeros.
2. ¿El paciente mejora?
3. Los alumnos entienden la lección.
4. Los análisis están listos.
5. Él no entiende los problemas de la economía.
6. ¿Tú aprendes español?
7. Yo compro las sábanas.
8. Uds. lo deciden el próximo mes.

9. Ellos escriben sobre la cultura y la civilización de México.
10. Ella va a clase sin falta.
11. Roberto habla con el profesor.
12. Los estudiantes comen en la cafetería.
13. Nosotros caminamos por la ciudad.
14. Tú no trabajas aquí.
15. ¿Van Uds. a la conferencia?

B. A small number of verbs are irregular in the future. These verbs use a modified form of the infinitive as a stem. The endings are the same.

Infinitive	Modified Form (Stem)	Future Tense		
decir	dir-	yo	dir-	é
hacer	har-	tú	har-	ás
saber	sabr-	Ud.	sabr-	á
haber	habr-	él	habr-	á
poder	podr-	ella	podr-	á
poner	pondr-	nosotros	pondr-	emos
venir	vendr-	Uds.	vendr-	án
tener	tendr-	ellos	tendr-	án
salir	saldr-	ellas	saldr-	án

¿Les has dicho la fecha de la reunión?	Have you told them the date of the meeting?
No, se la **diré** después.	No, I'll tell (it to) them later.
¿Cuándo **sabrán** Uds. el resultado de los análisis?	When will you know the result of the tests?
Lo **sabremos** la semana próxima.	We will know it next week.
¿**Vendrá** hoy el mecánico a arreglar el coche?	Will the mechanic come today to fix the car?
Sí, **vendrá** por la tarde.	Yes, he will come in the afternoon.

Exercise

Complete the following sentences with the future tense of the verbs in parentheses:

1. ¿Qué les _____ Ud. a sus pacientes? (decir)
2. Los padres de ella _____ después. (salir)
3. Nosotros _____ con el director del banco. (venir)
4. Yo _____ los resultados mañana. (tener)
5. El mecánico no _____ arreglar el coche. (poder)

6. ¿Cuándo _____ Ud. la fecha del examen? (saber)
7. ¿Qué _____ tú en el verano? (hacer)
8. Mañana _____ una reunión. (haber)
9. ¿_____ Uds. el dinero en el banco? (poner)
10. ¿Crees tú que él _____ con nosotros? ¡Yo creo que sí! (venir)

2. THE CONDITIONAL TENSE

A. The Spanish conditional tense is equivalent in meaning to the English conditional (*should* or *would*). Like the future, the conditional has only one ending for all three conjugations. It also uses the infinitive as the stem.

The Conditional Tense			
Infinitive		*Stem*	*Endings*
trabajar	yo	trabajar-	ía
aprender	tú	aprender-	ías
escribir	Ud.	escribir-	ía
ir	él	ir-	ía
ser	ella	ser-	ía
dar	nosotros	dar-	íamos
servir	Uds.	servir-	ían
estar	ellos	estar-	ían
preferir	ellas	preferir-	ían

¿**Vendería** Ud. su casa por cincuenta mil dólares?

Would you sell your house for fifty thousand dollars?

No, yo no la **vendería** a ese precio.

No, I wouldn't sell it at that price.

¿**Preferirían** Uds. ir conmigo a Europa?

Would you prefer to go to Europe with me?

Sí, **preferiríamos** ir contigo.

Yes, we would prefer going with you.

The conditional is also used to describe a future action in relation to the past:

Mi sobrino **dijo** que **trabajaría** en una estación de servicio el verano próximo.
¡Buena idea!

My nephew said he would work at a service station next summer.
Good idea!

Exercise

Item substitution:

1. Yo no vendería mi casa a ese precio. (Uds., Tú, Ella, Nosotros)
2. Nosotros no le escribiríamos. (Yo, Tú, Ellos, Él, Uds.)
3. Ellas serían felices. (Nosotros, Yo, Ud., Tú, Ella)
4. Mi sobrino trabajaría en la estación de servicio. (Yo, Nosotros, Uds., Tú, Ud., Ellos)
5. Ud. dijo que serviría el café. (Yo, Nosotros, Tú, Ella, Ellos)

B. The same verbs that have irregular stems in the future tense are also irregular in the conditional. The endings are the same as the ones for regular verbs.

Infinitive	Modified Form (Stem)	Conditional Tense		
decir	dir-	yo	**dir-**	ía
hacer	har-	tú	**har-**	ías
saber	sabr-	Ud.	**sabr-**	ía
haber	habr-	él	**habr-**	ía
poder	podr-	ella	**podr-**	ía
poner	pondr-	nosotros	**pondr-**	íamos
venir	vendr-	Uds.	**vendr-**	ían
tener	tendr-	ellos	**tendr-**	ían
salir	saldr-	ellas	**saldr-**	ían

¿Lo **harían** Uds.?	*Would you do it?*
No, no lo **haríamos.**	*No, we wouldn't do it.*
¿**Saldrías** conmigo?	*Would you go out with me?*
No, no **saldría** contigo.	*No, I wouldn't go out with you.*
¿**Podría** él llegar a tiempo?	*Would he be able to arrive on time?*
No, no **podría** llegar a tiempo.	*No, he wouldn't be able to arrive on time.*

Exercises

A. Change the following sentences according to the model:

Modelo: Dice que lo **hará.** (Dijo)
   Dijo que lo haría.

1. Digo que vendré. (Dije)
2. Decimos que saldremos. (Dijimos)
3. Dices que lo pondrás en el banco. (Dijiste)
4. Ud. dice que lo sabrá mañana. (Ud. dijo)
5. Dicen que se lo dirán hoy. (Dijeron)

6. Dice que habrá una reunión. (Dijo)
7. Digo que no podré ir. (Dije)
8. Dices que lo tendrás listo hoy. (Dijiste)

B. Give the Spanish equivalent:

1. Would the men arrive on time?
2. My mother wouldn't do it.
3. They wouldn't know what to say.
4. Would you like to go to Europe?
5. Would the mechanic be at the service station?
6. We wouldn't tell (it to) him.
7. Did she say there would be a meeting?
8. She said she wouldn't be able to work.

3. THE PRESENT SUBJUNCTIVE

Use of the Present Subjunctive

A. The present subjunctive is used almost exclusively in subordinate clauses when the speaker has doubts, uncertainty, or strong feelings about an action or assertion. For example, it is used when a contrary-to-fact supposition is made. The subjunctive expresses the subjectivity or mental uncertainty of the speaker.

B. The subjunctive is also used in English, although not as often as in Spanish. For example:

*I suggest that he **arrive** tomorrow.*

As in Spanish, the expression that requires the use of the subjunctive is in the main clause (*I suggest*). The subjunctive itself appears in the subordinate clause (*that he **arrive** tomorrow*).

C. There are three main concepts that call for the use of the subjunctive in Spanish:

1. Command: indirect or implied:

Ella quiere que yo le **escriba.**

2. Emotion: pity, joy, fear, surprise, hope, desire, etc.:

Espero que Uds. **puedan** venir.

3. Unreality: indefiniteness, doubt, uncertainty, nonexistence:

No hay nadie que **sepa** hacerlo.

Formation of the Present Subjunctive

The present subjunctive is formed by adding the following endings to the stem of the first person singular of the present indicative, after dropping the **-o**:

The Present Subjunctive of Regular Verbs		
-ar *Verbs*	-er *Verbs*	-ir *Verbs*
trabajar	**comer**	**vivir**
trabaj- **e**	com- **a**	viv- **a**
trabaj- **es**	com- **as**	viv- **as**
trabaj- **e**	com- **a**	viv- **a**
trabaj- **emos**	com- **amos**	viv- **amos**
trabaj- **en**	com- **an**	viv- **an**

ATENCIÓN: Notice that the endings for the **-er** and **-ir** verbs are the same.

The following table shows you how to form the first person singular of the present subjunctive from the infinitive of the verb:

Verb	First Person Singular (Indicative)	Stem	First Person Singular (Present Subjunctive)
ha**blar**	hablo	habl-	hable
apr**ender**	aprendo	aprend-	aprenda
escr**ibir**	escribo	escrib-	escriba
decir	digo	dig-	diga
hacer	hago	hag-	haga
traer	traigo	traig-	traiga
venir	vengo	veng-	venga
conocer	conozco	conozc-	conozca

Exercise

Give the present subjunctive of the following verbs:

1. **yo:**   comer, venir, hablar, hacer, salir, ponerse
2. **tú:**   decir, ver, traer, trabajar, escribir, acostarse
3. **él:**   vivir, aprender, salir, estudiar, levantarse
4. **nosotros:** escribir, caminar, poner, desear, tener, afeitarse
5. **ellos:**   salir, hacer, llevar, conocer, ver, bañarse

Subjunctive Forms of Stem-changing Verbs

1. **-ar** and **-er** verbs maintain the basic pattern of the present indicative. That is, their stems undergo the same changes in the present subjunctive:

recomendar *(to recommend)*		**recordar** *(to remember)*	
recomiende	recomendemos	recuerde	recordemos
recomiendes		recuerdes	
recomiende	recomienden	recuerde	recuerden

entender *(to understand)*		**mover** *(to move)*	
entienda	entendamos	mueva	movamos
entiendas		muevas	
entienda	entiendan	mueva	muevan

2. **-ir** verbs change the unstressed **e** to **i** and the unstressed **o** to **u** in the first and second person plural:

mentir *(to lie)*		**dormir** *(to sleep)*	
mienta	mintamos	duerma	durmamos
mientas		duermas	
mienta	mientan	duerma	duerman

Verbs That Are Irregular in the Subjunctive

dar	estar	haber	saber	ser	ir
dé	esté	haya	sepa	sea	vaya
des	estés	hayas	sepas	seas	vayas
dé	esté	haya	sepa	sea	vaya
demos	estemos	hayamos	sepamos	seamos	vayamos
den	estén	hayan	sepan	sean	vayan

Exercise

Give the present subjunctive of the following verbs:

1. **yo:**   dormir, mover, cerrar, sentir, ser
2. **tú:**   mentir, volver, ir, dar, recordar
3. **ella:**   estar, saber, perder, dormir, ser
4. **nosotros:** pensar, recordar, dar, morir, cerrar
5. **ellos:**   ver, preferir, dar, ir, saber

STUDY OF COGNATES

1. Spanish word ending in **-ción** instead of English *-tion:*

   la civilización   civilization

2. Approximate cognates:

la cultura	culture
Europa	Europe
el mecánico	mechanic
el paciente	patient
el resultado	result

NEW VOCABULARY

NOUNS

el análisis	test
la estación de servicio	service station
la fecha	date
el precio	price
la sobrina	niece
el sobrino	nephew

VERBS

arreglar	to fix, to arrange
mejorar	to improve
vender	to sell

OTHER WORDS AND EXPRESSIONS

a tiempo	on time
después	later, afterwards
estar listo(a)	to be ready
sin falta	without fail
yo creo que sí	I think so
pronto	soon

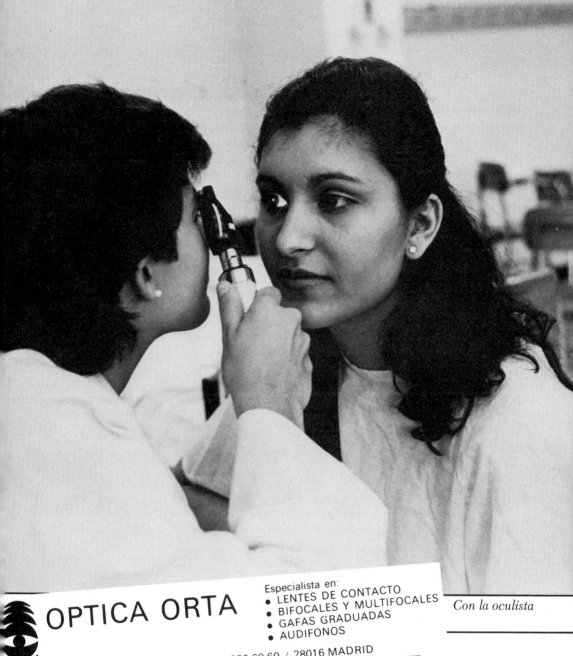

Con la oculista

Lesson **17**

1. THE SUBJUNCTIVE IN INDIRECT OR IMPLIED COMMANDS

A. All indirect and implied commands use the present subjunctive. In this type of sentence, there must be a different subject in the subordinate clause in order to maintain the indirect command in the main clause. Some common verbs used in the indirect command are: **querer, aconsejar** (*to advise*), **sugerir** (*to suggest*), etc. Notice the structure in the use of the subjunctive:

I want	you to study.
Yo quiero que	**Ud. estudie.**
main clause	subordinate clause

Mañana tengo examen de geografía física.	*I have an exam in physical geography tomorrow.*
Pues te aconsejo que **estudies.**	*Well, I advise you to study.*
¿Qué quiere que yo **haga?**	*What do you want me to do?*
Quiero que Ud. me **traiga** esos paquetes.	*I want you to bring me those packages.*

ATENCIÓN: If there is no change of subject, the infinitive is used:

¿Qué quiere **hacer** Ud.?	*What do you want to do?*
Yo quiero **traer** esos paquetes.	*I want to bring those packages.*

Exercise

Complete the following sentences with the present subjunctive of the verbs in parentheses:

1. Yo te sugiero que _____ (hacer) el trabajo hoy.
2. Nosotros queremos que Ud. _____ (sentarse).
3. Ud. me aconseja que yo _____ (venir) temprano.
4. Ellos necesitan que él _____ (traer) los paquetes.
5. Él me pide que yo lo _____ (ayudar).
6. Uds. les dicen a ellas que _____ (abrir) la puerta.
7. Ellos prefieren que nosotros _____ (ir) a la oficina.
8. La doctora Rivas quiere que Ud. _____ (venir) por la tarde.
9. El profesor nos dice que _____ (estudiar) geografía física.
10. Yo no quiero que Uds. me _____ (dar) nada.

B. Sometimes the main clause in which the command is expressed is omitted in Spanish, but the expression of the speaker's will is easily understood:

¿Qué quiere Ud. que **hagan** los muchachos?	*What do you want the boys to do?*

(Quiero) Que **estudien.**	*I want them to study.*
¿Va Ud. a hacer el trabajo?	*Are you going to do the work?*
No. Que lo **haga** Jorge.	*No. Let George do it.*

Exercise

Respond, following the models:

Modelo: ¿Quién va a hacerlo? ¿Ud.?
¡Yo no! ¡Que lo haga ella!

1. ¿Quién va a salir? ¿Ud.?
2. ¿Quién va a comer? ¿Ud.?
3. ¿Quién va a ir? ¿Ud.?
4. ¿Quién va a hablar? ¿Ud.?
5. ¿Quién va a traerlo? ¿Ud.?

Modelo: ¿No va a entrar Ud.?
No, ¡que entren ellos!

1. ¿No va a dormir Ud.?
2. ¿No va a volver Ud.?
3. ¿No va a trabajar Ud.?
4. ¿No va a venir Ud.?
5. ¿No va a beber Ud.?

2. THE SUBJUNCTIVE TO EXPRESS EMOTION

In Spanish the subjunctive is always used in the subordinate clause when the verb in the main clause expresses any kind of emotion, such as fear, joy, pity, hope, pleasure, surprise, anger, regret, and sorrow. Some of the verbs that call for the subjunctive are **temer** (*to fear*), **alegrarse (de)**, (*to be glad*), **sentir** (*to regret*), **esperar** (*to hope*).

¿Vas a ir a cortarte el pelo hoy?	*Are you going to get a haircut today?*
No. **Temo** que el barbero **tenga** muchos clientes.	*No. I'm afraid the barber will have many customers.*
¿Cuándo vienen tus padres?	*When are your parents coming?*
Espero que ellos **lleguen** mañana.	*I hope they will arrive tomorrow.*

ATENCIÓN: The subject of the subordinate clause must be different from that of the main clause. If there is no change of subject, the infinitive is used instead:

¿Vas a terminar el trabajo para las cinco?	*Are you going to finish the work by five?*

¿Vas a terminar el trabajo para
  las cinco?
Temo no **poder** terminarlo tan
  pronto.
(**Yo temo** in main clause. **Yo no
  puedo** in subordinate clause.)

*Are you going to finish the
  work by five?*
*I'm afraid I can't finish it so
  soon.*

¿Cuándo se van Uds.?
Esperamos **irnos** esta noche.
(**Nosotros esperamos** in main
  clause. **Nosotros nos vamos** in
  subordinate clause.)

When are you leaving?
We hope to leave tonight.

Exercise

Complete the following sentences with the subjunctive or infinitive of
the verbs in parentheses, as needed:

1. Espero que los niños _____ (cortarse) el pelo hoy.
2. Me alegro de _____ (estar) aquí.
3. Temen no _____ (poder) terminar para la una.
4. Ella espera _____ (salir) mañana.
5. Uds. esperan que el barbero no _____ (tener) muchos clientes.
6. Siento que ellos no _____ (volver) tan pronto.
7. Espero que no _____ (llover) hoy pues tengo que salir.
8. Espero que ellos lo _____ (traer).
9. Siento _____ (estar) tan enferma.
10. Temo que Ud. no _____ (tener) trabajo pronto.
11. Temo no _____ (recordar) su dirección.
12. Me alegro de que nosotros _____ (poder) salir mañana.

3. THE SUBJUNCTIVE WITH IMPERSONAL EXPRESSIONS

Certain impersonal expressions indicate emotion, doubt, uncertainty,
unreality, or an indirect or implied command. These expressions require the subjunctive in the subordinate clause if a subject is expressed in the
subordinate clause. The most common of these expressions are:

conviene	it is advisable
es difícil	it is unlikely
es importante	it is important
es (im)posible	it is (im)possible
es lástima	it is a pity

es mejor	it is better.
es necesario	it is necessary
¡ojalá!	if only . . .! *or* I hope
puede ser	it may be

¿Viene hoy el plomero?	*Is the plumber coming today?*
Es difícil que **venga** hoy.	*It is unlikely that he'll come today.*

¿Cuándo quiere Ud. que escriba las cartas?	*When do you want me to write the letters?*
Es importante que las **escriba** hoy.	*It is important that you write them today.*

¿Cuándo quiere que los estudiantes tomen el examen?	*When do you want the students to take the exam?*
Es mejor que lo **tomen** en seguida.	*It is better that they take it right away.*

Es lástima que Ud. no **pueda** hacerlo.	*It is a pity you can't do it.*
Lo sé, pero no tengo tiempo.	*I know, but I don't have time.*

¿Lloverá mañana?	*Will it rain tomorrow?*
Espero que no llueva porque **es posible** que Enrique me **lleve** a la playa.	*I hope it won't rain, because it's possible that Henry will take me to the beach.*

ATENCIÓN:

1. When the impersonal expression implies certainty, the indicative is used:

¿Vienen ellos hoy?	*Are they coming today?*
Sí, **es seguro** que **vienen** hoy.	*Yes, it is certain that they'll come today.*

2. Impersonal expressions that are *not* followed by a subordinate clause containing a specific subject are followed by an infinitive construction:

¿Cuándo vamos a firmar el contrato?	*When are we going to sign the contract?*
Conviene **firmarlo** esta semana.	*It is advisable to sign it this week.*

Exercise

Give the Spanish equivalent:

1. It is unlikely that the plumber will come today.
2. It is important that the students take the test right away.
3. It's a pity that your mother is sick.
4. It is necessary to finish the job this week.
5. I hope he doesn't say anything.
6. It is certain that it is going to rain tonight.
7. It is better to see the client now.
8. It is advisable to sign the contract this week.
9. Well, is it possible to do it today?
10. It is better to go to the beach now than later.

STUDY OF COGNATES

1. These words are the same in Spanish and English, except for a final vowel or a single consonant:

el barbero	barber
importante	important
posible	possible

2. Approximate cognates:

el contrato	contract
la geografía	geography
físico(a)	physical

NEW VOCABULARY

Nouns

el cliente	customer
el paquete	package
la playa	beach
el plomero	plumber

Verbs

aconsejar	to advise
alegrarse (de)	to be glad
esperar	to hope
firmar	to sign
sentir (e > ie)	to regret

sugerir (e > ie)	to suggest
temer	to fear

Other words and expressions

conviene	it is advisable
cortarse el pelo	to get a haircut
es difícil	it's unlikely
es lástima	it is a pity
en seguida	right away
es seguro	it is certain
¡ojalá!	if only . . . !
pues	well

La hora de cenar

MENU

PAPITAS RELLENAS

Ingredientes:

1 kilo de papas
1 huevo
1/8 de queso mantecoso
1/2 taza de harina
1/2 taza de leche caliente
/2 cucharada de polvos
e hornear

Preparación:

ele las papas y cuézalas en agua con sal. Páselas
el prensa-puré. Haga un puré firme con la leche y el
vo. Agregue la harina y polvos de hornear. Deje una
cla suave que no se pegue en los dedos. Tome un
ito de puré, ponga al medio un trocito de queso y
e bolitas. Fríalas en aceite o manteca bien caliente.

Lesson 18

1. THE SUBJUNCTIVE TO EXPRESS DOUBT AND UNREALITY

A. The subjunctive is always used in the subordinate clause when the verb in the main clause expresses doubt, uncertainty, denial, negation, disbelief, indefiniteness, or nonexistence:

1. Uncertainty or doubt:

¿Viene tu hermana a la oficina hoy? — *Is your sister coming to the office today?*
Dudo que ella **venga** hoy. — *I doubt whether she's coming today.*

¿Está Ud. seguro de que el jefe sale mañana? — *Are you sure (that) the boss is leaving tomorrow?*
No, **no estoy seguro** de que **salga** mañana. — *No, I'm not sure (that) he's leaving tomorrow.*

ATENCIÓN: The verb **dudar** (in the affirmative) takes the subjunctive in the subordinate clause even when there is no change of subject:

¿Puedes ir conmigo al médico? — *Can you go to the doctor's with me?*

(Yo) dudo que **(yo) pueda** ir contigo hoy. — *I doubt whether I can go with you today.*

● When no doubt is expressed, and the speaker is certain of the reality, the indicative is used:

¿Viene tu hermana hoy? — *Is your sister coming today?*
No dudo (de) que ella **viene.** — *I don't doubt that she's coming.*

¿Está Ud. seguro de que él sale mañana? — *Are you sure (that) he's leaving tomorrow?*
Sí, estoy seguro de que él **sale** mañana. — *Yes, I'm sure (that) he's leaving tomorrow.*

2. The verb **creer** (*to believe, to think*) is followed by the indicative when used in affirmative sentences, and by the subjunctive when used in negative sentences:

¿Cuántos cuartos tiene la casa? — *How many rooms does the house have?*

Creo que **tiene** veinte y cinco cuartos. — *I think it has twenty-five rooms.*
¡Vamos! **No creo** que **tenga** veinte y cinco cuartos. — *Come on! I don't believe it has twenty-five rooms.*

3. When the main clause negates the statement made in the subordinate clause, the subjunctive is used:

¿Es verdad que tu padre está preso?

Is it true that your father is in jail?

No, **no es verdad** que mi padre **esté** preso.

No, it isn't true that my father is in jail.

ATENCIÓN: When the main clause does not negate the statement made in the subordinate clause, the indicative is used:

¿Es verdad que tu padre está preso?

Is it true that your father is in jail?

Sí, **es verdad** que mi padre **está** preso.

Yes, it is true that my father is in jail.

B. The subjunctive is always used when the subordinate clause refers to someone or something that is indefinite, unspecified, or nonexistent:

¿Qué clase de casa necesitan ellos?

What kind of house do they need?

Ellos necesitan una casa que **sea** grande y que **quede** cerca del centro.

They need a house that is big and (that is) located near the downtown area.

Buscamos un profesor que **hable** tres idiomas.

We're looking for a professor who speaks three languages.

Pues yo busco un profesor que **sepa** inglés.

Well, I'm looking for a professor who knows English.

¿Hay alguien aquí que **sepa** hacer traducciones?

Is there anybody here who knows how to do translations?

No, no hay nadie que **sepa** hacer traducciones.

No, there is no one who knows how to do translations.

ATENCIÓN: If the subordinate clause refers to existent, definite, or specific persons or things, the indicative is used:

¿Dónde viven ellos?

Where do they live?

Ellos viven en una casa que **es** grande y que **queda** cerca del centro.

They live in a house that is big and that is located near the downtown area.

¿Tienen Uds. secretaria?	*Do you have a secretary?*
Sí, tenemos una secretaria que **habla** tres idiomas y que **sabe** escribir muy bien a máquina.	*Yes, we have a secretary who speaks three languages and who can (knows how to) type very well.*
Aquí hay alguien que **sabe** hacer traducciones.	*There is someone here who knows how to do translations.*
¡Fantástico!	*Fantastic!*

Exercise

Complete the sentences using either the present indicative or the present subjunctive of the verbs in the following list, as needed. Read each sentence aloud:

tener	saber	querer
poder	ser	escribir
entender	servir	venir
salir	hablar	estar
abrirse	quedar	ir

1. Dudo que la maestra _____ a la escuela hoy, niños, porque está muy enferma.
2. No estoy seguro de que (nosotros) _____ terminar el trabajo para esta tarde.
3. Dudo que (yo) _____ a la reunión esta noche.
4. Estamos seguros de que Uds. _____ la situación.
5. No creo que el avión _____ el sábado por la noche.
6. Creo que el banco _____ a las nueve de la mañana.
7. ¡Vamos! No es verdad que el jefe _____ preso.
8. Es verdad que la casa de Tomás _____ sólo tres cuartos.
9. Tengo una secretaria que _____ cuatro idiomas.
10. ¿Hay alguien aquí que _____ escribir a máquina?
11. María busca una casa que _____ cerca del centro.
12. Busca una esposa que _____ inteligente.
13. En esta ciudad no hay ningún restaurante que _____ comida italiana.
14. Aquí hay tres personas que _____ hacer traducciones del inglés al español. ¡Fantástico!
15. Necesito una pluma que _____ bien.

2. THE FAMILIAR COMMAND (**tú** FORM)

The Affirmative Command

The affirmative command for **tú** has exactly the same form as the third person singular of the present indicative.

Verb	Present Indicative Third Person Singular	Familiar Command (tú Form)
hablar	él habla	habla
comer	él come	come
abrir	él abre	abre
cerrar	él cierra	cierra
volver	él vuelve	vuelve
pedir	él pide	pide
traer	él trae	trae

¿Qué pido?
Pide un coctel para mí y una limonada para ti.

What shall I order?
Order a cocktail for me and a lemonade for you.

Cierra las ventanas y **apaga** las luces antes de salir.

Close the windows and turn off the lights before going out.

Muy bien. **Espérame** en el coche.

Very well. Wait for me in the car.

¿Puedo jugar afuera?
No, **quédate** adentro. Hace mucho frío.

May I play outside?
No, stay inside. It's very cold.

ATENCIÓN: Notice that direct, indirect, and reflexive pronouns are always placed *after* an affirmative command.

• Eight Spanish verbs have irregular forms for the affirmative command of **tú:**

decir:	**di** (*say, tell*)	salir:	**sal** (*go out, leave*)
hacer:	**haz** (*do, make*)	ser:	**sé** (*be*)
ir:	**ve** (*go*)	tener:	**ten** (*have*)
poner:	**pon** (*put*)	venir:	**ven** (*come*)

Carlitos, **ven** aquí. **Haz**me un favor. **Ve** y **di**le a tu mamá que quiero hablar con ella.

Charlie, come here. Do me a favor. Go and tell your mom I want to speak with her.

¿Dónde pongo las plantas? **Pon**las en la mesa.

Where shall I put the plants? Put them on the table.

Marcos, **sé** bueno y **sal** con los niños esta tarde. Necesito trabajar.
Bueno. Pero ¿cuándo vas a terminar ese trabajo?
Ten paciencia. Estará listo mañana por la tarde.

Mark, be nice (kind) and go out with the kids this afternoon. I need to work.
Okay. But, when are you going to finish that job?
Have patience. It will be ready tomorrow afternoon.

The Negative Command

The negative command for **tú** uses the corresponding form of the present subjunctive:

Tengo mil dólares para gastar durante mis vacaciones.
No lleves dinero. Lleva cheques de viajeros.

I have a thousand dollars to spend during my vacation.
Don't take money. Take travelers' checks.

Tengo que ir a la oficina de correos. **No me esperes** para cenar.
No vayas hoy. Ve mañana.

I have to go to the post office. Don't wait for me to (have) dinner.
Don't go today. Go tomorrow.

No te bañes todavía. No hay agua caliente.
No me digas que otra vez no tenemos agua caliente.

Don't bathe yet. There is no hot water.
Don't tell me that we don't have hot water again.

ATENCIÓN: All object pronouns are placed *before* a negative command.

Exercises

A. Answer the following questions, according to the model:

Modelo: ¿Traigo las plantas?
Sí, tráelas, por favor.

1. ¿Pido el coctel?
2. ¿Hago la limonada?
3. ¿Apago la luz?
4. ¿Te espero en el coche?
5. ¿Me quedo aquí?
6. ¿Juego afuera?
7. ¿Vengo con Eva?
8. ¿Lo pongo adentro?
9. ¿Se lo digo?
10. ¿Voy con Alberto?
11. ¿Salgo temprano?
12. ¿Llevo las plantas?
13. ¿Abro las ventanas?
14. ¿Cierro las puertas?
15. ¿Traigo los cheques de viajeros?

B. Make the following commands negative:

1. Gasta todo el dinero.
2. Vete.
3. Dile que venga con nosotros.
4. Sal con Roberto.
5. Ven esta tarde.
6. Pídele que salga con los chicos.
7. Dile que necesitas trabajar.
8. Báñate con agua caliente.
9. Hazlo otra vez.
10. Pon las plantas en la mesa.
11. Sé bueno.
12. Ten paciencia.
13. Quédate con ella.
14. Dale el dinero al médico.
15. Llévala al cine.

C. Give the Spanish equivalent (Use the **tú** form.):

1. Tell him what kind of house you want.
2. Go to the post office.
3. Don't have supper now.
4. Do me a favor.
5. Wash your hands before going out.

STUDY OF COGNATES

1. Exact cognate:

   el favor   favor

2. The following words are the same in Spanish and English except for a final vowel or an accent:

   fantástico(a)   fantastic

3. Spanish word ending in **-ción,** instead of English *-tion:*

   las vacaciones[1]   vacation

4. Approximate cognates:

   el coctel   cocktail
   el cheque   check
   la limonada   lemonade
   la paciencia   patience

NEW VOCABULARY

NOUNS

el agua (f.)[2]	water
el centro	downtown
la clase	kind, type
el cuarto	room
el jefe	boss, chief
la luz	light
el médico	medical doctor
la oficina de correos	post office
la traducción	translation
el viajero	traveler

VERBS

apagar	to turn off
buscar	to look for
cenar	to have supper, to dine
dudar	to doubt
jugar[3]	to play (a game)
quedar	to be located
quedarse	to stay, to remain

ADJECTIVES

caliente	hot
seguro(a)	sure

OTHER WORDS AND EXPRESSIONS

adentro	inside
afuera	outside
antes de	before
cerca (de)	near, next to
estar preso(a)	to be in jail
otra vez	again
¡vamos!	come on!

---

[1] **Vacaciones** is always used in the plural form in Spanish.
[2] When a singular, feminine noun begins with a stressed **a** or **ha,** the masculine article is used.
[3] Present indicative: juego, juegas, juega, jugamos, juegan

FARMACIAS

INFORMACION FARMACIAS DE GUARDIA 098

CALLE DE AGUSTIN DE FOXA	215 28 35
Numero 25	733 63 10
Numero 31	413 75 32
CALLE DE ALBERTO ALCOCER	
Numero 22	257 54 28
Numero 111	
Numero 166	
CALLE DE POLONIO MORALES	
Numero 4	259 06 65
CALLE DEL AVIA	
Numero 1 y 3	458 28 14
CALLE DE BOLIVIA	
Numero 8	455 57 81
Numero 16	279 11 86
Numero 38	279 68 13
PASEO DE LA CASTELLANA	259 10 38
Numero 113	279 11 87
Numero 123	250 04 44
Numero 151	
Numero 176	
Numero 181	
Numero 198	
Numero 264	

En la farmacia

Lesson **19**

1. THE SUBJUNCTIVE AFTER CONJUNCTIONS IMPLYING UNCERTAINTY OR UNFULFILLMENT

A. Certain conjunctions of time, such as **tan pronto como, en cuanto** (both meaning *as soon as*), **hasta que** (*until*), and **cuando** (*when*), may take the indicative or the subjunctive. They take the subjunctive when the action in the subordinate clause has not yet been completed. This is because there is always some uncertainty as to whether a future action will be completed:

Eva, ¿cuándo va a llamarte el doctor?	*Eva, when is the doctor going to call you?*
Me llamará **tan pronto como sepa** el resultado de los análisis.	*He is going to call me as soon as he finds out the result of the tests.*
Carlos, ¿a qué hora vamos a empezar la asamblea?	*Charles, at what time are we going to begin the assembly?*
La vamos a empezar **en cuanto lleguen** todos los empleados.	*We are going to start it as soon as all the employees arrive.*
Tomás, ¿cuándo vamos a salir para el aeropuerto?	*Thomas, when are we going to leave for the airport?*
No podemos salir **hasta que** el carro **esté** arreglado.	*We can't leave until the car is fixed.*
Cuando llegue Carlos dígale que saque copia de estas cartas y las eche al correo.	*When Charles arrives tell him to photocopy these letters and mail them.*
Muy bien, se lo diré **cuando venga.**	*OK, I'll tell him when he arrives.*

If there is no indication of a future action, the indicative is used after the conjunction of time:

Eva, ¿cuándo te llamó el doctor?	*Eva, when did the doctor call you?*
Me llamó **tan pronto como supo** el resultado de los análisis.	*He called me as soon as he found out the result of the tests.*
Carlos, ¿a qué hora vamos a empezar la asamblea?	*Charles, at what time are we going to begin the assembly?*
Siempre empezamos **en cuanto llegan** todos los empleados.	*We always begin as soon as all the employees arrive.*

Pedro, ¿cuándo salieron Uds. para el aeropuerto?

Peter, when did you leave for the airport?

No pudimos salir **hasta que** el coche **estuvo** arreglado.

We were not able to leave until the car was fixed.

B. There are some conjunctions that by their very meaning imply uncertainty or condition, such as **sin que** (*without*) and **a menos que** (*unless*). These conjunctions are always followed by the subjunctive:

¿Va Ud. a firmar el testamento hoy?

Are you going to sign the will today?

No puedo firmarlo **sin que** mi abogado lo **lea.**

I can't sign it without my lawyer reading it.

¿Piensa Ud. vender su casa?

Are you thinking of selling your house?

Voy a venderla **a menos que** **pueda** alquilarla.

I'm going to sell it unless I can rent it.

Exercise

Complete the sentences with the subjunctive or the indicative of the following verbs, as needed: **venir, dar, llegar, pedir, firmar, llover, salir, preguntar, ver, estar.** Use each verb only once.

1. Vamos a echar las cartas al correo tan pronto como el jefe las _____ .
2. Siempre cierro las ventanas cuando _____ .
3. Me llamó tan pronto como _____ de la asamblea.
4. No puede salir sin que ellos lo _____ .
5. No me lo dirán a menos que se lo _____ .
6. No podré alquilarlo hasta que Ud. me _____ el dinero.
7. Le dimos el carro tan pronto como nos lo _____ .
8. Dígale al empleado que saque copia del testamento en cuanto _____ terminado.
9. Siempre espero hasta que él _____ del trabajo.
10. Te llamaré por teléfono cuando _____ a casa.

2. THE PRESENT PERFECT SUBJUNCTIVE

The present perfect subjunctive is formed with the present subjunctive of the auxiliary verb **haber** plus the past participle of the main verb.

Present Perfect Subjunctive		
Present Subjunctive of **haber**	+	*Past Participle of the Main Verb*
yo haya		amado
tú hayas		comido
él haya		vivido
ella haya		conseguido
nosotros hayamos		hecho
ellos hayan		puesto
ellas hayan		traducido

Exercise

Conjugate the following verbs in the present perfect subjunctive for each subject given:

1. **yo:**   hacer, venir, comer, levantarse
2. **tú:**   trabajar, poner, decir, acostarse
3. **ella:**   escribir, cerrar, abrir, sentarse
4. **nosotros:** morir, hablar, llegar, vestirse
5. **ellos:**   romper, vender, alquilar, bañarse

3. USES OF THE PRESENT PERFECT SUBJUNCTIVE

The present perfect subjunctive is used in the same way as the present perfect in English, but only in sentences that call for the subjunctive in the subordinate clause:

¿Ya han pagado Uds. la cuenta del teléfono?	*Have you already paid the phone bill?*
No recuerdo . . . no, **no creo** que la **hayamos pagado** todavía.	*I don't remember . . . No, I don't think we've paid it yet.*
Estoy tan ocupado que no he tenido tiempo de revisar los informes.	*I'm so busy (that) I haven't had time to check the reports.*
Espero que por lo menos su ayudante los **haya visto.**	*I hope at least your assistant has seen them.*
Hubo un accidente en la autopista. Chocaron dos autobuses, y **temo** que **hayan muerto** todos los pasajeros.	*There was an accident on the freeway. Two buses collided and I'm afraid all the passengers have died.*
¡Qué horrible![1] **Ojalá** que algunos **hayan sobrevivido.**	*How horrible! I hope some (of them) have survived.*

[1] The Spanish equivalent of *"how"* + *adjective* is **qué** + *adjective.*

Exercise

Complete the sentences with the present perfect subjunctive of the verbs in the following list, as needed: **estar, ir, sobrevivir, conseguir, pagar, chocar, poder, revisar, morir, llegar.** Use each verb only once.

1. No creo que ellos _____ la cuenta.
2. Siento que tú _____ tan ocupado.
3. Espero que Uds. _____ los informes.
4. Ojalá que mi ayudante _____ a la oficina.
5. No es verdad que _____ dos autobuses.
6. Temo que ninguno de los pasajeros del avión _____. ¡Qué horrible!
7. Dudo que él _____ vender la casa a ese precio.
8. Ojalá que no _____ todos los pasajeros en el accidente de la autopista.
9. No creo que todos los empleados _____ a la reunión.
10. Siento que tú no _____ el puesto.

STUDY OF COGNATES

1. Exact cognates:

   horrible   horrible

2. These words are the same in Spanish and English, except for a written accent or a final vowel:

   el autobús   bus, autobus
   el testamento   will, testament

3. Approximate cognates:

   la asamblea   assembly
   el pasajero   passenger

NEW VOCABULARY

NOUNS		VERBS	
la autopista	freeway	**alquilar**	to rent
el, la ayudante	assistant	**revisar**	to check
el carro	car	**sobrevivir**	to survive
el empleado	employee		
el informe	report	OTHER WORDS AND EXPRESSIONS	
		echar al correo	to mail
		sacar copia	to photocopy
		por lo menos	at least

Restaurante
MESON TXISTU
LA COCINA
VASCA
Pza. Angel Carbajo, 6 • (Antes Rosa de Silva, 25)
Teléfono 270 96 51 • MADRID-20

ASADOR !!! DONOSTIARRA
ASADOR
TIPICO VASCO
Infanta Mercedes, 79
Teléf. 279 73 40 • MADRID-20

Con unos amigos en un restaurante

Lesson 20

1. THE IMPERFECT SUBJUNCTIVE

The imperfect subjunctive is the simple past tense of the subjunctive. It is formed in the same way for all verbs, regular and irregular: the **-ron** ending of the third person plural of the preterit is dropped and the following endings are added to the stem: **-ra, -ras, -ra, -ramos, -ran.**

	Formation of the Imperfect Subjunctive			
Verb	*Preterit, Third Person Plural*	*Stem*	*Imperfect Subjunctive*	
hablar	hablaron	habla-	que yo habla-	**ra**
comer	comieron	comie-	que tú comie-	**ras**
vivir	vivieron	vivie-	que Ud. vivie-	**ra**
traer	trajeron	traje-	que él traje-	**ra**
ir	fueron	fue-	que ella fue-	**ra**
saber	supieron	supie-	que nosotros supié-	**ramos**
decir	dijeron	dije-	que Uds. dije-	**ran**
poner	pusieron	pusie-	que ellos pusie-	**ran**
estar	estuvieron	estuvie-	que ellas estuvie-	**ran**

• Notice the written accent mark in the first person plural form.

Exercise

Conjugate the following verbs in the imperfect subjunctive for each subject given:

1. **yo:**   caminar, aprender, abrir, cerrar, acostarse
2. **tú:**   salir, sentir, temer, recordar, ponerse
3. **Ud.:**   llevar, romper, morir, terminar, volar, alegrarse
4. **nosotros:** esperar, traer, pedir, volver, servir, vestirse
5. **ellos:**   tener, ser, dar, estar, poder, irse

2. USES OF THE IMPERFECT SUBJUNCTIVE

A. The imperfect subjunctive is always used in a subordinate clause when the verb of the main clause is in the past:

Señorita Peña, ayer le **dije** que **archivara** las solicitudes de empleo.

Miss Peña, yesterday I told you to file the job applications.

Pero el jefe de personal me **pidió** que las **dejara** en su escritorio.

But the personnel director asked me to leave them on his desk.

| Carlitos, te **dije** que **te lavaras** la cara y las manos antes de hacer la tarea. | *Charlie, I told you to wash your face and hands before doing your (the) homework.* |
| Ya me las lavé. | *I already washed them.* |

B. The imperfect subjunctive is also used when the verb of the main clause is in the present, but the subordinate clause refers to the past:

| **Es** una lástima que no **asistieras ayer** a la conferencia de la Dra. Ruiz. | *It's a pity that you didn't attend Dr. Ruiz's lecture yesterday.* |
| No pude, porque tuve que ir al consulado a recoger mi pasaporte. | *I wasn't able to (make it) because I had to go to the consulate to pick up my passport.* |

Exercises

A. Complete the sentences with the imperfect subjunctive of the following verbs, as needed: **escribir, asistir, sacar, archivar, lavarse, venir, recoger, firmar.** Use each verb once.

1. El jefe de personal nos dijo que _____ los documentos.
2. Sentí mucho que Ud. no _____ a la conferencia el sábado pasado.
3. Le pedí a papá que _____ mi pasaporte en el consulado.
4. Ella no les dijo que _____ las cartas.
5. Es una lástima que el plomero no _____ ayer.
6. El director me pidió que _____ copias de las solicitudes de empleo.
7. El profesor quería que nosotros _____ a máquina las lecciones.
8. Tú no me dijiste que _____ la cara y las manos antes de hacer la tarea.

B. Give the Spanish equivalent:

1. They wanted me to leave my car.
2. I told you not to play with him, Robert.
3. I'm sorry you were sick yesterday, Mr. Vera.
4. We asked them to attend the lecture.
5. He told us to get dressed.
6. I'm glad you were able to come last Friday.

3. "IF" CLAUSES

In Spanish, as in English, the imperfect subjunctive is used when a contrary-to-fact statement is made:

If I were you . . .
Si yo fuera Ud. . . .

Si yo **tuviera** dinero iría de vacaciones con Uds.	*If I had money I would go on vacation with you.*
¿No te lo puede prestar tu padre?	*Can't your father lend it to you?*
No, porque si mi padre me lo **prestara,** tendría que devolvérselo antes de septiembre, y yo necesito el dinero para pagar la matrícula.	*No, because if my father were to lend it to me, I would have to give it back to him before September and I need the money to pay for registration.*
Si los muchachos **vinieran** hoy, podríamos ir a la playa o al parque.	*If the boys (young men) came today, we could go to the beach or to the park.*
Sí, pero ellos no llegan hasta mañana por la tarde.	*Yes, but they are not arriving until tomorrow afternoon.*

ATENCIÓN: When an "if" clause is *not* contrary to fact, the indicative is used.

Si los muchachos **vienen** hoy, podemos ir a la playa.

● The present subjunctive is *never* used with an "if" clause.

Exercises

A. Complete the following sentences with the present indicative or the imperfect subjunctive of the verbs in parentheses, as needed:

1. Si yo _____ (tener) tiempo, te llevaré al cine.
2. Si tú _____ (poder), ¿lo harías?
3. Si Federico me _____ (devolver) el dinero, podré pagar la matrícula.
4. Si ella _____ (venir) iríamos a la playa.
5. Si el jefe me _____ (dar) una semana de vacaciones, iría a Francia.
6. Nosotros visitaríamos a nuestros abuelos si (nosotros) no _____ (estar) enfermos.
7. Compraré la casa si _____ (conseguir) el dinero.
8. Si yo _____ (ser) tú, no conduciría a esa velocidad.
9. Mamá dice que me va a comprar el vestido si _____ (salir) temprano de la oficina.
10. Si ellos lo _____ (saber), te lo dirían.

B. Give the Spanish equivalent:

1. I would help you if I could, Charlie.
2. If she has time, she'll take you to the movies.
3. If you study, you will learn.
4. We would go on vacation if we had the money.
5. I would attend the lecture if I weren't sleepy.
6. We are going to go to the park if she comes back early.

STUDY OF COGNATES

Approximate cognates:

el consulado	consulate
Francia	France
el parque	park
el pasaporte	passport
el personal	personnel

NEW VOCABULARY

NOUNS

la cara	face
el empleo	job
la matrícula	registration
la solicitud	application

VERBS

archivar	to file
asistir	to attend
dejar	to leave (behind)

devolver (o > ue)	to return, to give back
lavarse	to wash oneself
recoger	to pick up

OTHER WORDS AND EXPRESSIONS

ir(se) de vacaciones	to go on vacation

Test Yourself: Lessons 16-20

A. The future tense

Answer the following questions, according to the model:

Modelo: ¿Cuándo comprarán Uds. un coche? (el año próximo)
Compraremos un coche el año próximo.

1. ¿Cuál será el tema de la conferencia? (la civilización y la cultura de México)
2. ¿Cuándo estarán listos los análisis? (la semana que viene)
3. ¿Qué idioma aprenderán Uds.? (el español)
4. ¿A dónde irán Uds. el verano próximo? (a Santiago)
5. ¿Qué le dirán Uds. a Raquel? (que sí)
6. ¿Qué harás tú el domingo? (nada)
7. ¿Cuándo sabremos el resultado? (el próximo mes)
8. ¿Quién abrirá las puertas? (el señor Reyes)
9. ¿Quiénes podrán venir? (María y Carlos)
10. ¿Dónde pondrás el dinero? (en el banco)
11. ¿Cuándo volverán Uds. de México? (el sábado próximo)
12. ¿Con quién vendrá Ud. a la reunión? (con la señorita Vargas)
13. ¿Qué tendrán que hacer Uds.? (estudiar para el examen)
14. ¿Cuándo me dará Ud. las cartas? (mañana)
15. ¿Con quiénes saldrán Uds. el sábado? (con Raúl y Mario)

B. The conditional tense

Complete the sentences with the conditional tense of the following verbs: **servir, poner, quejarse, haber, trabajar, seguir, vender, levantarse, preferir, ir.** Use each verb once:

1. Él dijo que nosotros _____ a Europa el verano próximo.
2. Ellos no _____ su casa a ese precio.
3. ¿Dijo Ud. que _____ una reunión esta tarde?
4. Yo no _____ el café en la terraza.
5. Tú no _____ en una estación de servicio.
6. ¿_____ Ud. su dinero en ese banco?
7. ¿Qué _____ Uds.: ir a México o ir a Guatemala?
8. ¿_____ Uds. estudiando español?
9. ¿_____ tú a las tres de la mañana?
10. Nosotros no _____ del profesor.

C. The subjunctive

Complete the sentences with the Spanish equivalent of the verbs in parentheses. Use the present subjunctive. Follow the model:

Modelo: . . . que yo _____ (speak)

    . . . que yo hable

1. . . . que nosotros _____ (*work*)
2. . . . que yo _____ (*eat*)
3. . . . que Uds. _____ (*write*)
4. . . . que tú _____ (*live*)
5. . . . que él _____ (*say*)
6. . . . que Ud. _____ (*close*)
7. . . . que ellos _____ (*come*)
8. . . . que ella _____ (*get up*)
9. . . . que yo _____ (*ask for, request*)
10. . . . que Uds. _____ (*do*)
11. . . . que Ana _____ (*bring*)
12. . . . que Ud. _____ (*recommend*)
13. . . . que nosotros _____ (*move*)
14. . . . que yo _____ (*go*)
15. . . . que Luis _____ (*shave*)
16. . . . que nosotros _____ (*sleep*)
17. . . . que ella _____ (*give*)
18. . . . que ellos _____ (*know*)
19. . . . que yo _____ (*go out*)
20. . . . que tú _____ (*have*)

LESSON 17

A. The subjunctive in indirect or implied commands

Give the Spanish equivalent:

1. She wants me to bring the packages.
2. I prefer that we go to your office, Miss Diaz.
3. At what time do you want me to be here tomorrow, Mr. Acevedo?
4. Ask him to help you, Mrs. Portillo.
5. Tell them not to be afraid.
6. (Let) Robert do it.
7. (Let) them come in.
8. She wants me to be her friend.
9. Do you need them to give you the money today, Mr. Ortiz?
10. I don't want you to do anything, Johnny.

B. The subjunctive to express emotion

Give the Spanish equivalent:

1. I hope you can get a haircut this afternoon, Robbie.
2. I'm glad your mother is feeling better, Mr. Gómez.
3. I'm afraid we can't meet next week, Miss Herrero.

4. We're glad to be here today.
5. She hopes to leave tomorrow morning.
6. I hope you can come to the meeting, Mr. Peña.
7. We're afraid we can't finish the job tonight.
8. I'm sorry you are sick, Mrs. Treviño.

C. The subjunctive with impersonal expressions

Complete the following sentences with the subjunctive, the indicactive, or the infinitive of the verb in parentheses, as needed:

1. Es difícil que ellos _____ (poder) venir hoy.
2. Es necesario _____ (estudiar) mucho.
3. Es mejor _____ (escribir) ahora mismo.
4. Es verdad que nosotros _____(terminar) mañana.
5. Es lástima que el plomero no _____(estar) aquí ahora.
6. Es importante _____ (hacer) bien el trabajo.
7. Es seguro que ellos _____ (llegar) el lunes.
8. Es posible _____ (firmar) los contratos hoy.

LESSON 18

A. The subjunctive to express doubt and unreality

Change the following sentences, according to the model:

Modelo: Estoy seguro de que el jefe *viene* hoy. (Dudo)
Dudo que el jefe venga hoy.

1. Dudo que ellos *puedan* venir. (Estoy seguro de que)
2. Creo que Pedro *va* con nosotros. (No creo que)
3. Es verdad que María *está* muy enferma. (No es verdad que)
4. Tengo una casa que *queda* cerca del centro. (Busco)
5. ¿Hay alguien aquí que *sepa* escribir a máquina? (Aquí hay una chica que)
6. Hay muchas personas que *quieren* hacer traducciones. (No hay muchas personas que)
7. No creo que él se *levante* a las cuatro de la mañana. (Creo que)
8. Necesito una casa que *tenga* seis cuartos. (Vivo en una casa que)

B. The affirmative familiar command (**tú** form)

Change the commands from the **Ud.** (formal) form to the **tú** (informal) form. Follow the model:

Modelo: Salga con los niños.
Sal con los niños.

1. Venga acá, por favor.
2. Hable con la maestra.
3. Dígame su dirección.
4. Escriba la carta.

5. Póngase el abrigo.
6. Tráiganos agua caliente.
7. Termine el trabajo.
8. Hágame el favor.
9. Apague la luz.
10. Vaya al centro.

11. Salga temprano.
12. Quédese afuera.
13. Tenga paciencia.
14. Sea buena.
15. Cene con nosotros.

C. The negative familiar command (**tú** form)

Give the Spanish equivalent:

1. Don't tell (it to) him.
2. Don't go out now.
3. Don't get up.
4. Don't do the translations.
5. Don't drink the lemonade.
6. Don't break it (*masc.*).
7. Don't talk to them.
8. Don't go downtown.
9. That dress? Don't put it on!
10. Don't do that.

LESSON 19

A. The subjunctive after conjunctions implying uncertainty or un-fulfillment:

Give the Spanish equivalent:

1. I'll speak to him as soon as I see him.
2. Stay here in case he calls, Miss Gonzalez.
3. He wrote to me as soon as he arrived.
4. We are going to wait until he comes.
5. I can't go without my parents knowing (it).
6. We'll buy the car when we have the money.

B. The present perfect subjunctive

Complete the following sentences with the Spanish equivalent of the verbs in parentheses. Use the present perfect subjunctive. Follow the model:

Modelo: . . . que él _____ (*speak*)
      que él haya hablado

1. . . . que yo _____ (*see*)
2. . . . que Uds. _____ (*do*)
3. . . . que tú _____ (*learn*)
4. . . . que ellos _____ (*sign*)
5. . . . que Ud. _____ (*fix*)
6. . . . que nosotros _____ (*file*)

7. . . . que Ana _____ (*return*)
8. . . . que Luis _____ (*go to bed*)

C. Uses of the present perfect subjunctive

Write sentences using the following items. Follow the model:

Modelo: Yo / alegrarse / tú / venir
        Yo me alegro de que tú hayas venido.

1. Ellos / sentir / Uds. / estar enfermos
2. Rosa / no creer / yo / hacerlo
3. Nosotros / temer / él / morir
4. No es verdad / nosotros / escribir / esa carta
5. Ojalá / papá / poder / venir

LESSON 20

A. The imperfect subjunctive (forms)

Complete the sentences with the Spanish equivalent of the verbs
in parentheses. Use imperfect subjunctive. Follow the model:

Modelo: . . . que yo _____ (*live*)
        que yo viviera

1. . . . que nosotros _____ (*attend*)
2. . . . que tú _____ (*leave behind*)
3. . . . que ellos _____ (*wash themselves*)
4. . . . que yo _____ (*pick up*)
5. . . . que Ud. _____ (*can*)
6. . . . que Carlos _____ (*bring*)
7. . . . que Uds. _____(*give back*)
8. . . . que ella _____ (*have*)

B. Uses of the imperfect subjunctive

Change the following sentences according to the models:

Modelo 1: Me dice que hable con él.
        Me dijo que hablara con él.

Modelo 2: Siento que tú estés enferma. (ayer)
        Siento que tú estuvieras enferma ayer.

1. Le pido que venga en seguida.
2. Me alegro de que puedas terminarlo. (anoche)
3. No creo que ella lo haga.
4. No es verdad que mi hermano esté preso. (el año pasado)
5. Tememos que ella no sepa escribir a máquina.
6. Dudo que la conferencia sea hoy. (el sábado pasado)

C. "If" clauses

Complete the following sentences:

1. Yo compraría una casa si . . .
2. Iremos a verte si . . .
3. Yo iría al médico si . . .
4. Mañana saldremos si . . .
5. Ellos nos ayudarían si . . .
6. Nosotros se lo diremos si . . .
7. Yo dormiría si . . .
8. Vamos a comer algo si . . .

En el centro, Buenos Aires

Lesson 21

1. THE FUTURE PERFECT TENSE

The future perfect in Spanish corresponds closely in meaning and formation to the compound future tense in English. The future perfect is formed in Spanish with the future tense of the auxiliary verb **haber** plus the past participle of the main verb.

Future Perfect		
Future of **haber**	+	*Past Participle of the Main Verb*
yo habré		terminado
tú habrás		vuelto
él habrá		comido
nosotros habremos		escrito
ellos habrán		salido

This tense is used, like its English equivalent, to indicate what *will have happened* by the time another action occurs:

¿Ya **habrán acabado** Uds. el trabajo para mañana?

Will you have (already) finished the job by tomorrow?

No, no lo **habremos terminado** todavía.

No, we will not have finished it yet.

¿Ya **se habrá secado** la ropa cuando yo vuelva?

Will the clothes have (already) dried when I return?

Sí, estoy segura de que para esa hora ya **se habrá secado**.

Yes, I'm sure that by that time they will have (already) dried.

¿**Te habrás graduado** para septiembre?

Will you have graduated by September?

Sí, me graduaré en junio.

Yes, I will graduate in June.

Exercise

Complete the following sentences, changing the verbs in parentheses to the future perfect tense:

1. Las hermanas de Ana (graduarse) _____ para agosto.
2. A esa hora Julio ya (escribir) _____ todas las cartas.
3. A esa hora tú no (volver) _____ todavía.
4. ¿(llegar) _____ ustedes a casa para las cinco?

5. Para el sábado, yo ya (vender) _____ el coche.
6. ¿Tú ya (hacer) _____ la tarea para las ocho de la noche?
7. Ud. ya (acostarse) _____ para las once de la noche, ¿verdad?
8. Adela y yo (poner) _____ el dinero en el banco para el jueves.

2. THE CONDITIONAL PERFECT TENSE

The conditional perfect is formed with the conditional of the auxiliary verb **haber** plus the past participle of the main verb.

Conditional Perfect		
Conditional of **haber**	+	*Past Participle of the Main Verb*
yo habría		vuelto
tú habrías		comido
él habría		salido
nosotros habríamos		estudiado
ellos habrían		muerto

The conditional perfect tense tells what *would have happened* if something else occurred:

Mamá sólo quería un sillón, pero no tenía dinero.	*Mom only wanted an armchair, but she didn't have money.*
Yo se lo **habría comprado,** pero ella no me dijo nada.	*I would have bought it for her, but she didn't tell me anything.*
¿Es su esposa? Yo le iba a preguntar si era su mamá . . .	*Is she his wife? I was going to ask him if she were his mom . . .*
¡Pues **habrías metido** la pata!	*Well, you would have put your foot in your mouth!*
¿María fue a la estación de ómnibus sola?	*Did Mary go to the bus station alone?*
Sí, insistió en ir sola.	*Yes, she insisted on going alone.*
Nosotros se lo **habríamos prohibido.**	*We would have forbidden it.*

Exercise

Finish each statement following the model:

Modelo: Tú no terminaste .el trabajo.   Nosotros . . .
Tú no terminaste el trabajo. Nosotros lo habríamos terminado.

1. Pedro no trajo el dinero.   Ud. . . .
2. Pedro no compró el sillón.   Yo . . .
3. Pedro no le prohibió que saliera.   Miguel y yo . . .
4. Pedro no metió la pata.   Luis . . .
5. Pedro no vendió la casa.   Nosotros . . .
6. Pedro no se lo dijo.   Tú . . .
7. Pedro no se levantó.   Uds. . . .
8. Pedro no me ayudó.   Marisa y Rosa . . .

3. ADJECTIVES WITH SHORTENED FORMS

The adjectives **bueno, malo, alguno, ninguno, primero,** and **tercero** drop the final -o when they are used before masculine, singular nouns.

Rodolfo es un **buen** abogado.	*Rodolfo is a good lawyer.*
Ése es un **mal** chiste.	*That's a bad joke.*
Algún[1] día sabremos la respuesta.	*Some day we'll know the answer.*
Ellos no recibieron **ningún**[1] premio.	*They didn't receive any prize.*
Adán fue el **primer** hombre en la tierra.	*Adam was the first man on earth.*
La discoteca está en el **tercer** piso.	*The discotheque is on the third floor.*

The adjective **grande** becomes **gran** in front of a masculine or feminine singular noun:

Lincoln fue un **gran** hombre.	*Lincoln was a great man.*
Susan B. Anthony fue una **gran** mujer.	*Susan B. Anthony was a great woman.*

Exercise

Give the Spanish equivalent:

1. We used to live on the first floor.

[1] **Algún** and **ningún** require written accents in order to maintain the stress on the last syllables.

2. He didn't eat any dessert.
3. Mr. Vigo said it was a good joke.
4. I am going to need the third book.
5. Some night we'll go to the discotheque.
6. He is a bad teacher.
7. I think San Francisco is a great city.

4. POSITION OF ADJECTIVES: CHANGE IN MEANING

Certain adjectives change their meanings depending on whether they precede or follow the nouns they describe. The following are among the more common:

pobre	un hombre **pobre**	*a poor (not rich) man*
	un **pobre** hombre	*a poor (unfortunate) man*
grande	un hombre **grande**	*a big man*
	un **gran** hombre	*a great man*
único	un libro **único**	*a unique book*
	mi **único** libro	*my only book*
viejo	un amigo **viejo**	*an old (elderly) friend*
	un **viejo** amigo	*an old friend (someone who has been a friend for a long time)*
mismo	el profesor **mismo**	*the teacher himself*
	el **mismo** profesor	*the same teacher*

Exercise

Complete the following sentences, placing the appropriate adjectives either before or after the nouns, as needed:

1. Tengo sólo un hermano. Es mi _____ hermano _____ .
2. Washington fue un _____ hombre _____ .
3. Hace 8 años que la conozco. Es una _____ amiga _____ .
4. El año que viene vamos a usar el _____ libro _____ . No tengo que comprar otro.
5. No tiene dinero. Es un _____ muchacho _____ .
6. No hay otra ciudad como París. Es una _____ ciudad _____ .

7. Gonzalo es muy alto y muy gordo. Es un _____ hombre _____.
8. Ramón Cifuentes tiene noventa años. Es un _____ hombre
   _____ .
9. Estoy segura de que mañana tenemos un examen. Me lo dijo la
   _____ profesora _____ .
10. El _____ Paco _____ tuvo un accidente y ahora tiene que estar
    un mes en el hospital.

NEW VOCABULARY

NOUNS

la abogada ⎫ el abogado ⎭	lawyer
el chiste	joke
la discoteca	discotheque
la estación de ómnibus	bus station
el premio	prize
la respuesta	answer
la ropa[1]	clothes
el sillón	armchair
la tierra	earth

VERBS

acabar	to finish
graduarse	to graduate
insistir (en)	to insist (on)

prohibir	to forbid, to prohibit
secarse	to dry, to get dry

ADJECTIVES

mismo(a)	same
único(a)	unique, only

OTHER WORDS AND EXPRESSIONS

estar seguro(a)	to be sure
gran	great
meter la pata	to put one's foot in one's mouth
sólo	only

---

[1] **Ropa** is singular in Spanish.

VIVA UN NUEVO
AMANECER

Unidad Residencial
Cuarto de Legua:
1a. etapa

Apartamentos de dos
y tres alcobas

Visite el apto. modelo
Todos los días,
hasta las 5 p.m.

n nuevo amanecer   Calle 4a. Cra. 60

usted se lo merece

La playa, Montevideo, Uruguay

Lesson **22**

1. PLUPERFECT SUBJUNCTIVE

The pluperfect subjunctive is formed with the imperfect subjunctive of the auxiliary verb **haber** plus the past participle of the main verb. It is used the same way that the past perfect is used in English but in sentences in which the main clause calls for the use of the subjunctive in the subordinate clause.

Pluperfect Subjunctive		
Imperfect Subjunctive of **haber**	+	*Past Participle of the Main Verb*
yo hubiera		estudiado
tú hubieras		salido
él hubiera		leído
nosotros hubiéramos		dicho
ellos hubieran		escrito

Uds. no quisieron ir a jugar al tenis con nosotros.

You didn't want (refused) to go play tennis with us.

Al contrario . . . si **hubiéramos tenido** las raquetas de tenis habríamos ido con Uds.

On the contrary . . . if we had had the tennis rackets we would have gone with you.

Fue una lástima que ella no **hubiera podido** evitar ese accidente . . .

It was a pity that she hadn't been able to avoid that accident . . .

Es verdad, pero la culpa fue del hombre. Si él no **hubiera cruzado** la calle de repente, ella habría tenido tiempo de parar el coche y no habrían chocado.

It's true, but it was the man's fault. If he hadn't crossed the street suddenly, she would have had time to stop the car and they wouldn't have collided.

Exercises

A. Item substitution. Change each sentence according to the new subject provided:

1. Él se alegró de que ella hubiera venido.
2. _____ nosotros _____ .
3. _____ yo _____ vuelto.
4. _____ tú _____ .
5. _____ Uds. _____ llegado.
6. _____ Ud. _____ .

B. Complete the following sentences with the pluperfect subjunctive of the verb in parentheses:

1. Sentían que tú no _____ (ir) a jugar al tenis con ellos.
2. Se alegraron de que yo _____ (poder) ir con ellos al baile.
3. Fue una lástima que _____ (empezar) a llover de repente.
4. Si ellos no _____ (cruzar) la calle tú los habrías visto.
5. Al contrario, si nosotros _____ (tener) dinero te habríamos comprado la raqueta de tenis.
6. Cuando vimos que ellos no llegaban, temíamos que _____ (ocurrir) un accidente.
7. ¿Dudabas que yo _____ (comprar) los dulces?
8. Ojalá que tú _____ (venir) ayer.

2. THE SUBJUNCTIVE AFTER THE EXPRESSION como si

As you recall, the imperfect subjunctive is used with an *if*-clause when a contrary-to-fact statement is made. The imperfect subjunctive or pluperfect subjunctive is always used after **como si** (*as if*) since this expression implies a contrary-to-fact-situation.

Adivina qué compró Carlos ayer . . .	*Guess what Carlos bought yesterday . . .*
Me doy por vencida . . . ¿Qué?	*I give up . . . What?*
¡Un TRANS-AM!	*A TRANS-AM!*
¡Qué barbaridad! Carlos gasta dinero **como si fuera** millonario . . .	*Gee! Carlos spends money as if he were a millionaire.*
Paco dice que está cansadísimo y que ya no quiere trabajar.	*Paco says he is extremely tired and that he no longer wants to work.*
Sí, él habla **como si hubiera hecho** todo el trabajo, pero no hizo nada.	*Yes, he talks as if he had done all the work, but he didn't do anything.*

Exercise

Respond, using **como si** + the imperfect subjunctive in your answers. Follow the model:

Modelo: José ya se afeita, ¿verdad?   (tener barba)
   Sí, se afeita como si tuviera barba.

1. Él gasta mucho dinero, ¿verdad?   (ser millonario)

2. Rodolfo y Mario están comiendo, ¿verdad?   (tener mucha hambre)
3. Álvaro está durmiendo, ¿verdad?   (estar muy cansado)
4. Ana está guardando cama, ¿verdad?   (estar enferma)
5. Silvia siempre habla de Juan, ¿verdad?   (conocerlo muy bien)

3. RELATIVE PRONOUNS que, quien, AND quienes

Que is the relative pronoun that is most commonly used in Spanish. It can refer to persons or things. Although *that* may sometimes be omitted in English, **que** must be included in Spanish.

¿Es ese muchacho **que** acaba de bajarse del ómnibus tu hermano?	*Is that boy who has just gotten off the bus your brother?*
No, es el hermano de Marta.	*No, he's Marta's brother.*
¿Dónde está la pelota **que** compré ayer?	*Where is the ball I bought yesterday?*
Se la di a Robertito porque estaba llorando.	*I gave it to Robbie because he was crying.*

With the prepositions **a, de, con,** and **en,** Spanish uses **que** when referring to things and **quien** (**quienes**) when referring to persons. In the latter case, **quien** (**quienes**) is the equivalent of *whom.* **Quien** (**quienes**) can replace **que**, but only when referring to persons:

La chica **con quien** salió Carlos ayer es muy mal educada.	*The girl with whom Carlos went out yesterday is very rude.*
Sí, ¡y es la chica más desagradable del mundo!	*Yes, and she is the most unpleasant girl in the world!*
¿Dónde está la chica **de quien** me hablaste?	*Where is the girl you spoke to me about?*
Está tomando el sol en la terraza.	*She's sunbathing on the terrace.*

Exercise

Give the Spanish equivalent:

1. The lady to whom you sold the books wants to talk to you, sir.
2. The two men who came last night were crying.
3. Hector didn't like the ball (that) I bought him.
4. The girls with whom you were talking have just gotten off the bus.
5. The clerk I spoke to you about is very rude and very unpleasant.
6. The girl who is sunbathing is very pretty.

4. OMISSION OF THE INDEFINITE ARTICLE

The indefinite article is used less frequently in Spanish than in English. It is omitted in the following situations:

A. With names of professions, religions, or nationalities after **ser:**

María Ibarra es abogada.	*Maria Ibarra is a lawyer.*
¿Tú eres católica?	*Are you a Catholic?*
Yo soy norteamericano.	*I'm a North American.*

If the nouns are modified by an adjective, the indefinite article is generally used:

María Ibarra es **una buena** abogada.	*Maria Ibarra is a good lawyer.*

B. With names of personal objects when the idea of quantity is not emphasized:

No tengo lápiz.	*I don't have a pencil.*
Él nunca usa sombrero.	*He never wears a hat.*

C. With the numbers **ciento** and **mil** and with the adjective **medio** (*half*):

Pagué cien pesos por esas tijeras.	*I paid a hundred pesos for those scissors.*
Cobran mil dólares por presentar el espectáculo.	*They charge a thousand dollars to present the show.*
Necesito media botella de leche.	*I need half a bottle (a half bottle) of milk.*

D. Before the adjective **otro** when followed by a noun and after **que** when it is used in exclamations:

¡Qué barbaridad! Me rompí otra uña.	*Gee! I broke another nail.*
¡Qué hermoso día!	*What a beautiful day!*

E. With some verbs like **buscar** and **tener** when the idea of quantity is not emphasized:

Ese payaso no tiene trabajo.	*That clown doesn't have a job.*
¿Buscan Uds. casa?	*Are you looking for a house?*

Exercise

Give the Spanish equivalent:

1. Are you going to buy another hat?

2. What a beautiful girl! —said the clown.
3. They said they didn't have a secretary.
4. I will have to look for an apartment.
5. He drank half a bottle of water.
6. I know she is a teacher, but is she a good teacher?
7. She gave me a thousand dollars.
8. She is a good Catholic.
9. Don't tell me (that) you broke another nail!
10. My father is an engineer.

STUDY OF COGNATES

1. This word is the same in Spanish and English, except for a single consonant:

   el tenis   tennis

2. Approximate cognates:

   el apartamento apartment
   la raqueta   racket

NEW VOCABULARY

NOUNS

la culpa	fault
el espectáculo	show
el mundo	world
el payaso	clown
la pelota	ball
el sombrero	hat
la(s) tijera(s)	scissors
la uña	fingernail

VERBS

adivinar	to guess
bajar(se) (de)	to get off
cruzar	to cross
llorar	to cry

ADJECTIVES

católico(a)	Catholic
desagradable	unpleasant
hermoso(a)	beautiful
medio(a)	half

OTHER WORDS AND EXPRESSIONS

al contrario	on the contrary
darse por vencido	to give up
de repente	suddenly
jugar al tenis	to play tennis
mal educado(a)	rude, ill-mannered
¡qué barbaridad!	gee!
tomar el sol	to sunbathe

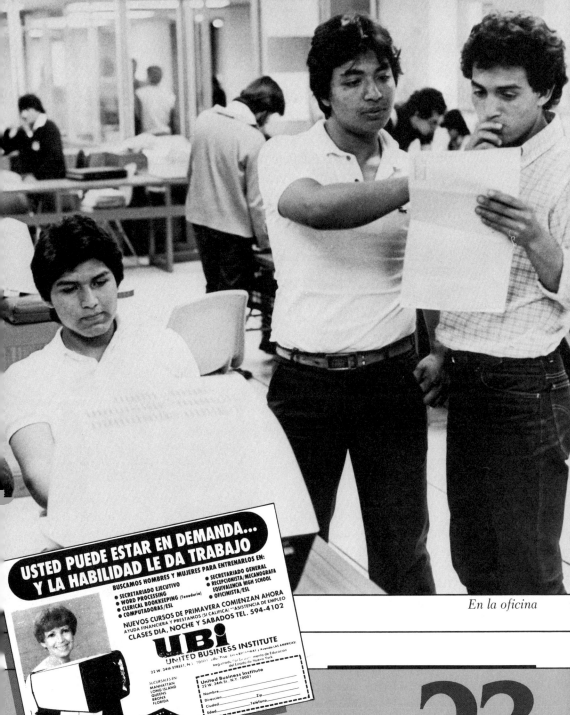

En la oficina

Lesson 23

1. THE SUBJUNCTIVE WITH **tal vez, quizá(s),** and **aunque**

A. With the adverbs **tal vez** and **quizá(s),**[1] which are equivalent to the English *perhaps*, the subjunctive is used when expressing doubt:

Quizás Héctor **pueda** hacer el papel de Romeo en la obra teatral que vamos a presentar, pero no sé si le gustará la idea.	*Perhaps Hector can play the role of Romeo in the play we're going to present, but I don't know if he'll like the idea.*
Yo creo que le gustará la idea a menos que tenga que estudiar para los exámenes.	*I think he'll like the idea unless he has to study for exams.*
¿Con quién vas a la fiesta?	*With whom are you going to the party?*
No sé . . . **tal vez vaya** con Luis.	*I don't know . . . perhaps I'll go with Luis.*

If no doubt is expressed, the indicative is used:

Yo creo que Tomás se enamoró de Ángela.	*I think Tomas fell in love with Angela.*
Bueno, **quizá** Tomás **se enamoró** de Ángela, pero ella está enamorada de Antonio.	*Well, perhaps Tomas fell in love with Angela, but she is in love with Antonio.*

B. With the conjunction **aunque,** equivalent to *even if* or *although*, the subjunctive is required when expressing uncertainty:

Yo te sugiero que no compres entradas para el partido de mañana; dicen que va a llover.	*I suggest you don't buy tickets for tomorrow's game; they say it's going to rain.*
No importa. Yo iré **aunque llueva.**	*It doesn't matter. I'll go even if it rains.*

The indicative is used with **aunque** when no uncertainty is expressed:

Margarita se va a casar con Ricardo, ¿verdad?	*Margarita is going to marry Ricardo, right?*
Sí, está muy enamorada de él, **aunque** él **tiene** muchos defectos . . .	*Yes, she's very much in love with him, although he has many faults . . .*
Sí, es haragán, vanidoso y tacaño . . .	*Yes, he is lazy, vain and stingy . . .*

[1] **Quizá** or **quizás** can be used.

Exercise

Give the Spanish equivalent:

1. Although they want him to play the role of Hamlet, he doesn't want to do it.
2. We are going to see that play tomorrow even if it rains.
3. Perhaps you can get that job . . . (doubt expressed)
4. Although Ernesto is in love with Ana, he will never say anything.
5. Are they going to present a play? Even if the students don't want to do it? (uncertainty expressed)
6. Unless she can come tomorrow, she can't work. Even if she can work more afterwards . . .
7. Well, perhaps you fell in love with her . . . but you can't get married now.
8. Perhaps they will tell you that I am lazy, stingy, and vain, but don't believe them. (no doubt expressed)
9. Perhaps my mother can suggest a few ideas to you, dear . . . (doubt expressed)
10. Although he doesn't have any faults, I don't want to marry him.

2. SEQUENCE OF TENSES WITH THE SUBJUNCTIVE

The tense used in the subordinate clause depends on the tense of the verb used in the main clause.

A. If the verb of the main clause is in the present, future, or present perfect or is a command form, the verb of the subordinate clause is in the present subjunctive or present perfect subjunctive.

Main Clause Indicative	Subordinate Clause Subjunctive
1. Present 2. Future 3. Present perfect 4. Command	Present Present perfect

Yo siempre le **digo** que no **toque** la bocina.

I always tell him not to honk the horn.

Le **diré** que lo **haga** de nuevo.

I'll tell him to do it over.

Le **he pedido** que no te **moleste**.

I have asked him not to bother you.

Pídele al profesor que lo **repita**.	*Ask the teacher to repeat it.*
Me alegro de que Roberto **haya llegado**.	*I'm happy that Roberto has arrived.*

B. If the verb of the main clause is in the preterit, imperfect, pluperfect, or conditional, the verb of the subordinate clause is in the imperfect subjunctive or the pluperfect subjunctive.

Main Clause Indicative	Subordinate Clause Subjunctive
1. Preterit 2. Imperfect 3. Pluperfect 4. Conditional	Imperfect Pluperfect

Les **dije** que no **se acercaran** al fuego.	*I told them not to get near the fire.*
Ella siempre nos **pedía** que **nos expresáramos** claramente.	*She always asked us to express ourselves clearly.*
Yo les **diría** que **se portaran** bien.	*I would tell them to behave themselves.*
Temió que no **hubieran venido** los demás.	*He was afraid that the others hadn't come.*
Había esperado que Juana **llegara** ayer.	*I had hoped that Juana would arrive yesterday.*

C. If the verb of the main clause is in the present indicative but the action of the subordinate clause refers to something that happened in the past, the verb of the subordinate clause should be in the imperfect.

Main Clause Indicative	Subordinate Clause Subjunctive
Present	Imperfect

Siento que tu padre no te **permitiera** venir ayer.	*I'm sorry your father didn't allow you to come yesterday.*
Es una lástima que no nos **presentaras** al campeón anoche.	*It's a pity that you didn't introduce us to the champion last night.*

Exercise

Complete the following sentences with the correct tense of the verbs in parentheses:

1. Dile a Marisa que (empezar) _____ de nuevo.
2. Me gustaría que tú (conocer) _____ a la campeona de tenis.
3. Siento que ellos no (haber visto) _____ las flores de mamá.
4. Le dijeron que (tocar) _____ la bocina.
5. Siento mucho que los chicos no (portarse) _____ bien ayer.
6. Les vamos a sugerir que ellos (repetir) _____ la lección.
7. Ellos siempre nos decían que no los (molestar) _____ .
8. Quiero que tú me (presentar) _____ a esa chica.
9. El profesor nos ha pedido que no (hablar) _____ en clase.
10. Raquel habló muy bien. Fue una lástima que los demás no (haberse expresado) _____ claramente.

3. USES OF **sino, sino que,** AND **pero**

Sino, meaning *but* in the sense of *on the contrary*, can only be used after a negative:

Ella trabaja para la ciudad, ¿verdad?	*She works for the city, right?*
No, no trabaja para la ciudad **sino** para el estado.	*No, she doesn't work for the city but for the state.*

Sino que is used in the same way as **sino** but to introduce a clause with a different verb:

¿Dónde trabaja Carlos?	*Where does Carlos work?*
Él no trabaja **sino que** estudia.	*He doesn't work; (but) he studies.*

Pero is used as the equivalent of *but* in all other cases:

¿Cuántos años tiene Anita?	*How old is Anita?*
No sé, **pero** creo que tiene más o menos quince años.	*I don't know, but I think she is about fifteen years old.*
¿No te vio Nicolás?	*Didn't Nicolas see you?*
Sí, me vio, **pero** no me reconoció.	*Yes, he saw me, but he didn't recognize me.*

Exercise

Complete the following sentences using **sino, sino que,** or **pero,** as needed:

1. Luis no va a vivir en el estado de Kansas _____ en el estado de Utah.
2. La culpa no fue mía _____ tuya.
3. Gerardo vino a hablarme, _____ yo no lo reconocí.
4. Marta no lo prohibió, _____ lo permitió.
5. No vivían en una casa, _____ en un apartamento.
6. Luis tiene muchos defectos, _____ Raquel lo quiere mucho.
7. María es bonita _____ no es simpática.
8. No me lo trajo Carlos _____ su esposa.
9. Elena no se dio por vencido, _____ lo hizo de nuevo.
10. No quieren flores _____ dulces.
11. Estudiaron mucho _____ no aprendieron nada.
12. Quiero ir a la playa _____ mis padres no me lo van a permitir.

4. NOMINALIZATION WITH THE NEUTER **lo**

In Spanish, the neuter **lo** is used with the masculine singular form of an adjective to form an abstract noun:

lo bueno	*the good thing*	**lo importante**	*the important thing*
lo malo	*the bad thing*	**lo interesante**	*the interesting thing*
lo mejor	*the best part*	**lo increíble**	*the incredible thing*
lo peor	*the worst part*	**lo imposible**	*the impossible thing*
lo triste	*the sad thing*		

¿Qué fue **lo mejor** del viaje a Brasil?

What was the best part about the trip to Brazil?

Para mí, **lo** más **impresionante** fue ver las cataratas del Iguazú.

For me, the most impressive thing was to see Iguazu Falls.

Beatriz no se lleva bien con sus hermanos.

Beatriz doesn't get along with her brothers.

No . . . y **lo peor** es que tampoco se lleva bien con sus padres.

No . . . and the worst part is that she doesn't get along with her parents either.

Exercise

Match the items in column A with those in column B:

A	B
1. Lo mejor	a. fue ver las cataratas del Niágara.
2. Lo triste	b. es tener una A sin estudiar.
3. Lo importante	c. es estar enfermo.
4. Lo impresionante	d. es aprender español.
5. Lo difícil	e. es que murieron todos.
6. Lo peor	f. es ser feliz.
7. Lo increíble	g. es que tiene dos años y habla dos idiomas.
8. Lo bueno	h. es llevarse bien con todo el mundo.

NEW VOCABULARY

NOUNS

la bocina	horn
el campeón } la campeona }	champion
las cataratas	falls
el defecto	fault
el estado	state
la flor	flower
la obra teatral	play

VERBS

acercarse (a)	to get near
enamorarse (de)	to fall in love (with)
expresar(se)	to express (oneself)
molestar(se)	to bother
permitir	to permit, to allow
portarse bien	to behave properly
presentar	to introduce, to present
reconocer	to recognize

repetir (e > i)	to repeat
sugerir (e > ie)	to suggest

ADJECTIVES

haragán(ana)	lazy
impresionante	impressive
increíble	incredible
tacaño(a)	stingy
triste	sad
vanidoso(a)	vain

OTHER WORDS AND EXPRESSIONS

a menos que	unless
de nuevo	again
hacer (algo) de nuevo	to do (something) over
hacer el papel de	to play the role of
los, las demás	the others
llevarse bien	to get along
más o menos	about, more or less

Para sus vacaciones ...

PUERTO RICO

El fin de semana en las
montañas de Puerto Rico

Lesson 24

1. FIRST PERSON PLURAL COMMAND ("LET'S" + VERB)

The first person plural of the affirmative command, which is translated *let's* + verb, may be expressed in Spanish in two different ways:

A. By using the first person plural of the present subjunctive:

¿Dónde vamos a comer hoy?	*Where are we going to eat today?*
Comamos en un restaurante italiano.	*Let's eat in an Italian restaurant.*
¿Dónde estudiamos?	*Where shall we study?*
Estudiemos en la biblioteca.	*Let's study in the library.*

An exception to this rule is the verb **ir**. With this verb, the subjunctive is not used in the affirmative:

¿A dónde vamos?	*Where shall we go?*
Vamos a la biblioteca.	*Let's go to the library.*
No . . . **no vayamos** a la biblioteca. **Vamos** a casa.	*No . . . let's not go to the library. Let's go home.*

B. By using the expression **vamos a** + the infinitive:[1]

Yo no creo que sea una buena idea tener el examen mañana.	*I don't think it's a good idea to have the exam tomorrow.*
Yo tampoco. **Vamos a hablar** con el profesor.	*I don't either. Let's talk to the professor.*

As in all direct affirmative commands the object pronouns are attached to the verb and a written accent is placed on the stressed syllable:

Tenemos que arreglar el techo porque gotea.	*We have to fix the roof because it's leaking.*
Pues **arreglémoslo** antes de que empiece la temporada de lluvias.	*Well, let's fix it before the rainy season starts.*

If the pronouns **nos** or **se** are attached to the verb, the final -s of the verb is dropped before adding the pronoun:

Estoy muy cansada.	*I'm very tired. Let's sit on this rock.*
Sentémonos en esta piedra.	
¿Está limpia?	*Is it clean?*

---

[1] This construction cannot be used in negative *let's* commands. For these, only the subjunctive is permitted: **No hablemos con el profesor.**

No, está llena de arena, pero no importa.

No, it's full of sand, but it doesn't matter.

¿A qué hora sale la excursión para el museo?
No sé, **preguntémoselo** al guía.

What time does the tour leave for the museum?
I don't know; let's ask the guide.

Exercise

Change the following sentences according to the model:

Modelo: Vamos a comer.
        Comamos.

1. Vamos a hacer comida italiana.
2. Vamos a arreglar el techo porque gotea.
3. Vamos a viajar antes de que empiece la temporada de lluvias.
4. Vamos a decírselo al guía.
5. Vamos a traer los vasos limpios.
6. Vamos a quitarle la arena a la piedra.
7. Vamos a desvestirnos.
8. Vamos a pedírselas a ellos.
9. Vamos a acostarnos temprano.
10. Vamos a darle la taza llena de café.

2. THE PASSIVE VOICE

In the active voice, the subject is the doer of the action. In the true passive voice, the subject of the sentence does not perform the action of the verb, but receives it. In Spanish the passive voice is formed in the same way as in English: English uses a form of *to be* + the past participle and Spanish uses a form of **ser** + the past participle.

Active Voice:	**Colón** descubrió América en 1492.	
	Subject Verb	

Columbus discovered America in 1492.
Subject   Verb

Passive Voice: **América fue descubierta** por Colón en 1492.
           Subject   Verb

America was discovered by Columbus in 1492.
Subject   Verb

In the true passive voice, the past participle always agrees with the subject in gender and number, and the agent (person performing the action) is preceded by **por** (*by*):

Esta iglesia es muy antigua . . .	*This church is very old . . .*
Sí, **fue construida** por los españoles en el siglo dieciocho.	*Yes, it was built by the Spaniards in the eighteenth century.*
¿Quién escribió estos libros?	*Who wrote these books?*
Creo que **fueron escritos** por Mark Twain.	*I believe they were written by Mark Twain.*

Exercise

Change these sentences from the active voice to the passive. Follow the model:

Modelo: Colón descubrió Cuba.
Cuba fue descubierta por Colón.

1. La compañía Sandoval construirá el edificio.
2. Cervantes escribió *Don Quijote* en el siglo 17.
3. El presidente ha recibido a los empleados.
4. El director envía las cartas de recomendación.
5. El presidente firmó los documentos.

3. THE PAST PARTICIPLE WITH ser OR estar

A. As you have seen, the past participle is used with the verb **ser** to express the passive voice. In this case the past participle agrees with the subject in gender and number:

El programa fue **desarrollado** por el gobierno federal.	*The program was developed by the federal government.*
Las cartas serán **escritas** por los estudiantes.	*The letters will be written by students.*

B. The past participle is used with the verb **estar** to describe a state or condition resulting from a previous action. The past participle, which is used as an adjective, agrees with the subject in gender and number:

¿Cómo entró el ladrón?	*How did the burglar get in?*
La **ventana** de mi cuarto **estaba abierta.**	*The window in my room was open.*
¿En qué idioma **está escrito** ese **libro**?	*What language is that book written in?*
Está escrito en inglés.	*It's written in English.*

Exercise

Give the Spanish equivalent:

1. The letters will be signed by the president.
2. Are all doors open?
3. She is sitting on her bed, reading a book.
4. America was discovered by Columbus.
5. The books are written in Italian.

4. CONJUNCTIONS e > y AND u > o

Spanish Equivalents of *and*	
When used directly before a word beginning with **i** or **hi:**	In other positions
e	y

Spanish Equivalents of *or*	
When used directly before a word beginning with **o** or **ho:**	In other positions
u	o

¿Para quién vas a tomar esos apuntes?

For whom are you going to take those notes?

Para Carlos **e** Hilda, que no vinieron a clase hoy.

For Carlos and Hilda, who didn't come to class today.

¿Quién te empujó, Carlos **u** Oscar?

Who pushed you, Carlos or Oscar?

Oscar, y por eso me peleé con él.

Oscar, that's why I fought with him.

Exercise

Rewrite the following sentences changing the order of the italicized words:

1. ¿Prefieres *oro* o *plata*?
2. Visité *Irán* y *España*.
3. Necesito *hilo* y *aguja*.
4. *Horacio* o *Víctor* van a tomar los apuntes.
5. *Isabel* y *Carmen* se pelearon con mi hija ayer.
6. Elsa es *inteligente* y *simpática*.

7. *¿Oeste* o *este?* ¿Hacia dónde vamos?
8. Pedimos *itinerarios de trenes* y *listas de hoteles.*

STUDY OF COGNATES

Exact cognate

federal   federal

NEW VOCABULARY

NOUNS

la arena	sand
el guía } **la guía**	guide
la piedra	rock, stone
el siglo	century
el techo	roof

VERBS

construir[1]	to build
desarrollar	to develop
descubrir	to discover
empujar	to push
gotear	to leak
pelear(se) (con)	to fight (with)

ADJECTIVES

italiano(a)	Italian
limpio(a)	clean
lleno(a)	full

OTHER WORDS AND EXPRESSIONS

temporada de lluvias	rainy season
tomar apuntes	to take notes

---

[1] Present indicative: **construyo, construyes, construye, construimos, construyen**

Test Yourself: Lessons 21-24

A. The future perfect tense

Give the Spanish equivalent:

1. By eight o'clock, we will have arrived at the bus station.
2. Will you have graduated by June, dear?
3. By Sunday I will have given him an answer.
4. The lawyers will have finished the job by next week.
5. I'm sure that he will have received the prize by tomorrow.

B. The conditional perfect tense

Write sentences with the verb in the conditional perfect, using the elements given. Add any necessary words. Follow the model:

Modelo: yo / no / hacerlo / todavía
Yo no lo habría hecho todavía.

1. nosotros / ir / discoteca
2. tú / no / comprar / ropa / esa tienda
3. ellos / prohibírmelo
4. ella / poner / sillón / su cuarto
5. ése / ser / mal / chiste
6. yo / no / secarse / esa toalla

C. Adjectives with shortened forms

Rewrite the following sentences using the new words provided in parentheses and making any necessary changes:

1. Vivimos en el segundo piso. (tercero)
2. Es una buena profesora. (profesor)
3. Insisten en que traigamos algunos periódicos. (dinero)
4. Adán fue el primer hombre sobre la tierra. (Eva)
5. No necesito ninguna clase. (libro)
6. Es mal profesor. (profesores)

D. Position of adjectives: change in meaning

Give the Spanish equivalent:

1. Poor Miguel! He always puts his foot in his mouth . . .
2. He is a poor man; he doesn't have (any) money.
3. He was a big man.

4. I met him ten years ago. He's an old friend.
5. Would you have brought the same clothes?
6. Lincoln was a great man.
7. She is an old woman. She is ninety-eight years old.
8. I have only one brother. He is my only brother.
9. I spoke to the president himself.
10. She is a unique woman.

LESSON 22

A. Pluperfect subjunctive

Write sentences with the verbs in the pluperfect subjunctive using the elements given. Add any necessary words. Follow the model:

Modelo: yo / sentir / tú / no / venir
   Yo sentí que tú no hubieras venido.

1. ser una lástima / ustedes / no ver / el espectáculo / los payasos
2. él / sentir / nosotros / ver / algo / tan desagradable
3. yo / alegrarme / tú / traerme / la pelota / la raqueta de tenis
4. ellos / alegrarse / yo / no / tener / la culpa
5. ojalá / ella / no / bajarse / esa estación
6. yo / no creer / ellos / darse por vencidos

B. The subjunctive after the expression **como si**

Fill in the blanks using the appropriate form of the verbs in the following list:

doler   poder   tener   ser   saber

1. Habla como si _____ jugar al tenis.
2. ¡Qué barbaridad! Gasta dinero como si _____ miles de dólares.
3. Ella está llorando como si le _____ mucho.
4. La mira como si ella _____ la mujer más hermosa del mundo.
5. Hablamos como si nosotros _____ adivinar el futuro.

C. Relative pronouns **que, quien,** and **quienes**

Complete the following sentences using **que, quien,** or **quienes,** as needed:

1. Ése es el hombre a _____ le alquilé el apartamento.
2. Las tijeras _____ me trajiste no son muy buenas.
3. Las señoras con _____ hablé ayer son católicas.

4. La chica con _____ estoy saliendo no es mal educada. Al contrario, es muy bien educada.
5. Ese chico _____ cruzó la calle de repente es mi hijo.
6. El sombrero _____ compré me costó treinta dólares.
7. ¿Quiénes son las chicas _____ están tomando el sol en el jardín?
8. La señora de _____ te hablamos ayer está aquí.

D. Omission of the indefinite article

Use the indefinite article when necessary:

1. Ella es _____ buena profesora.
2. Roberto no es _____ católico.
3. ¡ _____ otra tragedia! Hubo _____ accidente terrible en la autopista.
4. Necesito _____ tijera para cortarme las uñas.
5. Tenía tanta hambre que se comió _____ medio pollo.
6. Roberto me regaló _____ sombrero, pero yo nunca uso _____ sombrero.
7. Tengo _____ secretaria que habla muy bien el español.
8. Ellos están buscando _____ casa.

LESSON 23

A. The subjunctive with **tal vez, quizá(s),** and **aunque**

Complete the following sentences using the verbs in parentheses in the indicative or the subjunctive, as needed:

1. Aunque ellos (estar) _____ en el Brazil el mes pasado, no vieron las impresionantes cataratas del Iguazú.
2. Tal vez Gerardo (enamorarse) _____ de ella cuando la conozca.
3. Quizás los niños (portarse) _____ mal anoche, pero casi siempre se portan bien.
4. Yo iré al cine mañana aunque ellos no me lo (querer) _____ permitir.
5. Quizás ustedes (tener) _____ que hacerlo de nuevo, pero ahora está mejor.

B. Sequence of tenses with the subjunctive

Give the Spanish equivalent:

1. She didn't want the others to think that she was lazy, vain, and stingy.
2. My mother doesn't want us to see that play unless she goes with us.

3. I'm sorry the children have bothered you.
4. Tell him to try to express himself clearly.
5. I would have told her not to get near the house.
6. They're sorry that the champion lost last night.
7. I'll ask her to repeat it.
8. They told me to introduce him to my parents.

C. Uses of **sino, sino que,** and **pero**

Match the items in column A with those in column B. Use **sino, sino que,** or **pero** to join each pair and read each sentence aloud:

A	B
1. Me vio	a. el de Otelo.
2. Se lo sugerí	b. es muy inteligente.
3. No quiere hacer el papel de Hamlet	c. dulces.
4. No lo vendió	d. no quiso hacerlo.
5. No vive en el estado de Oregón	e. trabajamos.
6. Tiene muchos defectos	f. lo compró.
7. No fue a la peluquería	g. en el de Wáshington.
8. No compré flores	h. no quiere gastarlos.
9. No estudiamos	i. no me reconoció.
10. Tiene más o menos 100 dólares	j. a la farmacia.

(pero / sino / sino que)

D. Nominalization with the neuter **lo**

Give the Spanish equivalent:

1. The sad thing is that I don't get along with my brother.
2. The incredible thing is that she is only six years old and she speaks three languages.
3. The best part is that we're going to have a vacation.
4. He said the important thing was to have a lot of money.
5. The bad thing is that they can't go.

LESSON 24

A. First person plural command (*Let's* + verb)

Respond, agreeing with all suggestions offered. Follow the model:

Modelo: ¿Por qué no comemos comida italiana?
   Sí, comamos comida italiana.

1. ¿Por qué no estudiamos el siglo diez y nueve?
2. ¿Por qué no pintamos el techo?
3. ¿Por qué no llamamos al guía?
4. ¿Por qué no tomamos apuntes?
5. ¿Por qué no bebemos Coca-Cola?
6. ¿Por qué no se lo pedimos a Hugo?
7. ¿Por qué no nos acostamos?
8. ¿Por qué no se lo escribimos en inglés?

B. The passive voice

Answer the following questions, using the passive voice. Use the words provided in parentheses. Follow the model:

Modelo: ¿Quién firmó las cartas? (la directora)
Las cartas fueron firmadas por la directora.

1. ¿Quién descubrió América? (Cristóbal Colón)
2. ¿Quién construirá los edificios? (la compañía Rivera)
3. ¿Quién ha desarrollado ese programa? (el gobierno federal)
4. ¿Quién recomendó a ese abogado? (el presidente de la compañía)
5. ¿Quién firma las cartas? (la jefa)

C. The past participle with **ser** or **estar**

Match the items in columns A, B, and C, and combine them to write sentences:

A	B	C
1. Las ventanas	fue	construido en enero.
2. La puerta	está	abiertas.
3. Las cartas	será	firmadas por él.
4. Cuba	fue	cerrada con llave.
5. El edificio	está	comprada ayer.
6. Los niños	estaban	pintada de rojo.
7. La piedra	están	parados en la esquina.
8. La arena	son	descubierta en 1492.

D. Conjunctions **e** > **y** and **u** > **o**

Give the Spanish equivalent:

1. Carlos or Osvaldo will fix the roof, because it leaks.
2. The rainy season starts in September or October.
3. The room was full of relatives and guests.
4. Raquel and Hilario fought with Rosa and pushed her.
5. Mariana and Ines said the house wasn't clean.

APPENDICES

Appendix A: Pronunciation

1. SPANISH SOUNDS

A. The Vowels

Spanish has five distinctive vowels: **a, e, i, o, u.** Each vowel has only one basic sound that is produced with considerable muscular tension. The pronunciation of each vowel is constant, clear, and brief. The sound is never prolonged; in fact, the length of the sound is almost the same whether it is produced in a stressed or an unstressed syllable.[1]

To produce the English stressed vowels that most closely resemble Spanish, the speaker changes the position of the tongue, lips, and lower jaw during the production of the sound, so that the vowel actually starts as one sound, and then *glides* into another. In Spanish, however, the tongue, lips, and jaw keep a constant position during the production of the sound.

English	*Spanish*
banana	banana

The stress falls on the same vowel and syllable in both Spanish and English, but the stressed English *a* is longer in comparison to Spanish stressed **a.**

English	*Spanish*
banana	banana

Also notice that the stressed English *a* has a sound different from the other *a*'s in the word, while the Spanish **a** sound remains constant and is similar to the other **a** sounds in the Spanish word.

a   in Spanish has a sound somewhat similar to the English *a* in the word *father:*

alta	palma	cama	alma
casa	Ana	Panamá	apagar

e   is pronounced like the English *e* in the word *met:*

mes	este	ese	teme
entre	deje	encender	prender

i   has a sound similar to the English *ee* in the word *see:*

fin	sí	dividir	difícil
ir	sin	Trini	

---

[1] In a stressed syllable the prominence of the vowel is indicated by its loudness.

231

o is similar to the English *o* in the word *know*, but without the glide:

toco	poco	corto	solo
como	roto	corro	loco

u is pronounced like the English *oo* sound in the word *shoot*, or the *ue* sound in the word *Sue:*

su	Úrsula	un	sucursal
Lulú	cultura	luna	Uruguay

Diphthongs and Triphthongs:

When unstressed **i** or **u** falls next to another vowel in a syllable, it unites with it to form a *diphthong*. Both vowels are pronounced as one syllable. Their sounds do not change; they are only pronounced more rapidly and with a glide. For example:

traiga	Lidia	treinta	siete	oigo	adiós
Aurora	agua	bueno	antiguo	ciudad	Luis

A *triphthong* is the union of three vowels, a stressed vowel between unstressed **i** or **u,** in the same syllable. For example:

Paraguay   estudiáis

NOTE: Stressed **i** and **u** do not form diphthongs with other vowels, except in the combinations **iu** and **ui.** For example:

rí-o   sa-bí-ais

In syllabication, diphthongs and triphthongs are considered as a single vowel. Their components cannot be separated.

B. The Consonants

Consonant sounds are produced by regulating the flow of air through the mouth with the aid of two speech organs. As the diagrams illustrate, different speech organs can be used to control the air flow. The point of articulation will differ accordingly.

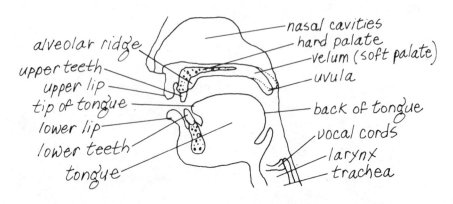

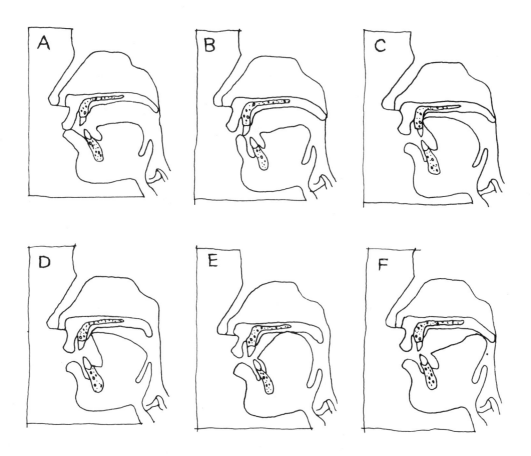

In Spanish the air flow can be controlled in different ways. One such way is called a *stop* because in the articulation of the sound the air is stopped at some point while passing through the oral cavity.

When we bring the speech organs close together, but without closing the air flow completely, we produce a friction sound called a *fricative*, such as the *ff* and the *th* in the English words *offer* and *other*.

p Spanish **p** is produced by bringing the lips together as a stream of air passes through the oral cavity (see diagram A). It is pronounced in a manner similar to the English *p* sound, but without the puff of air that comes out after the English sound is produced:

pesca	pude	puedo	parte	papá
postre	piña	puente	Paco	

k Spanish **k** sound, represented by the letters **k, c** (before **a, o, u,** or *a consonant*), and **qu,** is produced by touching the velum with the back of the tongue, as in diagram B. The sound is somewhat similar to the English *k* sound but without the puff of air:

casa   comer   cuna   clima   acción   que
quinto   queso   aunque   kiosko   kilómetro

t   The Spanish **t** sound is produced by touching the back of the upper front teeth with the tip of the tongue, as in diagram C. It has no puff of air as in the English *t:*

todo   antes   corto   Guatemala   diente
resto   tonto   roto   tanque

d   The Spanish consonant **d** has two different sounds depending on its position. At the beginning of an utterance and after **n** or **l**, the tip of the tongue presses the back of the upper front teeth to produce what is called a *voiced dental stop* (see diagram C):

día   doma   dice   dolor   dar
anda   Aldo   caldo   el deseo   un domicilio

In all other positions the sound of **d** is similar to the *th* sound in the English word *they*, but softer. This sound is called a *voiced dental fricative* (see diagram C). To produce it, place the tip of the tongue behind the front teeth:

medida   todo   nada   nadie   medio
puedo   moda   queda   nudo

g   The Spanish consonant **g** also represents two sounds. At the beginning of an utterance or after **n**, it is a *voiced velar stop* (see diagram B), identical to the English *g* sound in the word *guy:*

goma   glotón   gallo   gloria
gorrión   garra   guerra   angustia

In all other positions, except before **e** or **i**, it is a *voiced velar fricative* (see diagram B), similar to the English *g* sound in the word *sugar*. To produce it, move the back of the tongue close to the velum, as in diagram F:

lago   alga   traga   amigo
algo   Dagoberto   el gorrión   la goma

j   The sound of Spanish **j** (or **g** before **e** and **i**) is called a *voiceless velar fricative*. To produce it, position the back of the tongue close to the velum (see diagram F). (In some Latin American countries the sound is similar to a strongly exaggerated English *h* sound.):

gemir   juez   jarro   gitano   agente
juego   giro   bajo   gente

b, v There is no difference in sound between Spanish **b** and **v**. Both letters are pronounced alike. At the beginning of an utterance or after **m** or **n**, **b** and **v** have a sound called a *voiced bilabial stop* (see diagram A), which is identical to the English *b* sound in the word *boy:*

vivir	beber	vamos	barco	enviar
hambre	batea	bueno	vestido	

In all other positions the Spanish **b** and **v** sound is a *voiced bilabial fricative* (see diagram A). To produce this sound, bring the lips together but do not close them, letting some air pass through.

y, ll At the beginning of an utterance or after **n** or **l**, Spanish **y** and **ll** have a sound similar to the English *dg* in the word *edge*, but somewhat softer (see diagram E):

el llavero	el yeso	llama
un yelmo	su yunta	yema

In all other positions the sound is a *voiced palatal fricative* (see diagram E), similar to the English *y* sound in the word *yes:*

oye	trayectoria	milla
trayecto	mayo	bella

NOTE: Spanish **y** when it stands alone or is at the end of a word is pronounced like the vowel **i:**

rey	doy	voy
hoy	buey	estoy
y	muy	soy

r, rr Spanish **r** is produced by tapping the alveolar ridge with the tongue only once and very briefly (see diagram D). The sound is similar to the English *tt* sound in the word *gutter* or the *dd* sound in the word *ladder:*

crema	aroma	cara	arena	aro
harina	toro	oro	eres	portero

Spanish **r** in an initial position and after **n, l,** or **s,** and also **rr** in the middle of a word are pronounced with a very strong trill. This trill is produced by bringing the tip of the tongue near the alveolar ridge and letting it vibrate freely while the air passes through the mouth:

rama	carro	Israel	cierra	roto
perro	alrededor	rizo	corre	Enrique

s Spanish **s** is represented in most of the Spanish world by the letters **s, z,** and **c** before **e** or **i**. The sound is very similar to the English sibilant *s* in the word *sink:*

sale	sitio	presidente	signo
salsa	seda	suma	vaso
sobrino	ciudad	cima	canción
zapato	zarza	cerveza	centro

When it is in final position, Spanish **s** is less sibilant than in other positions. In many regions of the Spanish world there is a tendency to aspirate word-final **s** and even to drop it altogether:

eres	somos	estas	mesas	libros
vamos	sillas	cosas	rezas mucho	

h The letter **h** is silent in Spanish, unless it is combined with the **c** to form **ch:**

hoy	hora	hidra	hemos
humor	huevo	horror	hortelano

ch Spanish **ch** is pronounced like the English *ch* in the word *chief:*

hecho	chico	coche	Chile
mucho	muchacho	salchicha	

f Spanish **f** is identical in sound to the English *f:*

difícil	feo	fuego	forma
fácil	fecha	foto	fueron

l To produce the Spanish **l** sound, touch the alveolar ridge with the tip of the tongue as for the English *l*. Try to keep the rest of the tongue fairly low in the mouth:

dolor	lata	ángel	lago	sueldo
los	pelo	lana	general	fácil

m Spanish **m** is pronounced like the English *m* in the word *mother:*

mano	moda	mucho	muy
mismo	tampoco	multa	cómoda

n In most cases, Spanish **n** has a sound similar to the English *n* (see diagram D):

nada	nunca	ninguno	norte
entra	tiene	sienta	

The sound of Spanish **n** is often affected by the sounds that occur around it. When it appears before **b, v,** or **p,** it is pronounced like an **m:**

| tan bueno | toman vino | sin poder |
| un pobre | comen peras | siguen bebiendo |

Before **k, g,** and **j,** Spanish **n** has a voiced velar nasal sound, similar to the English *ng* in the word *sing:*

| un kilómetro | incompleto | conjunto | mango |
| tengo | enjuto | un comedor | |

ñ   Spanish **ñ** is a voiced palatal sound (see diagram E), similar to the English *ny* sound in the word *canyon:*

| señor | otoño | ñoño | uña |
| leña | dueño | niños | años |

x   Spanish **x** has two pronunciations depending on its position. Between vowels the sound is similar to an English *gs:*

| examen | exacto | boxeo | éxito |
| oxidar | oxígeno | existencia | |

When Spanish **x** occurs before a consonant it sounds like *s:*

| expresión | explicar | extraer | excusa |
| expreso | exquisito | extremo | |

NOTE: When the x appears in the word **México** or in other words of Mexican origin that are associated with historical or legendary figures or name places, it is pronounced like the letter **j.**

2. RHYTHM

Rhythm is the melodic variation of sound intensity that we usually associate with music. Spanish and English each regulate these variations in speech differently, because they have different patterns of syllable length. In Spanish the length of the stressed and unstressed syllables remains almost the same, while in English stressed syllables are considerably longer than unstressed ones:

student	**estudiante**
composition	**composición**
police	**policía**

Since the length of the Spanish syllables remains constant, the greater the number of syllables in a given word or phrase, the longer the phrase will be.

Pronounce the following words trying to keep stressed and unstressed syllables the same length, and enunciating each syllable clearly. (Remember that stressed and unstressed vowels are pronounced alike.)

Úr-su-la	los-za-pa-tos
la-su-cur-sal	bue-no
Pa-ra-guay	di-fí-cil
la-cul-tu-ra	ba-jan-to-dos
el-ci-ne	ki-ló-me-tro

3. LINKING

In spoken Spanish the different words in a phrase or a sentence are not pronounced as isolated elements but combined together. This is called *linking:*

Pe-pe-co-me-pan	Pepe come pan
To-más-to-ma-le-che	Tomás toma leche
Luis-tie-ne-la-lla-ve	Luis tiene la llave
la-ma-no-de-Ro-ber-to	La mano de Roberto

1. The last consonant of a word is pronounced together with the initial vowel of the following word:

Car-lo-san-da	Carlos anda
u-nán-gel	un ángel
e-lo-to-ño	el otoño
u-no-ses-tu-dio-sin-te-re-san-tes	unos estudios interesantes

2. A diphthong is formed between the last vowel of a word and the initial vowel of the following word. A triphthong is formed when there is a three vowel combination:

suher-ma-na	su hermana
tues-co-pe-ta	tu escopeta
Ro-ber-toy-Luis	Roberto y Luis
ne-go-cioim-por-tan-te	negocio importante
llu-viay-nie-ve	lluvia y nieve
ar-duaem-pre-sa	ardua empresa

3. When the last vowel of a word and the initial vowel of the following word are the same, they are pronounced slightly longer than one vowel:

A-nal-can-za	Ana alcanza	tie-ne-so	tiene eso
lol-vi-do	lo olvido	Ada-tien-de	Ada atiende

The same rule applies when two equal vowels appear within a word:

cres	crees
Te-rán	Teherán
cor-di-na-ción	coordinación

4. When the last consonant of a word and the initial consonant of the following word are the same, they are pronounced like one consonant with slightly longer than normal duration:

e-la-do   el lado   tie-ne-sed tienes sed
Car-lo-sal-ta Carlos salta

4. INTONATION

Intonation is the rise and fall of pitch in the delivery of a phrase or a sentence. In most languages intonation is one of the most important devices used to express differences of meaning between otherwise identical phrases or sentences. In general, Spanish pitch tends to change less than English pitch, giving the impression that the language is less emphatic.

As a rule, the intonation for normal statements in Spanish starts in a low tone, raises to a higher one on the first syllable, maintains that tone until the last stressed syllable, and then goes back to the initial low tone, with still another drop at the very end:

5. THE ALPHABET

Letter	Name	Letter	Name	Letter	Name	Letter	Name
a	a	g	ge	m	eme	rr	erre
b	be	h	hache	n	ene	s	ese
c	ce	i	i	ñ	eñe	t	te
ch	che	j	jota	o	o	u	u
d	de	k	ka	p	pe	v	ve
e	e	l	ele	q	cu	w	doble ve
f	efe	ll	elle	r	ere	x	equis
						y	i griega
						z	zeta

6. SYLLABLE FORMATION IN SPANISH

General rules for dividing words into syllables:

A. Vowels

1. A vowel or a vowel combination can constitute a syllable:

   a-lum-no   a-bue-la   Eu-ro-pa

2. Diphthongs and triphthongs are considered single vowels and cannot be divided:

   bai-le   puen-te   Dia-na   es-tu-diáis   an-ti-guo

3. Two stressed vowels do not form a diphthong and are separated into two syllables:

   em-ple-ar   vol-te-ar   lo-a

4. A written accent on unstressed **i** or **u** breaks the diphthong, thus the vowels are separated into two syllables:

   trí-o   dí-a   Ma-rí-a

B. Consonants

1. A single consonant forms a syllable with the vowel which follows it:

   po-der   ma-no   mi-nu-to

   NOTE: **ch, ll,** and **rr** are considered single consonants, for example:

   a-ma-ri-llo   co-che   pe-rro

2. Consonant clusters composed of **b, c, d, f, g, p,** or **t** with **l** or **r** are considered single consonants and cannot be separated:

   ha-blar   cla-vo   a-tlán-ti-co   Glo-ria

3. When two consonants appear between two vowels, they are separated into two syllables:

   al-fa-be-to   cam-pe-ón   me-ter-se   mo-les-tia

   EXCEPTION: When a consonant cluster appears between two vowels, we apply rule 2, and the cluster joins the following vowel, for example:

   so-bre   o-tros   ca-ble   te-lé-gra-fo

4. When three consonants appear between two vowels, only the last one goes with the following vowel:

ins-pec-tor   trans-por-te   trans-for-mar

EXCEPTION: When a consonant cluster appears, the first consonant joins the preceding vowel and the cluster joins the following vowel, for example:

es-cri-bir   ex-tran-je-ro   im-plo-rar   es-tre-cho

7. ACCENTUATION

In Spanish all words are stressed according to specific rules. Words that do not follow the rules must have a written accent to indicate the change of stress. The basic rules for accentuation are as follows:

1. Words ending in a vowel, **n**, or **s** are stressed on the next to the last syllable:

hi-jo   **ca**-lle   **me**-sa   fa-**mo**-sos
flo-**re**-cen   **pla**-ya   **ve**-ces

2. Words ending in a consonant, except **n** or **s**, are stressed on the last syllable:

ma-**yor**   na-**riz**
a-**mor**   re-**loj**
tro-pi-**cal**   co-rre-**dor**

3. All words that do not follow these rules, and also those that are stressed on the second syllable from the last, must have the written accent:

ca-**fé**   sa-**lió**   rin-**cón**   fran-**cés**   sa-**lón**   ma-**má**
án-gel   **lá**-piz   **dé**-bil   a-**zú**-car   **Víc**-tor
sim-**pá**-tico **lí**-qui-do **mú**-si-ca e-**xá**-me-nes de-**mó**-cra-ta

4. Pronouns and adverbs of interrogation and exclamation have a written accent to distinguish them from the relatives:

¿**Qué** comes? *What are you eating?*
La pera que no comió. *The pear that he did not eat.*

¿**Quién** está ahí? *Who is there?*
El hombre a quien vi. *The man whom I saw.*

¿**Dónde** está? *Where is he?*
El lugar donde él trabaja. *The place where he works.*

5. Words that are spelled the same but have a different meaning take a written accent to differentiate one from the other:

el	the	**él**	he, him
mi	my	**mí**	me
tu	your	**tú**	you
te	you (pronoun)	**té**	tea
si	if	**sí**	yes
mas	but	**más**	more

6. The demonstrative adjectives have a written accent when they are used as pronouns:

éste	ésta	éstos	éstas	ése	ésa
ésos	ésas	aquél	aquélla	aquéllos	aquéllas

Prefiero **aquél.**   *I prefer that one.*

8. COGNATES

When learning a foreign language, being able to recognize cognates is of great value. Let's study some of them:

1. Some exact cognates (only the pronunciation is different):

general	mineral	central	natural
idea	musical	cultural	banana
terrible	horrible	humor	terror

2. Some cognates are almost the same, except for a written accent mark, a final vowel, or a single consonant in the Spanish word:

región	península	México	conversión
persona	arte	importante	potente
comercial	oficial	posible	imposible

3. Most nouns ending in *-tion* in English end in **-ción** in Spanish:

conversación   solución   operación   cooperación

4. English words ending in -ce and -ty end in **-cia, -cio,** and **-dad** in Spanish:

importancia	competencia	precipicio
universidad	frivolidad	popularidad

5. The English ending *-ous* is often equivalent to the Spanish ending **-oso:**

famoso   amoroso   numeroso   malicioso

6. S consonant is often equivalent to **es** consonant in Spanish:

escuela   estado   estudio   especial

7. Finally, there are less approximate cognates that are still easily recognizable:

millón	norte	millonario	monte
ingeniero	estudiar	artículo	ordenar
deliberadamente	enemigo	mayoría	centro

Appendix B: Pronouns

SUBJECT PRONOUNS

yo I	**nosotros, -as** we
tú you (*fam.*)	**vosotros, -as** you (*fam.*)
usted you (*form.*)	**ustedes** you (*form.*)
él he	**ellos** they (*masc.*)
ella she	**ellas** they (*fem.*)

DIRECT OBJECT PRONOUNS

me me	**nos** us
te you (*fam.*)	**os** you (*fam.*)
lo you (*masc. form.*), him, it	**los** you (*masc. form.*), them (*masc.*)
la you (*fem. form.*), her, it	**las** you (*fem. form.*), them (*fem.*)

INDIRECT OBJECT PRONOUNS

me me	**nos** us
te you (*fam.*)	**os** you (*fam.*)
le you (*form.*), him, her	**les** you (*form.*), them

OBJECTS OF PREPOSITIONS

mí me	**nosotros, -as** us
ti you (*fam.*)	**vosotros, -as** you (*fam.*)
usted you (*form.*)	**ustedes** you (*form.*)
él him	**ellos** them (*masc.*)
ella her	**ellas** them (*fem.*)

REFLEXIVE PRONOUNS

me myself	**nos** ourselves
te yourself (*fam.*)	**os** yourselves (*fam.*)
se yourself (*form.*), himself, herself	**se** yourselves (*form.*), themselves

POSSESSIVE PRONOUNS

el mío mine	**el nuestro** ours
el tuyo yours (*fam.*)	**el vuestro** yours (*fam.*)
el suyo yours (*form.*), his, hers	**el suyo** yours (*form.*)

Appendix C: Verbs

Regular verbs

Model **-ar, -er, -ir** verbs

	INFINITIVE	
amar (*to love*)	**comer** (*to eat*)	**vivir** (*to live*)

	PRESENT PARTICIPLE	
amando (*loving*)	**comiendo** (*eating*)	**viviendo** (*living*)

	PAST PARTICIPLE	
amado (*loved*)	**comido** (*eaten*)	**vivido** (*lived*)

SIMPLE TENSES

Indicative Mood

	PRESENT	
(*I love*)	(*I eat*)	(*I live*)
am**o**	com**o**	viv**o**
am**as**	com**es**	viv**es**
am**a**	com**e**	viv**e**
am**amos**	com**emos**	viv**imos**
am**áis**	com**éis**	viv**ís**
am**an**	com**en**	viv**en**

	IMPERFECT	
(*I used to love*)	(*I used to eat*)	(*I used to live*)
am**aba**	com**ía**	viv**ía**
am**abas**	com**ías**	viv**ías**
am**aba**	com**ía**	viv**ía**
am**ábamos**	com**íamos**	viv**íamos**
am**abais**	com**íais**	viv**íais**
am**aban**	com**ían**	viv**ían**

PRETERIT

(*I loved*)	(*I ate*)	(*I lived*)
amé	comí	viví
amaste	comiste	viviste
amó	comió	vivió
amamos	comimos	vivimos
amasteis	comisteis	vivisteis
amaron	comieron	vivieron

FUTURE

(*I will love*)	(*I will eat*)	(*I will live*)
amaré	comeré	viviré
amarás	comerás	vivirás
amará	comerá	vivirá
amaremos	comeremos	viviremos
amaréis	comeréis	viviréis
amarán	comerán	vivirán

CONDITIONAL

(*I would love*)	(*I would eat*)	(*I would live*)
amaría	comería	viviría
amarías	comerías	vivirías
amaría	comería	viviría
amaríamos	comeríamos	viviríamos
amaríais	comeríais	viviríais
amarían	comerían	vivirían

Subjunctive Mood

PRESENT

([*that*] I [*may*] love)	([*that*] I [*may*] eat)	([*that*] I [*may*] live)
ame	coma	viva
ames	comas	vivas
ame	coma	viva
amemos	comamos	vivamos
améis	comáis	viváis
amen	coman	vivan

IMPERFECT

(two forms: ara, ase)

([*that*] I [*might*] love)	([*that*] I [*might*] eat)	([*that*] I [*might*] live)
amara -ase	comiera -iese	viviera -iese
amaras -ases	comieras -ieses	vivieras -ieses
amara -ase	comiera -iese	viviera -iese
amáramos -ásemos	comiéramos -iésemos	viviéramos -iésemos
amarais -aseis	comierais -ieseis	vivierais -ieseis
amaran -asen	comieran -iesen	vivieran -iesen

IMPERATIVE MOOD

(*love*)	(*eat*)	(*live*)
am**a** (tú)	com**e** (tú)	viv**e** (tú)
am**e** (Ud.)	com**a** (Ud.)	viv**a** (Ud.)
am**emos** (nosotros)	com**amos** (nosotros)	viv**amos** (nosotros)
am**ad** (vosotros)	com**ed** (vosotros)	viv**id** (vosotros)
am**en** (Uds.)	com**an** (Uds.)	viv**an** (Uds.)

COMPOUND TENSES

PERFECT INFINITIVE

haber amado	**haber comido**	**haber vivido**

PERFECT PARTICIPLE

habiendo amado	**habiendo comido**	**habiendo vivido**

Indicative Mood

PRESENT PERFECT

(*I have loved*)	(*I have eaten*)	(*I have lived*)
he amado	he comido	he vivido
has amado	has comido	has vivido
ha amado	ha comido	ha vivido
hemos amado	hemos comido	hemos vivido
habéis amado	habéis comido	habéis vivido
han amado	han comido	han vivido

PLUPERFECT

(*I had loved*)	(*I had eaten*)	(*I had lived*)
había amado	había comido	había vivido
habías amado	habías comido	habías vivido
había amado	había comido	había vivido
habíamos amado	habíamos comido	habíamos vivido
habíais amado	habíais comido	habíais vivido
habían amado	habían comido	habían vivido

FUTURE PERFECT

(*I will have loved*)	(*I will have eaten*)	(*I will have lived*)
habré amado	habré comido	habré vivido
habrás amado	habrás comido	habrás vivido
habrá amado	habrá comido	habrá vivido
habremos amado	habremos comido	habremos vivido
habréis amado	habréis comido	habréis vivido
habrán amado	habrán comido	habrán vivido

CONDITIONAL PERFECT

(*I would have loved*)	(*I would have eaten*)	(*I would have lived*)
habría amado	habría comido	habría vivido
habrías amado	habrías comido	habrías vivido
habría amado	habría comido	habría vivido
habríamos amado	habríamos comido	habríamos vivido
habríais amado	habríais comido	habríais vivido
habrían amado	habrían comido	habrían vivido

Subjunctive Mood

PRESENT PERFECT

([*that*] *I* [*may*] have loved)	([*that*] *I* [*may*] have eaten)	([*that*] *I* [*may*] have lived)
haya amado	haya comido	haya vivido
hayas amado	hayas comido	hayas vivido
haya amado	haya comido	haya vivido
hayamos amado	hayamos comido	hayamos vivido
hayáis amado	hayáis comido	hayáis vivido
hayan amado	hayan comido	hayan vivido

PLUPERFECT

(two forms: **-ra**, **-se**)

([*that*] *I* [*might*] have loved)	([*that*] *I* [*might*] have eaten)	([*that*] *I* [*might*] have lived)
hubiera(-iese) amado	hubiera(-iese) comido	hubiera(-iese) vivido
hubieras(-ieses) amado	hubieras(-ieses) comido	hubieras(-ieses) vivido
hubiera(-iese) amado	hubiera(-iese) comido	hubiera(-iese) vivido
hubiéramos(-iésemos) amado	hubiéramos(-iésemos) comido	hubiéramos(-iésemos) vivido
hubierais(-ieseis) amado	hubierais(-ieseis) comido	hubierais(-ieseis) vivido
hubieran(-iesen) amado	hubieran(-iesen) comido	hubieran(-iesen) vivido

Stem-changing verbs

The **-ar** and **-er** stem-changing verbs

Stem-changing verbs are those that have a change in the root of the verb. Verbs that end in **-ar** and **-er** change the stressed vowel **e** to **ie**, and the stressed **o** to **ue**. These changes occur in all persons, except the first and second persons plural, of the present indicative, present subjunctive, and imperative.

INFINITIVE	PRESENT INDICATIVE	IMPERATIVE	PRESENT SUBJUNCTIVE
perder (*to lose*)	pierdo	——	pierda
	pierdes	pierde	pierdas
	pierde	pierda	pierda
	perdemos	perdamos	perdamos
	perdéis	perded	perdáis
	pierden	pierdan	pierdan
cerrar (*to close*)	cierro	——	cierre
	cierras	cierra	cierres
	cierra	cierre	cierre
	cerramos	cerremos	cerremos
	cerráis	cerrad	cerréis
	cierran	cierren	cierren
contar (*to count, to tell*)	cuento	——	cuente
	cuentas	cuenta	cuentes
	cuenta	cuente	cuente
	contamos	contemos	contemos
	contáis	contad	contéis
	cuentan	cuenten	cuenten
volver (*to return*)	vuelvo	——	vuelva
	vuelves	vuelve	vuelvas
	vuelve	vuelva	vuelva
	volvemos	volvamos	volvamos
	volvéis	volved	volváis
	vuelven	vuelvan	vuelvan

Verbs that follow the same pattern are:

acordarse to remember
acostar(se) to go to bed
almorzar to have lunch
atravesar to go through
cocer to cook
colgar to hang
comenzar to begin
confesar to confess
costar to cost
demostrar to demonstrate, to show
despertar(se) to wake up
empezar to begin
encender to light, turn on
encontrar to find
entender to understand

llover to rain
mover to move
mostrar to show
negar to deny
nevar to snow
pensar to think, to plan
probar to prove, to taste
recordar to remember
rogar to beg
sentar(se) to sit down
soler to be in the habit of
soñar to dream
tender to stretch, to unfold
torcer to twist

The -ir stem-changing verbs

There are two types of stem-changing verbs that end in -ir: one type changes stressed e to ie in some tenses and to i in others, and stressed o to ue or u; the second type changes stressed e to i only in all the irregular tenses.

Type I   -ir: e > ie / o > ue or u

These changes occur as follows:

Present Indicative: all persons except the first and second plural change e to ie and o to ue. Preterit: third person, singular and plural, changes e to i and o to u. Present Subjunctive: all persons change e to ie and o to ue, except the first and second persons plural which change e to i and o to u. Imperfect Subjunctive: all persons change e to i and o to u. Imperative: all persons except the second person plural change e to ie and o to ue, and first person plural changes e to i and o to u. Present Participle: changes e to i and o to u.

	Indicative		Imperative	Subjunctive	
INFINITIVE	PRESENT	PRETERIT		PRESENT	IMPERFECT
sentir	siento	sentí	——	sienta	sintiera (-iese)
(*to feel*)	sientes	sentiste	siente	sientas	sintieras
	siente	sintió	sienta	sienta	sintiera
PRESENT	sentimos	sentimos	sintamos	sintamos	sintiéramos
PARTICIPLE	sentís	sentisteis	sentid	sintáis	sintierais
sintiendo	sienten	sintieron	sientan	sientan	sintieran
dormir	duermo	dormí	——	duerma	durmiera (-iese)
(*to sleep*)	duermes	dormiste	duerme	duermas	durmieras
	duerme	durmió	duerma	duerma	durmiera
PRESENT	dormimos	dormimos	durmamos	durmamos	durmiéramos
PARTICIPLE	dormís	dormisteis	dormid	durmáis	durmierais
durmiendo	duermen	durmieron	duerman	duerman	durmieran

Other verbs that follow the same pattern are:

advertir to warn   **mentir** to lie
arrepentir(se) to repent   **morir** to die
consentir to consent, to pamper   **preferir** to prefer
convertir(se) to turn into   **referir** to refer
divertir(se) to amuse oneself   **sugerir** to suggest
herir to wound, to hurt

Type II   -ir: e > i

The verbs in this second category are irregular in the same tenses as those of the first type. The only difference is that they only have one change: **e > i** in all irregular persons.

	Indicative		Imperative	Subjunctive	
INFINITIVE	PRESENT	PRETERIT		PRESENT	IMPERFECT
pedir	pido	pedí	——	pida	pidiera (-iese)
(*to ask for,*	pides	pediste	pide	pidas	pidieras
request)	pide	pidió	pida	pida	pidiera
PRESENT	pedimos	pedimos	pidamos	pidamos	pidiéramos
PARTICIPLE	pedís	pedisteis	pedid	pidáis	pidierais
pidiendo	piden	pidieron	pidan	pidan	pidieran

Verbs that follow this pattern are:

concebir to conceive
competir to compete
despedir(se) to say goodbye
elegir to choose
impedir to prevent
perseguir to pursue

reir(se) to laugh
repetir to repeat
reñir to fight
seguir to follow
servir to serve
vestir(se) to dress

Orthographic-changing verbs

Some verbs undergo a change in the spelling of the stem in some tenses, in order to keep the sound of the final consonant. The most common ones are those with the consonants **g** and **c**. Remember that **g** and **c** in front of **e** or **i** have a soft sound, and in front of **a, o,** or **u** have a hard sound. In order to keep the soft sound in front of **a, o,** and **u,** we change **g** and **c** to **j** and **z,** respectively. And in order to keep the hard sound of **g** and **c** in front of **e** and **i,** we add a **u** to the **g** (**gu**) and change the **c** to **qu**. Following are the most important verbs of this type:

1. Verbs ending in **-gar** change **g** to **gu** before **e** in the first person of the preterit and in all persons of the present subjunctive.

   pagar (*to pay*)
   Preterit: pagué, pagaste, pagó, etc.
   Pres. Subj.:   pague, pagues, pague, paguemos, paguéis, paguen

   Verbs with the same change: **colgar, llegar, navegar, negar, regar, rogar, jugar.**

2. Verbs ending in **-ger** and **-gir** change **g** to **j** before **o** and **a** in the first person of the present indicative and in all the persons of the present subjunctive.

proteger (*to protect*)
Pres. Ind.:   protejo, proteges, protege, etc.
Pres. Subj.:   proteja, protejas, proteja, protejamos, protejáis, protejan

Verbs that follow the same pattern: **coger, dirigir, escoger, exigir, recoger, corregir.**

3. Verbs ending in **-guar** change **gu** to **gü** before **e** in the first persons of the preterit and in all persons of the present subjunctive.

averiguar (*to find out*)
Preterit: averigüé, averiguaste, averiguó, etc.
Pres. Subj.:   averigüe, averigües, averigüe, averigüemos, averigüéis, averigüen

The verb **apaciguar** has the same changes.

4. Verbs ending in **-guir** change **gu** to **g** before **o** and **a** in the first person of the present indicative and in all persons of the present subjunctive.

conseguir (*to get*)
Pres. Ind.:   consigo, consigues, consigue, etc.
Pres. Subj.:   consiga, consigas, consiga, consigamos, consigáis, consigan

Verbs with the same change: **distinguir, perseguir, proseguir, seguir.**

5. Verbs ending in **-car** change **c** to **qu** before **e** in the first person of the preterit and in all persons of the present subjunctive.

tocar (*to touch, to play* [*a musical instrument*])
Preterit: toqué, tocaste, tocó, etc.
Pres. Subj.:   toque, toques, toque, toquemos, toquéis, toquen

Verbs with the same pattern: **atacar, buscar, communicar, explicar, indicar, sacar, pescar.**

6. Verbs ending in **-cer** and **-cir** preceded by a consonant change **c** to **z** before **o** and **a** in the first person of the present indicative and in all persons of the present subjunctive.

torcer (*to twist*)
Pres. Ind.:   tuerzo, tuerces, tuerce, etc.
Pres. Subj.:   tuerza, tuerzas, tuerza, torzamos, torzáis, tuerzan

Verbs with the same change: **convencer, esparcir, vencer.**

7. Verbs ending in **-cer** and **-cir** preceded by a vowel change **c** to **zc** before **o** and **a** in the first person of the present indicative and in all persons of the present subjunctive.

conocer (*to know, to be acquainted with*)
Pres. Ind.:   conozco, conoces, conoce, etc.
Pres. Subj.:   conozca, conozcas, conozca, conozcamos, conozcáis, conozcan

Verbs with the same change: **agradecer, aparecer, carecer, establecer, entristecer** (*to sadden*), **lucir, nacer, obedecer, ofrecer, padecer, parecer, pertenecer, relucir, reconocer**.

8. Verbs ending in **-zar** change **z** to **c** before **e** in the first person of the preterit and in all persons of the present subjunctive.

rezar (*to pray*)
Preterit: recé, rezaste, rezó, etc.
Pres. Subj.:   rece, reces, rece, recemos, recéis, recen

Verbs with the same pattern: **alcanzar, almorzar, comenzar, cruzar, empezar, forzar, gozar, abrazar.**

9. Verbs ending in **-eer** change the unstressed **i** to **y** between vowels in the third person singular and plural of the preterit, in all persons of the imperfect subjunctive, and in the present participle.

creer (*to believe*)
Preterit: creí, creíste, creyó, creímos, creísteis, creyeron
Imp. Subj.:   creyera, creyeras, creyera, creyéramos, creyerais, creyeran
Pres. Part.:   creyendo
Past Part.:   creído

Leer and **poseer** follow the same change pattern.

10. Verbs ending in **-uir** change the unstressed **i** to **y** between vowels (except **-quir** which has the silent **u**) in the following tenses and persons:

huir (*to escape, to flee*)
Pres. Part.:   huyendo
Pres. Ind.:   huyo, huyes, huye, huimos, huís, huyen
Preterit: huí, huiste, huyó, huimos, huisteis, huyeron
Imperative: huye, huya, huyamos, huid, huyan
Pres. Subj.:   huya, huyas, huya, huyamos, huyáis, huyan
Imp. Subj.:   huyera(ese), huyeras, huyera, huyéramos, huyerais, huyeran

Verbs with the same change: **atribuir, concluir, constituir, cons-truir, contribuir, destituir, destruir, disminuir, distribuir, excluir, incluir, influir, instruir, restituir, sustituir.**

11. Verbs ending in **-eír** lose one **e** in the third person singular and plural of the preterit, in all persons of the imperfect subjunctive, and in the present participle.

reír (*to laugh*)
Preterit: reí, reíste, rio, reímos, reísteis, rieron
Imp. Subj.: riera(ese), rieras, riera, rieramos, rierais, rieran
Pres. Part.: riendo

Sonreír and **freír** have the same pattern.

12. Verbs ending in **-iar** add a written accent to the **i**, except in the first and second persons plural of the present indicative and subjunctive.

fiar(se) (*to trust*)
Pres. Ind.:   fío (me), fías (te), fía (se), fiamos (nos), fiais (os), fían (se)
Pres. Subj.: fíe (me), fíes (te), fíe (se), fiemos (nos), fiéis (os), fíen (se)

Other verbs with the same change: **enviar, ampliar, criar, desviar, enfriar, guiar, telegrafiar, vaciar, variar.**

13. Verbs ending in **-uar** (except **-guar**) add a written accent to the **u**, except in the first and second persons plural of the present indicative and subjunctive.

actuar (*to act*)
Pres. Ind.:   actúo, actúas, actúa, actuamos, actuáis, actúan
Pres. Subj.: actúe, actúes, actúe, actuemos, actuéis, actúen

Verbs with the same pattern: **continuar, acentuar, efectuar, excep-tuar, graduar, habituar, insinuar, situar.**

14. Verbs ending in **-ñir** remove the **i** of the diphthongs **ie** and **ió** in the third person singular and plural of the preterit and in all persons of the imperfect subjunctive. They also change the **e** of stem to **i** in the same persons.

teñir (*to dye*)
Preterit: teñí, teñiste, tiñó, teñimos, teñisteis, tiñeron
Imp. Subj.: tiñera (ese), tiñeras, tiñera, tiñéramos, tiñerais, tiñe-ran

Verbs with the same change: **ceñir, constreñir, desteñir, estreñir, reñir.**

Some common irregular verbs

Only those tenses with irregular forms will be given.

acertar (*to guess right*)
Pres. Ind.: acierto, aciertas, acierta, acertamos, acertáis, aciertan
Pres. Subj.: acierte, aciertes, acierte, acertemos, acertéis, acierten
Imperative: acierta, acierte, acertemos, acertad, acierten

adquirir (*to acquire*)
Pres. Ind.: adquiero, adquieres, adquiere, adquirimos, adquirís, adquieren
Pres. Subj.: adquiera, adquieras, adquiera, adquiramos, adquiráis, adquieran
Imperative: adquiere, adquiera, adquiramos, adquirid, adquieran

andar (*to walk*)
Preterit: anduve, anduviste, anduvo, anduvimos, anduvisteis, anduvieron
Imp. Subj.: anduviera (anduviese), anduvieras, anduviera, anduviéramos, anduvierais, anduvieran

avergonzarse (*to be ashamed, to be embarrassed*)
Pres. Ind.: me avergüenzo, te avergüenzas, se avergüenza, nos avergonzamos, os avergonzáis, se avergüenzan
Pres. Subj.: me avergüence, te avergüences, se avergüence, nos avergoncemos, os avergoncéis, se avergüencen
Imperative: avergüénzate, avergüéncese, avergoncémonos, avergonzaos, avergüenzense

caber (*to fit, to have enough room*)
Pres. Ind.: quepo, cabes, cabe, cabemos, cabéis, caben
Preterit: cupe, cupiste, cupo cupimos, cupisteis, cupieron
Future: cabré, cabrás, cabrá, cabremos, cabréis, cabrán
Conditional: cabría, cabrías, cabría, cabríamos, cabríais, cabrían
Imperative: cabe, quepa, quepamos, cabed, quepan
Pres. Subj.: quepa, quepas, quepa, quepamos, quepáis, quepan
Imp. Subj.: cupiera (cupiese), cupieras, cupiera, cupiéramos, cupierais, cupieran

caer (*to fall*)
Pres. Ind.: caigo, caes, cae, caemos, caéis, caen
Preterit: caí, caíste, cayó, caímos, caísteis, cayeron
Imperative: cae, caiga, caigamos, caed, caigan
Pres. Subj.: caiga, caigas, caiga, caigamos, ciagáis, caigan
Imp. Subj.: cayera (cayese), cayeras, cayera, cayéramos, cayerais, cayeran
Past Part.: caído

cegar (*to blind*)
Pres. Ind.:   ciego, ciegas, ciega, cegamos, cegáis, ciegan
Imperative: ciega, ciegue, ceguemos, cegad, cieguen
Pres. Subj.: ciegue, ciegues, ciegue, ceguemos, ceguéis, cieguen

conducir (*to guide, to drive*)
Pres. Ind.:   conduzco, conduces, conduce, conducimos, conducís, conducen
Preterit: conduje, condujiste, condujo, condujimos, condujisteis, condujeron
Imperative: conduce, conduzca, conduzcamos, conducid, conduzcan
Pres. Subj.: conduzca, conduzcas, conduzca, conduzcamos, conduzcáis, conduzcan
Imp. Subj.: condujera (condujese), condujeras, condujera, condujéramos, condujerais, condujeran

(All verbs ending in **-ducir** follow this pattern)

convenir (*to agree*) See **venir**.

dar (*to give*)
Pres. Ind.:   doy, das, da, damos, dais, dan
Preterit: di, diste, dio, dimos, disteis, dieron
Imperative: da, dé, demos, dad, den
Pres. Subj.: dé, des, dé, demos, deis, den
Imp. Subj.: diera (diese), dieras, diera, diéramos, dierais, dieran

decir (*to say, to tell*)
Pres. Ind.:   digo, dices, dice, decimos, decís, dicen
Preterit: dije, dijiste, dijo, dijimos, dijisteis, dijeron
Future: diré, dirás, dirá, diremos, diréis, dirán
Conditional: diría, dirías, diría, diríamos, diríais, dirían
Imperative: di, diga, digamos, decid, digan
Pres. Subj.: diga, digas, diga, digamos, digáis, digan
Imp. Subj.: dijera (dijese), dijeras, dijera, dijéramos, dijerais, dijeran
Pres. Part.: diciendo
Past. Part.: dicho

detener (*to stop, to hold, to arrest*) See **tener**.

elegir (*to choose*)
Pres. Ind.:   elijo, eliges, elige, elegimos, elegís, eligen
Preterit: elegí, elegiste, eligió, elegimos, elegisteis, eligieron
Imperative: elige, elija, elijamos, elegid, elijan
Pres. Subj.: elija, elijas, elija, elijamos, elijáis, elijan
Imp. Subj.: eligiera (eligiese), eligieras, eligiera, eligiéramos, eligierais, eligieran

entender (*to understand*)
Pres. Ind.:   entiendo, entiendes, entiende, entendemos, entendéis, entienden
Imperative: entiende, entienda, entendamos, entended, entiendan
Pres. Subj.:   entienda, entiendas, entienda, entendamos, entendáis, entiendan

entretener (*to entertain, to amuse*) See **tener**.

extender (*to extend, to stretch out*) See **tender**.

errar (*to err, to miss*)
Pres. Ind.:   yerro, yerras, yerra, erramos, erráis, yerran
Imperative: yerra, yerre, erremos, errad, yerren
Pres. Subj.:   yerre, yerres, yerre, erremos, erréis, yerren

estar (*to be*)
Pres. Ind.:   estoy, estás, está, estamos, estáis, están
Preterit: estuve, estuviste, estuvo, estuvimos, estuvisteis, estuvieron
Imperative: está, esté, estemos, estad, estén
Pres. Subj.:   esté, estés, esté, estemos, estéis, estén
Imp. Subj.:   estuviera (estuviese), estuvieras, estuviera, estuviéramos, estuvierais, estuvieran

haber (*to have*)
Pres. Ind.:   he, has, ha, hemos, habéis, han
Preterit: hube, hubiste, hubo, hubimos, hubisteis, hubieron
Future: habré, habrás, habrá, habremos, habréis, habrán
Conditional: habría, habrías, habría, habríamos, habríais, habrían
Imperative: he, haya, hayamos, habed, hayan
Pres. Subj.:   haya, hayas, haya, hayamos, hayáis, hayan
Imp. Subj.:   hubiera (hubiese), hubieras, hubiera, hubiéramos, hubierais, hubieran

hacer (*to do, to make*)
Pres. Ind.:   hago, haces, hace, hacemos, hacéis, hacen
Preterit: hice, hiciste, hizo, hicimos, hicisteis, hicieron
Future: haré, harás, hará, haremos, haréis, harán
Conditional: haría, harías, haría, haríamos, haríais, harían
Imperative: haz, haga, hagamos, haced, hagan
Pres. Subj.:   haga, hagas, haga, hagamos, hagáis, hagan
Imp. Subj.:   hiciera (hiciese), hicieras, hiciera, hiciéramos, hicierais, hicieran
Past Part.:   hecho

imponer (*to impose, to deposit*) See **poner**.

introducir (*to introduce, to insert, to gain access*) See **conducir**.

ir (*to go*)
Pres. Ind.:   voy, vas, va, vamos, vais, van
Imp. Ind.:   iba, ibas, iba, íbamos, ibais, iban
Preterit: fui, fuiste, fue, fuimos, fuisteis, fueron
Imperative: ve, vaya, vayamos, id, vayan
Pres. Subj.:   vaya, vayas, vaya, vayamos, vayáis, vayan
Imp. Subj.:   fuera (fuese), fueras, fuera, fuéramos, fuerais, fueran

jugar (*to play*)
Pres. Ind.:   juego, juegas, juega, jugamos, jugáis, juegan
Imperative: juega, juegue, juguemos, jugad, jueguen
Pres. Subj.:   juegue, juegues, juegue, juguemos, juguéis, jueguen

obtener (*to obtain*) See **tener**.

oír (*to hear*)
Pres. Ind.:   oigo, oyes, oye, oímos, oís, oyen
Preterit: oí, oíste, oyó, oímos, oísteis, oyeron
Imperative: oye, oiga, oigamos, oid, oigan
Pres. Subj.:   oiga, oigas, oiga, oigamos, oigáis, oigan
Imp. Subj.:   oyera (oyese), oyeras, oyera, oyéramos, oyerais, oyeran
Pres. Part.:   oyendo
Past Part.:   oído

oler (*to smell*)
Pres. Ind.:   huelo, hueles, huele, olemos, oléis, huelen
Imperative: huele, huela, olamos, oled, huelan
Pres. Subj.:   huela, huelas, huela, olamos, oláis, huelan

poder (*to be able*)
Pres. Ind.:   puedo, puedes, puede, podemos, podéis, pueden
Preterit: pude, pudiste, pudo, pudimos, pudisteis, pudieron
Future: podré, podrás, podrá, podremos, podréis, podrán
Conditional: podría, podrías, podría, podríamos, podríais, podrían
Imperative: puede, pueda, podamos, poded, puedan
Pres. Subj.:   pueda, puedas, pueda, podamos, podáis, puedan
Imp. Subj.:   pudiera (pudiese), pudieras, pudiera, pudiéramos, pudierais, pudieran
Pres. Part.:   pudiendo

poner (*to place, to put*)
Pres. Ind.:   pongo, pones, pone, ponemos, ponéis, ponen
Preterit: puse, pusiste, puso, pusimos, pusisteis, pusieron
Future: pondré, pondrás, pondrá, pondremos, pondréis, pondrán
Conditional: pondría, pondrías, pondría, pondríamos, pondríais, pondrían
Imperative: pon, ponga, pongamos, poned, pongan
Pres. Subj.:   ponga, pongas, ponga, pongamos, pongáis, pongan

Imp. Subj.:   pusiera (pusiese), pusieras, pusiera, pusiéramos, pusierais, pusieran
Past Part.:   puesto

querer *(to want, to wish, to like)*
Pres. Ind.:   quiero, quieres, quiere, queremos, queréis, quieren
Preterit: quise, quisiste, quiso, quisimos, quisisteis, quisieron
Future: querré, querrás, querrá, querremos, querréis, querrán
Conditional: querría, querrías, querría, querríamos, querríais, querrían
Imperative: quiere, quiera, queramos, quered, quieran
Pres. Subj.:   quiera, quieras, quiera, queramos, queráis, quieran
Imp. Subj.:   quisiera (quisiese), quisieras, quisiera, quisiéramos, quisierais, quisieran

resolver *(to decide on)*
Pres. Ind.:   resuelvo, resuelves, resuelve, resolvemos, resolvéis, resuelven
Imperative: resuelve, resuelva, resolvamos, resolved, resuelvan
Pres. Subj.:   resuelva, resuelvas, resuelva, resolvamos, resolváis, resuelvan
Past Part.:   resuelto

saber *(to know)*
Pres. Ind.:   sé, sabes, sabe, sabemos, sabéis, saben
Preterit: supe, supiste, supo, supimos, supisteis, supieron
Future: sabré, sabrás, sabrá, sabremos, sabréis, sabrán
Conditional: sabría, sabrías, sabría, sabríamos, sabríais, sabrían
Imperative: sabe, sepa, sepamos, sabed, sepan
Pres. Subj.:   sepa, sepas, sepa, sepamos, sepáis, sepan
Imp. Subj.:   supiera (supiese), supieras, supiera, supiéramos, supierais, supieran

salir *(to leave, to go out)*
Pres. Ind.:   salgo, sales, sale, salimos, salís, salen
Future: saldré, saldrás, saldrá, saldremos, saldréis, saldrán
Conditional: saldría, saldrías, saldría, saldríamos, saldríais, saldrían
Imperative: sal, salga, salgamos, salid, salgan
Pres. Subj.:   salga, salgas, salga, salgamos, salgáis, salgan

ser *(to be)*
Pres. Ind.:   soy, eres, es, somos, sois, son
Imp. Ind.:   era, eras, era, éramos, erais, eran
Preterit: fui, fuiste, fue, fuimos, fuisteis, fueron
Imperative: sé, sea, seamos, sed, sean
Pres. Subj.:   sea, seas, sea, seamos, seáis, sean
Imp. Subj.:   fuera (fuese), fueras, fuera, fuéramos, fuerais, fueran

suponer *(to assume)* See **poner**.

tener (*to have*)
Pres. Ind.:   tengo, tienes, tiene, tenemos, tenéis, tienen
Preterit: tuve, tuviste, tuvo, tuvimos, tuvisteis, tuvieron
Future: tendré, tendrás, tendrá, tendremos, tendréis, tendrán
Conditional: tendría, tendrías, tendría, tendríamos, tendríais, tendrían
Imperative: ten, tenga, tengamos, tened, tengan
Pres. Subj.: tenga, tengas, tenga, tengamos, tengáis, tengan
Imp. Subj.: tuviera (tuviese), tuvieras, tuviera, tuviéramos, tuvierais, tuvieran

tender (*to spread out, to hang out*)
Pres. Ind.:   tiendo, tiendes, tiende, tendemos, tendéis, tienden
Imperative: tiende, tienda, tendamos, tended, tiendan
Pres. Subj.: tienda, tiendas, tienda, tendamos, tendáis, tiendan

traducir (*to translate*)
Pres Ind.:   traduzco, traduces, traduce, traducimos, traducís, traducen
Preterit: traduje, tradujiste, tradujo, tradujimos, tradujisteis, tradujeron
Imperative: traduce, traduzca, traduzcamos, traducid, traduzcan
Pres. Subj.: traduzca, traduzcas, traduzca, traduzcamos, traduzcáis, traduzcan
Imp. Subj.: tradujera (tradujese), tradujeras, tradujera, tradujéramos, tradujerais, tradujeran

traer (*to bring*)
Pres. Ind.:   traigo, traes, trae, traemos, traéis, traen
Preterit: traje, trajiste, trajo, trajimos, trajisteis, trajeron
Imperative: trae, traiga, traigamos, traed, traigan
Pres. Subj.: traiga, traigas, traiga, traigamos, traigáis, traigan
Imp. Subj.: trajera (trajese), trajeras, trajera, trajéramos, trajerais, trajeran
Pres. Part: trayendo
Past Part.: traído

valer (*to be worth*)
Pres. Ind.:   valgo, vales, vale, valemos, valéis, valen
Future: valdré, valdrás, valdrá, valdremos, valdréis, valdrán
Conditional: valdría, valdrías, valdría, valdríamos, valdríais, valdrían
Imperative: vale, valga, valgamos, valed, valgan
Pres. Subj.: valga, valgas, valga, valgamos, valgáis, valgan

venir (*to come*)
Pres. Ind.:   vengo, vienes, viene, venimos, venís, vienen
Preterit: vine, viniste, vino, vinimos, vinisteis, vinieron
Future: vendré, vendrás, vendrá, vendremos, vendréis, vendrán

Conditional:	vendría, vendrías, vendría, vendríamos, vendríais, vendrían
Imperative:	ven, venga, vengamos, venid, vengan
Pres. Subj.:	venga, vengas, venga, vengamos, vengáis, vengan
Imp. Subj.:	viniera (viniese), vinieras, viniera, viniéramos, vinierais, vinieran
Pres. Part.:	viniendo

ver (*to see*)

Pres. Ind.:	veo, ves, ve, vemos, veis, ven
Imp. Ind.:	veía, veías, veía, veíamos, veíais, veían
Preterit:	vi, viste, vio, vimos, visteis, vieron
Imperative:	ve, vea, veamos, ved, vean
Pres. Subj.:	vea, veas, vea, veamos, veáis, vean
Imp. Subj.:	viera (viese), vieras, viera, viéramos, vierais, vieran
Past Part.:	visto

Appendix D: Glossary of Grammatical Terms

adjective: A word that is used to describe a noun: *tall* girl, *difficult* lesson.

adverb: A word that modifies a verb, an adjective, or another adverb. It answers the questions "How?", "When?", "Where?": She walked *slowly*. She'll be here *tomorrow*. She is *here*.

agreement: A term usually applied to adjectives. An adjective is said to show agreement with the noun it modifies when its ending changes in accordance with the gender and number of the noun. In Spanish, a feminine plural noun requires a feminine plural ending in the adjective that describes it (**casas amarillas**) and a masculine singular noun requires a masculine singular ending in the adjective (**libro negro**).

article: See *definite article* and *indefinite article*.

auxiliary verb: A verb that helps in the conjugation of another verb: I *have* finished. He *was* called. She *will* go. He *would* eat.

command form: The form of the verb used to give an order or a direction: *Go! Come back! Turn* to the right!

conjugation: The process by which the forms of the verb are presented in their different moods and tenses: I *am*, you

are, he *is*, she *was*, we *were*, etc.

contraction: The combination of two or more words into one: *isn't, don't, can't*.

definite article: A word used before a noun indicating a definite person or thing: *the* woman, *the* money.

demonstrative: A word that refers to a definite person or object: *this, that, these, those*.

diphthong: A combination of two vowels forming one syllable. In Spanish, a diphthong is composed of one *strong* vowel (**a, e, o**) and one *weak* vowel (**u, i**) or two weak vowels: **ei, au, ui**.

exclamation: A word used to express emotion: *How* strong! *What* beauty!

gender: A distinction of nouns, pronouns, and adjectives, based on whether they are masculine or feminine.

indefinite article: A word used before a noun that refers to an indefinite person or object: *A* child. *An* apple.

infinitive: The form of the verb generally preceded in English by the word *to* and showing no subject or number: *to do, to bring*.

interrogative: A word used in asking a question: *Who? What? Where?*

main clause: A group of words that includes a subject and a verb and by itself has complete meaning: *They saw me. I go now.*

noun: A word that names a person, place, thing, etc.: *Ann, London, pencil,* etc.

number: Number refers to singular and plural: *chair, chairs.*

object: Generally a noun or a pronoun that is the receiver of the verb's action. A direct object answers the question "*What?*" or "*Whom?*": We know *her.* Take *it.* An indirect object answers the question "*To whom?*" or "*To what?*": Give *John* the money. Nouns and pronouns can also be objects of prepositions: The letter is *from Rick.* I'm thinking *about you.*

past participle: Past forms of a verb: *gone, worked, written,* etc.

person: The form of the pronoun and of the verb that shows the person referred to: *I* (first person singular), *you* (second person singular), *she* (third person singular), etc.

possessive: A word that denotes ownership or possession: This is *our* house. The book isn't *mine.*

preposition: A word that introduces a noun, pronoun, adverb, infinitive, or present participle and indicates its function in the sentence: They were *with* us. She is *from* Nevada.

pronoun: A word that is used to replace a noun: *she, them, us,* etc. A **subject pronoun** refers to the person or thing spoken of: *They* work. An **object pronoun** receives the action of the verb: They arrested *us* (direct object pronoun). She spoke to *him* (indirect object pronoun). A pronoun can also be the object of a preposition: The children stayed with *us.*

reflexive pronoun: A pronoun that refers back to the subject: *myself, yourself, himself, herself, itself, ourselves,* etc.

subject: The person, place, or thing spoken of: *Robert* works. *Our car* is new.

subordinate clause: A clause that has no complete meaning by itself but depends on a main clause: They knew *that I was here.*

tense: The group of forms in a verb that show the time in which the action of the verb takes place: *I go* (present indicative), *I'm going* (present progressive), *I went* (past), *I was going* (past progressive), *I will go* (future), *I would go* (conditional), *I have gone* (present perfect), *I had gone* (past perfect), *that I may go* (present subjunctive), etc.

verb: A word that expresses an action or a state: We *sleep.* The baby *is* sick.

Appendix E: Careers and Occupations

accountant **contador**
actor **actor**
actress **actriz**
administrator **administrador**
agent **agente**
architect **arquitecto**
baker **panadero**
bank officer **empleado bancario**
bank teller **cajero**
banker **banquero**
barber **barbero**
bartender **barman, cantinero**
bill collector **cobrador**
bookkeeper **tenedor de libros**
brickmason (bricklayer) **albañil**
buyer **comprador**
cameraman **camarógrafo**
carpenter **carpintero**
cashier **cajero**
chiropractor **quiropráctico**
clerk **dependiente**
computer operator **computista**
contractor **contratista**
construction worker **obrero de
la construcción**
constructor **constructor**
cook **cocinero**
copilot **copiloto**
counselor **consejero**
craftsman **artesano**
dancer **bailarín**
decorator **decorador**
dental hygienist **higienista dental**
dentist **dentista**
designer **diseñador**
detective **detective**
dietician **especialista en
dietética**
diplomat **diplomático**

dockworker **obrero portuario**
doctor **doctor**
draftsman **dibujante**
dressmaker **modista**
driver **conductor**
economist **economista**
editor **editor**
electrician **electricista**
engineer **ingeniero**
engineering technician
ingeniero técnico
farmer **agricultor**
fashion designer **diseñador de
alta costura, modisto**
fireman **bombero**
fisherman **pescador**
flight attendant **azafata,
sobrecargo**
foreman **capataz, encargado**
funeral director **empresario de
pompas fúnebres**
garbage collector **basurero**
gardener **jardinero**
guard **guardia**
hairdresser **peluquero**
home economist **economista
doméstico**
housekeeper **ama de llaves**
inspector **inspector**
insurance agent **agente de
seguros**
interior designer **diseñador de
interiores**
interpreter **intérprete**
investigator **investigador**
janitor **conserje**
jeweler **joyero**
journalist **periodista**
judge **juez**
lawyer **abogado**

librarian **bibliotecario**
machinist **maquinista**
maid **criada**
mail carrier **cartero**
manager **gerente**
meat cutter **carnicero**
mechanic **mecánico**
midwife **comadrona, partera**
military **militar**
miner **minero**
model **modelo**
musician **músico**
night watchman **sereno, guardián**
nurse **enfermero**
optician **óptico**
optometrist **optometrista**
painter **pintor**
pharmacist **farmacéutico**
photographer **fotógrafo**
physical therapist **terapista física**
physician **médico**
pilot **piloto, aviador**
plumber **plomero**
policeman **policia**
printer **impresor**
psychologist **psicólogo**
public relations agent **agente de relaciones públicas**
real estate agent **agente de bienes raices**
receptionist **recepcionista**
reporter **reportero, periodista**
sailor **marinero**
salesman **vendedor**
scientist **científico**
seamstress **costurera, modista**

secretary **secretario**
social worker **trabajador social**
sociologist **sociólogo**
stenographer **estenógrafo**
stewardess **azafata**
stockbroker **bolsista**
supervisor **supervisor**
surgeon **cirujano**
systems analyst **analista de sistemas**
tailor **sastre**
taxi driver **chofer de taxi, conductor**
teacher **maestro** (*elem. school*), **profesor** (*high school and college*)
technician **técnico**
telephone operator **telefonista**
therapist **terapista**
television and radio technician **técnico de radio y televisión**
television and radio announcer **locutor**
teller **cajero**
travel agent **agente de viajes**
traveling salesman **viajante de comercio**
truck driver **camionero**
typist **mecanógrafa, dactilógrafa**
undertaker **director de pompas fúnebres**
veterinarian **veterinario**
waiter **mozo, camarero**
waitress **camarera**
watchmaker **relojero**
watchman **sereno, guardián**
worker **obrero**

Appendix F: Answer Key to Self-Testing Sections

Lesson 1

A. 1. nosotros 2. ellos 3. ustedes 4. ellas 5. nosotras

B. 1. Yo hablo español. 2. Nosotros hablamos español.
3. Nosotros hablamos inglés. 4. Tú hablas inglés. 5. Tú
trabajas en Lima. 6. Ellos trabajan en Lima. 7. Usted trabaja
en Lima. 8. Usted estudia en Lima. 9. Yo estudio en Lima.
10. Yo necesito dinero. 11. Él necesita dinero. 12. Nosotros
necesitamos dinero.

C. *Interrogative:* 1. ¿Trabaja Elena en Buenos Aires?
2. ¿Hablan ustedes inglés? 3. ¿Necesitas dinero tú?
4. ¿Juan y María estudian español? 5. ¿Trabaja usted en Los
Ángeles?

Negative: 1. Elena no trabaja en Buenos Aires. 2. Ustedes
no hablan inglés. 3. Tú no necesitas dinero. 4. Juan y María
no estudian español. 5. Ud. no trabaja en Los Ángeles.

D. *Masculine:* 1. programa 2. telegrama 3. señor 4. teléfono
5. libro 6. día 7. sistema 8. dinero 9. problema
10. idioma 11. número 12. tema

Feminine: 1. televisión 2. señora 3. banana 4. mano
5. silla 6. casa 7. mesa 8. libertad 9. lección
10. ciudad 11. calle 12. nacionalidad

E. 1. sesenta y seis 2. trece 3. noventa y uno 4. setenta y
tres 5. diez y nueve 6. ciento cincuenta

Lesson 2

A. 1. las casas verdes 2. los lápices negros 3. los profesores
inteligentes 4. las sillas grandes 5. los libros blancos 6. las
señoritas felices

B. 1. ¿Dónde vive usted, Sra. Vera? 2. Ellos beben café. Yo
bebo té. 3. Nosotros leemos las lecciones. 4. Él decide

267

estudiar inglés.   5. ¿Comprendes?   6. Ustedes comen
temprano.   7. Ella escribe en español.   8. Nosotros abrimos
los libros.   9. Yo aprendo español.   10. Ellos no reciben el
dinero.

C.   1. ___   2. a   3. ___   4. a   5. a

Lesson 3

A.   1. Nosotros recibimos el dinero de Carlos.   2. Ella lee la
lección de la profesora.   3. Los estudiantes visitan a la esposa
de Enrique.   4. ¿Tú esperas a la profesora de Teresa?   5. Ud.
no necesita la silla de María.

B.   1. tu   2. sus   de ella   3. nuestro   4. su   de usted   5. mis
6. tus   7. nuestras   8. su   de él

C.   1. un   2. una   3. unas   4. un   5. una   6. unos   7. unas
8. un   9. un   10. una

D.   1. Sí, yo soy alto(a).   2. Sí, yo soy de California.   3. Sí, somos
felices.   4. Sí, usted es (el)/(la) profesor(a).   5. Sí, mi lección
de español es difícil.   6. Sí, ellos son de México.

E.   1. Ellos dan su número de teléfono. Nosotros damos nuestro
número de teléfono. Tú das tu número de teléfono. Uds. dan su
número de teléfono. Ella da su número de teléfono.
2. Yo estoy en mi casa. Ellos están en su casa. Nosotros
estamos en nuestra casa. Ella está en su casa. Tú estás en tu
casa. Uds. están en su casa.
3. Nosotros vamos a nuestras clases. Ud. va a sus clases. Tú vas
a tus clases. Yo voy a mis clases. Ellos van a sus clases.

Lesson 4

A.   1. La botella es de plástico.   2. La señorita López está
enferma.   3. Las casas son de Jorge.   4. Los estudiantes son
mexicanos.   5. El profesor está en el hospital.   6. Yo soy de
Arizona.   7. Nosotros estamos bien.   8. María es alta.
9. Gustavo y yo somos casados.   10. Mañana es sábado.
11. Yo estoy en la calle Universidad.   12. El hijo de la señora
Nieto es ingeniero.

B. 1. Esperamos al señor Peña. 2. Ella visita al señor Linares y a la señora Viera. 3. El dinero es del señor Díaz. 4. Él va al hospital. 5. Necesitamos el número de teléfono del doctor Mena.

C. 1. No, yo no soy tan alto(a) como el profesor (la profesora). 2. No, el profesor no llega más tarde que los estudiantes. 3. No, yo no soy el (la) estudiante menos inteligente de la clase. 4. No, yo no soy la persona más feliz de la clase. 5. No, yo no soy el (la) peor estudiante. 6. No, nosotros no somos mayores que nuestros amigos. 7. No, usted no es el (la) mejor de la clase. 8. No, la casa de mi amigo no es más grande que mi casa.

D. 1. Nosotros venimos con nuestro hijo. Tú vienes con tu hijo. Ellos vienen con su hijo. Ud. viene con su hijo. Uds. vienen con su hijo. Él viene con su hijo. 2. Yo tengo mis libros. Ella tiene sus libros. Tú tienes tus libros. Uds. tienen sus libros. Ud. tiene sus libros.

E. 1. quinientos 2. mil 3. quinientos cincuenta 4. doscientos 5. novecientos 6. cuatrocientos cincuenta

Lesson 5

A. 1. Carlos tiene miedo. 2. Él tiene frío. 3. Yo tengo prisa. 4. Ellas tienen calor. 5. Ud. tiene sueño. 6. Tú tienes sed. 7. Nélida tiene cuatro años.

B. (*Possibilities*): 1. Mi clase de español es a las ocho de la mañana. 2. Nosotros comemos a las doce. 3. Yo voy a la universidad a las siete de la mañana. 4. Yo estudio por la noche. 5. El profesor llega a clase a las ocho menos cinco.

C. (*Possibilities*): 1. Nosotros preferimos estudiar francés. 2. No, no quiero ir al cine hoy. 3. La clase de español empieza a las once de la mañana. 4. Sí, nosotros entendemos las lecciones. 5. No, nosotros no perdemos mucho dinero en Las Vegas. 6. Cierran la biblioteca a las diez de la noche. 7. Mi programa de televisión favorito comienza a las ocho de la noche.

D. 1. vamos a comer 2. va a comprar 3. va a empezar 4. vas a visitar 5. va a llegar 6. voy a venir 7. vamos a necesitar 8. van a ir

E. 1. ¿Cuántos estudiantes hay? 2. No hay dinero. 3. Hay dos vuelos para Lima. 4. Hay una reunión hoy. 5. ¿Cuántas sillas hay?

Lesson 6

A. 1. Hoy es miércoles. 2. Las mujeres quieren igualdad con los hombres. 3. La libertad es importante. 4. Nosotros vamos a estudiar la semana próxima. 5. Yo no tengo clases los viernes.

B. (*Possibilities*): 1. Yo vuelvo a mi casa a las cinco y media. 2. Cuando nosotros vamos a México, volamos. 3. Sí, nosotros recordamos los verbos irregulares. 4. Yo duermo ocho horas. 5. No, nosotros no podemos ir al cine hoy.

C. 1. Ellos recuerdan algo. 2. Hay alguien en el cine. 3. Yo quiero volar también. 4. Recibimos algunos regalos. 5. Siempre tiene éxito.

D. cinco: quinto   ocho: octavo   diez: décimo   uno: primero   tres: tercero   nueve: noveno   dos: segundo   seis: sexto   cuatro: cuarto   siete: séptimo

E. 1. Para tener éxito, hay que trabajar. 2. Ud. tiene que volver la semana próxima, señor Vega. 3. Ella tiene que trabajar mañana. 4. Hay que comenzar temprano. 5. ¿Tenemos que empezar a los ocho?

Lesson 7

A. (*Possibilities*): 1. Nosotros servimos sopa. 2. Yo pido Coca-Cola para beber. 3. No, yo no digo mi edad. 4. Sí, yo sigo en la clase de español. 5. Sí, nosotros siempre pedimos postre.

B. 1. conduzco 2. salgo 3. pongo 4. traduzco 5. conozco 6. quepo 7. hago 8. veo 9. sé 10. traigo

C. 1. Yo conozco a su hijo. 2. Él no sabe francés. 3. ¿Sabe usted nadar, señorita Vera? 4. ¿Conoce usted al embajador? 5. ¿Conocen los estudiantes las novelas de Cervantes?

D. 1. Yo las conozco. 2. Uds. van a comprarlo. 3. Nosotros no queremos verte. 4. Ella la sirve. 5. ¿Ud. no me conoce? 6. Él los escribe. 7. Carlos va a traernos. 8. Nosotros no lo vemos.

E. 1. felizmente 2. especialmente 3. rápidamente 4. fácilmente 5. lenta y cuidadosamente

Lesson 8

A. 1. Necesito estas revistas y aquéllas. 2. ¿Quiere usted este cuaderno o ése? 3. Yo prefiero estos periódicos, no aquéllos. 4. ¿Quiere usted comprar esta corbata o ésa? 5. No quiero comer en este restaurante. Prefiero aquél. 6. Yo no entiendo eso.

B. 1. está estudiando 2. está comiendo 3. estamos leyendo 4. estás diciendo 5. estoy comprando

C. 1. Me va a comprar los pasajes. 2. Le doy las revistas. 3. Nos habla en español. 4. Les voy a decir la verdad. 5. Les pregunto la dirección de la oficina. 6. Le estamos escribiendo a nuestro profesor. 7. Le escribo los lunes. 8. Le doy la información al señor Vera. 9. Te hablo en inglés. 10. No me compran nada.

D. 1. ¿El dinero? Se lo doy mañana, señor Peña. 2. Ya sé que necesitas un diccionario, Anita, pero no puedo prestártelo. 3. Necesito mi abrigo. ¿Puede traérmelo, señorita López? 4. ¿Las plumas? Ella nos las trae. 5. Cuando yo necesito zapatos nuevos, mi mamá me los compra.

E. 1. Voy a preguntarle dónde vive. 2. Yo siempre le pido dinero a mi esposo. 3. Ella siempre pregunta cómo está usted, señora Nieto. 4. Me van a pedir los libros de química. 5. No vamos a preguntarle nada, señor.

Lesson 9

A. 1. No, no son mías. 2. No, no son de ella. 3. No, no es mío. 4. No, no es nuestra. 5. No, no es de ellos. 6. No, no son míos. 7. No, no es nuestro. 8. No, no es de ustedes.

B. 1. Yo me levanto a las siete, me baño, me visto y salgo a las
    siete y media.   2. ¿A qué hora se despiertan los niños?
    3. Ella no quiere sentarse.   4. Ud. siempre se preocupa por su
    hijo, señora Cruz.   5. ¿Te acuerdas de tus maestros, Carlitos?
    6. Siempre se están quejando.   7. Primero ella acuesta a los
    niños. Ella se acuesta a las diez.   8. ¿Quiere probarse este
    abrigo, señorita?   9. ¿Dónde ponen ustedes el dinero, señoras?
    10. Los estudiantes siempre se duermen en esta clase.

C. 1. Abra 2. Hablen 3. Traiga 4. Vengan 5. Cierre
    6. Doblen 7. Siga 8. Den 9. Estén 10. Sean 11. Vaya
    12. Vuelva 13. Sirva 14. Pongan 15. Escriban

D. 1. Dígales que sí, señor Mena.   2. ¿El postre? No me lo traiga
    ahora, señorita Ruiz.   3. No se lo diga a Ana, por favor.
    4. Traigan las sillas, señores. Tráiganlas a la terraza.   5. No se
    levante, señora Miño.   6. ¿El té? Tráigaselo a las cuatro de la
    tarde, señor Vargas.

Lesson 10

A. 1. Ayer ella entró en la cafetería y comió una ensalada.
    2. Ayer María le escribió a Pedro.   3. Anoche ella me prestó
    su bicicleta.   4. El año pasado ellos fueron los mejores
    estudiantes.   5. El sábado pasado ellos te esperaron cerca del
    cine.   6. El verano pasado mis hermanos fueron a Buenos
    Aires.   7. Ayer le di el dinero.   8. El lunes pasado nosotros
    decidimos comprar la bicicleta.   9. Anoche le pregunté la
    hora.   10. Ayer tú no entendiste la lección.   11. El jueves
    pasado fuimos los primeros.   12. Ayer me dieron muchos
    problemas.   13. Anoche Marta no bebió café.   14. El
    miércoles pasado yo no fui a la clase.   15. Ayer por la mañana
    te dimos té.

B. 1. Sí, acabamos de comer.   2. Sí, acaba de levantarse.   3. Sí,
    acabo de hablar con ella.   4. Sí, acaban de comprarla.   5. Sí,
    acabo de bañarme.   6. Sí, acaban de llegar.

C. 1. ¡Ah, sí! Es altísimo.   2. ¡Ah, sí! Estamos ocupadísimas.
    3. ¡Ah, sí! Son lentísimos. 4. ¡Ah, sí! Es buenísima. 5. ¡Ah,
    sí! Es dificilísima.   6. ¡Ah, sí! Es bellísima.   7. ¡Ah, sí! Es
    facilísimo.   8. ¡Ah, sí! Estoy ocupadísimo.

D. 1. Hace mucho frío.   2. Hace viento.   3. Llueve.   4. Hace
    mucho calor.   5. Nieva.   6. Hace sol.

Lesson 11

A. 1. (a) ¿Cuánto tiempo hace que trabaja en Lima? (b) ¿Cuánto tiempo lleva trabajando en Lima? 2. (a) Hace cinco años que trabajamos en Lima. (b) Llevamos cinco años trabajando en Lima. 3. (a) ¿Cuánto tiempo hace que esperan? (b) ¿Cuánto tiempo llevan esperando? 4. (a) Hace tres horas que esperan. (b) Llevan tres horas esperando. 5. (a) ¿Cuánto tiempo hace que estudia español? (b) ¿Cuánto tiempo lleva estudiando español? 6. (a) Hace dos años que ella estudia español. (b) Ella lleva dos años estudiando español.

B. 1. Ayer María estuvo muy ocupada. 2. Anoche no pudieron venir. 3. La semana pasada puse el dinero en el banco. 4. El domingo pasado no hiciste nada. 5. Ayer ella vino con Juan. 6. La semana pasada no quisimos venir a clase. 7. Anoche yo no dije nada. 8. Ayer trajimos la máquina de escribir. 9. Anoche yo conduje mi coche. 10. Ayer ellos tradujeron las lecciones.

C. 1. ¿De quién es ese paraguas? 2. ¿De quiénes son esos revólveres? 3. ¿De quién son estos zapatos? 4. ¿De quién es este dinero? 5. ¿De quién es aquella silla?

D. 1. Vivíamos en Alaska. 2. Hablaba inglés. 3. Veía a mi abuela. 4. Depositábamos el dinero en el Banco de América. 5. Se acostaban a las nueve. 6. Iba al cine. 7. Compraba café. 8. Gastábamos nuestro dinero en libros.

Lesson 12

A. 1. estábamos comiendo 2. estaban haciendo 3. estaba escribiendo 4. estaba hablando 5. estabas pensando 6. estaba leyendo 7. estaban estudiando 8. estaba trabajando

B. 1. Nos acostamos a las once anoche. 2. Ella estaba muy ocupada cuando la vi. 3. Íbamos a Buenos Aires. 4. Eran las diez y media cuando lo llamé. 5. Ella dijo que quería leer.

C. 1. Nosotros llegamos al aeorpuerto a las seis y media. 2. Mi hermana está en casa. 3. Ellos están en la esquina de Unión y Figueroa. 4. El accidente fue a las doce. 5. Yo estuve en la estación de policía ayer.

D. 1. conocía conocí 2. sabíamos supimos 3. podía
4. pudieron 5. quiso (pudo) 6. quería supe

Lesson 13

A. 1. Ayer él sintió mucho calor. 2. Anoche Marta no durmió
bien. 3. Ayer no le pedí nada. 4. La semana pasada ella te
mintió. 5. El sábado pasado ellos sirvieron los refrescos.
6. Ayer no lo repetí. 7. Anoche ella siguió estudiando. 8. El
lunes pasado tú no conseguiste nada.

B. 1. El ladrón entró por la ventana. 2. Ella pasó por mi casa.
3. No pudo venir por la lluvia. 4. Hay vuelos para México los
sábados. 5. Vamos por avión. 6. Él necesita la camisa para
mañana. 7. Iba a noventa millas por hora. 8. ¿Para quién es
el periódico? 9. Necesito el dinero para pagar la cuenta.
10. Ella pagó doscientos dólares por ese vestido.

C. 1. me gustan 2. le hace falta 3. le duele 4. nos hace falta
5. le gusta 6. Me hacen falta 7. Me duele 8. le (te) gusta

D. 1. ¿Puede venir conmigo? 2. ¿Va a trabajar con ellos? 3. ¿A
quién le dio las toallas? ¿A usted? 4. El regalo no es para mí.
Es para ella. 5. No, Carlitos. No puedo ir contigo.

Lesson 14

A. 1. ¿Qué es la libertad? 2. ¿Qué está haciendo usted aquí?
3. ¿Qué piensa el profesor de él? 4. ¿Cuál es su número de
teléfono? 5. ¿Cuáles son sus ideas acerca de esto?

B. 1. (a) Hace tres meses que nosotros llegamos a California. (b)
Nosotros llegamos a California hace tres meses. 2. (a) Hace
doce horas que Ud. comió. (b) Ud. comió hace doce horas.
3. (a) Hace dos días que ellos terminaron el trabajo. (b) Ellos
terminaron el trabajo hace dos días. 4. (a) Hace veinte años
que ella lo vio. (b) Ella lo vio hace veinte años. 5. (a) Hace
quince días que tú viniste a esta ciudad. (b) Tú viniste a esta
ciudad hace quince días.

C. 1. Hacía diez horas que yo no comía. 2. Hacía media hora que
lo esperábamos. 3. Hacía dos meses que yo estudiaba español. 4. Hacía cuatro años que él vivía en Quito. 5. Hacía
quince años que nosotros trabajábamos para el gobierno.

D. 1. Ana está en la escuela. 2. Ella se lava las manos. 3. Tú te quitas el abrigo. 4. Mamá va a la iglesia los domingos. 5. Felipe está en la cárcel. 6. Nosotros visitamos a la señorita García.

E. 2. recibido 3. volver 4. hablado 5. escrito 6. ir 7. aprendido 8. abrir 9. cubierto 10. comido 11. ver 12. hecho 13. sido 14. decir 15. cerrado 16. morir 17. romper 18. dormido 19. estado 20. poner

Lesson 15

A. 1. he venido 2. han terminado 3. hemos hablado 4. han dicho 5. has escrito 6. hemos hecho hemos tenido 7. ha abierto 8. ha puesto

B. 1. Yo ya había traído las sábanas. 2. Nosotros le habíamos escrito sobre nuestros experimentos con plantas tropicales. 3. Ellos habían roto los lápices. 4. Él ya había visto al administrador. 5. ¿Había cubierto usted las mesas, señorita Peña?

C. 1. El artículo está escrito. 2. Éstas son las sillas rotas. 3. La puerta está abierta. 4. ¿Están cerrados los libros? 5. El trabajo está terminado.

D. 1. arbolito 2. hermanita Teresita 3. vestidito hijita 4. Juancito 5. cochecito

Lesson 16

A. 1. El tema de la conferencia será "la civilización y la cultura de México." 2. Los análisis estarán listos la semana que viene. 3. Nosotros aprenderemos el español. 4. Iremos a Santiago el verano próximo. 5. Le diremos que sí. 6. No haré nada el domingo. 7. Sabremos el resultado el próximo mes. 8. El señor Reyes abrirá las puertas. 9. María y Carlos podrán venir. 10. Pondré el dinero en el banco. 11. Volveremos de México el sábado próximo. 12. Vendré a la reunión con la señorita Vargas. 13. Tendremos que estudiar para el examen. 14. Le daré las cartas mañana. 15. Saldremos con Raúl y Mario.

B.   1. iríamos   2. venderían   3. habría   4. serviría
5. trabajarías   6. pondría   7. preferirían   8. seguirían   9. te
levantarías   10. nos quejaríamos

C.   1. trabajemos   2. coma   3. escriban   4. vivas   5. diga
6. cierre   7. vengan   8. se levante   9. pida   10. hagan
11. traiga   12. recomiende   13. movamos   14. vaya   15. se
afeite   16. durmamos   17. dé   18. sepan (conozcan)
19. salga   20. tengas

Lesson 17

A.   1. Ella quiere que yo traiga los paquetes.   2. Prefiero que
vayamos a su oficina, señorita Díaz.   3. ¿A qué hora quiere
que esté aquí mañana, Señor Acevedo?   4. Pídale que la
ayude, señora Portillo.   5. Dígales que no tengan miedo.
6. Que lo haga Roberto.   7. Que pasen (entren).   8. Ella
quiere que yo sea su amiga.   9. ¿Necesita que le den el dinero
hoy, señor Ortiz?   10. No quiero que hagas nada, Juancito.

B.   1. Espero que puedas cortarte el pelo esta tarde, Robertito.
2. Me alegro de que su mamá se sienta mejor, Sr. Gómez.
3. Temo que no podamos reunirnos la semana próxima,
señorita Herrero.   4. Nos alegramos de estar aquí hoy.
5. Ella espera salir mañana por la mañana.   6. Espero que
pueda venir a la reunión, señor Peña.   7. Tememos no poder
terminar el trabajo esta noche.   8. Siento que esté enferma,
señora Treviño.

C.   1. puedan   2. estudiar   3. escribir   4. terminaremos   5. esté
6. hacer   7. llegan   8. firmar

Lesson 18

A.   1. Ellos pueden venir.   2. Pedro vaya con nosotros.   3. María
esté muy enferma.   4. una casa que quede cerca del centro
5. Sabe escribir a máquina.   6. Quieran hacer traducciones.
7. Él se levanta a las cuatro de la mañana.   8. Tiene seis
cuartos.

B.   1. Ven acá, por favor.   2. Habla con la maestra.   3. Dime tu
dirección.   4. Escribe la carta.   5. Ponte el abrigo.

6. Tráenos agua caliente. 7. Termina el trabajo. 8. Hazme el favor. 9. Apaga la luz. 10. Ve al centro. 11. Sal temprano. 12. Quédate afuera. 13. Ten paciencia. 14. Sé bueno. 15. Cena con nosotros.

C. 1. No se lo digas (a él). 2. No salgas ahora. 3. No te levantes. 4. No hagas las traducciones. 5. No bebas la limonada. 6. No lo rompas. 7. No les hables. 8. No vayas al centro. 9. ¿Ese vestido? ¡No te lo pongas! 10. No hagas eso.

Lesson 19

A. 1. Le hablaré tan pronto como lo vea. 2. Quédese aquí en caso de que él llame, señorita González. 3. Él me escribió en cuanto llegó. 4. Vamos a esperar hasta que él venga. 5. No puedo ir sin que lo sepan mis padres. 6. Compraremos el coche cuando tengamos el dinero.

B. 1. haya visto 2. hayan hecho 3. hayas aprendido 4. hayan firmado 5. haya arreglado 6. hayamos archivado 7. haya vuelto 8. se haya acostado

C. 1. Ellos sienten que ustedes hayan estado enfermos. 2. Rosa no cree que yo lo haya hecho. 3. Nosotros tememos que él haya muerto. 4. No es verdad que nosotros hayamos escrito esa carta. 5. Ojalá que papá haya podido venir.

Lesson 20

A. 1. asistiéramos 2. dejaras 3. se lavaran 4. recogiera 5. pudiera 6. trajera 7. devolvieran 8. tuviera

B. 1. Le pedí que viniera en seguida. 2. Me alegro de que pudieras terminarlo anoche. 3. No creí que ella lo hiciera. 4. No es verdad que mi hermano estuviera preso el año pasado. 5. Temíamos que ella no supiera escribir a máquina. 6. Dudo que la conferencia fuera el sábado pasado.

C. (*Possibilities*): 1. tuviera dinero 2. tenemos tiempo 3. estuviera enfermo 4. no llueve 5. pudieran 6. lo vemos 7. tuviera sueño 8. tenemos hambre

Lesson 21

A. 1. Para las ocho, habremos llegado a la estación de ómnibus.
2. ¿Te habrás graduado para junio, querido(a)? 3. Para el
domingo le habré dado una respuesta. 4. Los abogados habrán
terminado (acabado) el trabajo para la semana próxima.
5. Estoy seguro(a) de que él habrá recibido el premio para mañana.

B. 1. Nosotros habríamos ido a la discoteca. 2. Tú no habrías
comprado la ropa en esa tienda. 3. Ellos me lo habrían
prohibido. 4. Ella habría puesto el sillón en su cuarto. 5. Ése
habría sido un mal chiste. 6. Yo no me habría secado con esa
toalla.

C. 1. Vivimos en el tercer piso. 2. Es un buen profesor.
3. Insisten en que traigamos algún dinero. 4. Eva fue la
primera mujer sobre la tierra. 5. No necesito ningún libro.
6. Son malos profesores.

D. 1. ¡Pobre Miguel! Siempre mete la pata. 2. Él es un hombre
pobre; no tiene dinero. 3. Él era un hombre grande. 4. Lo
conocí hace diez años. Es un viejo amigo. 5. ¿Habrías traído
(Habría traído usted) la misma ropa? 6. Lincoln fue un gran
hombre. 7. Ella es una mujer vieja. Tiene noventa y ocho
años. 8. Yo tengo sólo un hermano. Es mi único hermano.
9. Yo le hablé al presidente mismo. 10. Ella es una mujer
única.

Lesson 22

A. 1. Fue una lástima que ustedes no hubieran visto el espectáculo
de los payasos. 2. Él sintió que nosotros hubiéramos visto algo
tan desagradable. 3. Yo me alegré de que tú me hubieras
traído la pelota y la raqueta de tenis. 4. Ellos se alegraron de
que yo no hubiera tenido la culpa. 5. Ojalá ella no se hubiera
bajado en esa estación. 6. Yo no creí que ellos se hubieran
dado por vencidos.

B. 1. supiera 2. tuviera 3. doliera 4. fuera
5. pudiéramos

C. 1. quien 2. que 3. quienes 4. quien 5. que
6. que 7. que 8. quien

D. 1. una   2. _____   3. _____ , un   4. una   5. _____
    6. un, _____   7. una   8. _____

Lesson 23

A. 1. estuvieron   2. se enamore   3. se portaron
    4. quieran   5. tuvieron

B. 1. Ella no quería que los demás pensaran que ella era haragana, vanidosa y tacaña.   2. Mi madre no quiere que nosotros veamos esa obra teatral a menos que ella vaya con nosotros.   3. Siento que los chicos te hayan molestado.   4. Dígale que trate de expresarse claramente.   5. Yo le habría dicho que no se acercara a la casa.   6. Ellos sienten que el campeón perdiera anoche.   7. Le pediré que lo repita.   8. Ellos me dijeron que se lo presentara a mis padres.

C. 1. Me vio pero no me reconoció.   2. Se lo sugerí pero no quiso hacerlo.   3. No quiere hacer el papel de Hamlet sino el de Otelo.   4. No lo vendió sino que lo compró.   5. No vive en el estado de Oregón sino en el de Wáshington.   6. Tiene muchos defectos pero es muy inteligente.   7. No fue a la peluquería sino a la farmacia.   8. No compré flores sino dulces.   9. No estudiamos sino que trabajamos.   10. Tiene más o menos 100 dólares pero no quiere gastarlos.

D. 1. Lo triste es que no me llevo bien con mi hermano.   2. Lo increíble es que ella tiene sólo seis años y habla tres idiomas.   3. Lo mejor es que vamos a tener vacaciones.   4. Él dijo que lo importante era tener mucho dinero.   5. Lo malo es que ellos no pueden ir.

Lesson 24

A. 1. Sí, estudiemos el siglo diez y nueve.   2. Sí, pintemos el techo.   3. Sí, llamemos al guía.   4. Sí, tomemos apuntes.   5. Sí, bebamos Coca-Cola.   6. Sí, pidámoselo a Hugo.   7. Sí, acostémonos.   8. Sí, escribámoselo en inglés.

B. 1. América fue descubierta por Cristóbal Colón.   2. Los edificios serán construidos por la compañía Rivera.   3. Ese programa ha sido desarrollado por el gobierno federal.   4. Ese abogado fue recomendado por el presidente de la compañía.   5. Las cartas son firmadas por la jefa.

C. 1. Las ventanas están abiertas.   2. La puerta está cerrada con llave (pintada de rojo) (fue comprada ayer).   3. Las cartas son firmadas por él.   4. Cuba fue descubierta en 1492.   5. El edificio será construido en enero.   6. Los niños estaban parados en la esquina.   7. La piedra está pintada de rojo.   8. La arena fue comprada ayer.

D. 1. Carlos u Osvaldo arreglarán el techo, porque gotea.   2. La temporada de lluvias comienza en septiembre u octubre.   3. El cuarto estaba lleno de parientes e invitados.   4. Raquel e Hilario se pelearon con Rosa y la empujaron.   5. Mariana e Inés dijeron que la casa no estaba limpia.

Vocabulary

Spanish — English

A

a at, to
a la derecha to the right
a la izquierda to the left
a menudo often
¿a quién? to whom?
a tiempo on time
a veces sometimes
abogado, -a (*m.f.*) lawyer
abrigo (*m.*) coat
abril April
abrir to open
abuela grandmother
abuelo grandfather
abuelos grandparents
acabar to finish; —— **de** to have just
accidente (*m.*) accident
acercarse (a) to get near
aconsejar to advise
acordarse (o:ue) (de) to remember
acostar(se) (o:ue) to put to bed, to go
  to bed
adentro inside
adiós good-bye
adivinar to guess
administrador, -a (*m.f.*) administrator
aeropuerto (*m.*) airport
afuera outside
agosto August
agua (*f.*) water
ahora now
ahorrar to save (*money*)
alegrarse (de) to be glad
alemán (*m.*) German (*language*)
algo something
alguien someone, somebody
alguno, -a any, some
alquilar to rent
alto, -a tall
allá over there
amigo, -a (*m.f.*) friend
análisis (*m.*) test

anoche last night
antes (de) before
año (*m.*) year
apagar to turn off
apellido (*m.*) surname; —— **de soltera** maiden name
aprender to learn
aquel(-los), aquella(-s) (*adj.*) that, those
  (*distant*)
aquél(-los), aquélla(-s) (*pron.*) that (one),
  those (*distant*)
aquello (*neuter pron.*) that
aquí here
árbol (*m.*) tree
archivar to file
archivo (*m.*) file
arena (*f.*) sand
argentino, -a (*m.f.*) Argentinian
artículo (*m.*) article
arreglar to fix, to repair
arroz (*m.*) rice; —— **con pollo** chicken
  and rice
asamblea (*f.*) assembly
asistir to attend
aspirina (*f.*) aspirin
atención (*f.*) attention
auto (*m.*) auto, automobile
autobús (*m.*) bus
autopista (*f.*) freeway
avenida (*f.*) avenue
avión (*m.*) plane
ayer yesterday
ayudante (*m.f.*) assistant
ayudar to help

B

bajar(se) (de) to get off
banana (*f.*) banana
banco (*m.*) bank
bañar(se) to bathe
barbero (*m.*) barber

281

beber   to drink
bello, -a   pretty
biblioteca (f.)   library
bicicleta (f.)   bicycle
bien   well, fine
blanco, -a   white
blusa (f.)   blouse
bocina (f.)   horn
bonito, -a   pretty
botella (f.)   bottle
brazo (m.)   arm
buenas noches   good evening, good night
buenas tardes   good afternoon
bueno, -a   good, kind, nice
buenos días   good morning, good day
buscar   to look for

C

caber   to fit
cabeza (f.)   head
caer   to fall
café (m.)   coffee
cafetería (f.)   cafeteria
caliente   hot
calle (f.)   street
cama (f.)   bed
caminar   to walk
camisa (f.)   shirt
campeón, -ona (m.f.)   champion
cansado, -a   tired
cara (f.)   face
cárcel (f.)   jail
carne (f.)   meat
carro (m.)   car
carta (f.)   letter
casa (f.)   house
casado, -a   married
casi nunca   hardly ever
cataratas (f.)   falls
católico, -a   Catholic
cenar   to have supper, to dine
centro (m.)   downtown (area)
cerca (de)   near, next to
cerrar (e:ie)   to close
cine (m.)   movie theater
ciudad (f.)   city
civilización (f.)   civilization

clase (f.)   class, kind, type
cliente (m.f.)   customer
coctel (m.)   cocktail
coche (m.)   car
comenzar (e:ie)   to begin
comer   to eat
comida (f.)   dinner, meal
¿cómo?   how?
comprar   to buy
comprender   to understand
con   with
¿con quién?   with whom?
concierto (m.)   concert
conducir   to drive
conferencia (f.)   lecture
conocer   to know, to be acquainted with
conseguir (e:i)   to obtain, to get
construir   to build
consulado (m.)   consulate
contador, -a (m.f.)   accountant
contrario: al ——   on the contrary
contrato (m.)   contract
conviene   it is advisable
copia (f.)   copy
corbata (f.)   tie
cortar   to cut
creer   to believe
cruzar   to cross
cuaderno (m.)   notebook
¿cuál?   which?, what?
¿cuándo?   when?
¿cuántos?, -as   how many?
cuarto (m.)   room
cuarto, -a   fourth
cubrir   to cover
cuenta (f.)   bill
cuidadoso, -a   careful
culpa (f.)   fault
cultura (f.)   culture

CH

cheque (m.)   check
chica   girl
chico   boy
chico, -a (adj.)   little, small
chiste (m.)   joke
chocar   to collide, to run into

D

dar to give
darse por vencido to give up
de of, from
de nada you're welcome
¿de quién? whose?
deber must
decidir to decide
décimo, -a tenth
decir (e:i) to say, to tell
defecto (m.) fault
dejar to leave (behind)
demás: los, las —— the others
dentista (m.f.) dentist
depositar to deposit
desagradable (adj.) unpleasant
desarrollar to develop
descubrir to discover
desear to wish, to want
despertar(se) (e:ie) to wake up
después afterwards, later
desvestir(se) (e:i) to get undressed
devolver (o:ue) to return
día (m.) day
diccionario (m.) dictionary
diciembre December
difícil difficult, unlikely
dinero (m.) money
dirección (f.) address
director, -a (m.f.) director
discoteca (f.) discotheque
divorciado, -a divorced
doblar to turn
doctor, -a (m.f.) doctor
documento (m.) document
dólar (m.) dollar
doler (o:ue) to hurt, to ache
dolor (m.) pain
domicilio (m.) address
domingo Sunday
¿dónde? where?
dormir(se) (o:ue) to sleep, to fall asleep
dormitorio (m.) bedroom
dudar to doubt

E

economía (f.) economics

echar al correo to mail
edad (f.) age
edificio (m.) building
educado, -a: mal —— rude
él he
ella she
ellas (f.) they
ellos (m.) they
embajador, -a ambassador
empezar (e:ie) to begin
empleado, -a (m.f.) employee
empleo (m.) job
empujar to push
en in, at, on
en casa at home
en seguida right away
enamorarse (de) to fall in love (with)
encontrar (o:ue) to find
enero January
enfermero, -a (m.f.) nurse
enfermo, -a sick
ensalada (f.) salad
entender (e:ie) to understand
entrar to enter
escribir to write; —— a máquina to type
escritorio (m.) desk
escuela (f.) school
ese (-os), esa (-as) (adj.) that, those (nearby)
ése (-os), ésa (-as) (pron.) that (one), those (nearby)
eso (neuter pron.) that
español, -a (m.f.) Spanish also adj.
español (m.) Spanish (language)
especial special
espectáculo (m.) show
esperar to wait, to hope, to wait for
esquina (f.) corner
estación (f.) station; —— de ómnibus (f.) bus station; —— de servicio (f.) service station
estado (m.) state; —— civil marital status
estar to be; —— listo, -a to be ready; —— preso, -a to be in jail
este (-os), esta (-as) (adj.) this, these
éste (-os), ésta (-as) (pron.) this (one), these, the latter

esto (*neuter pron.*)   this
estómago (*m.*)   stomach
estudiante (*m.f.*)   student
estudiar   to study
examen (*m.*)   exam
experimento (*m.*)   experiment
expresar(se)   to express (oneself)

F

fácil   easy
fantástico, -a   fantastic
favor (*m.*)   favor
favorito, -a   favorite
febrero   February
fecha (*f.*)   date; —— **de nacimiento**
    date of birth
feliz   happy
femenino, -a   feminine
fichero (*m.*)   file
fiesta (*f.*)   party
firmar   to sign
físico, -a   physical
flor (*f.*)   flower
francés (*m.*)   French (*language*)

G

gastar   to spend (*money*)
generoso, -a   generous
geografía (*f.*)   geography
gerente (*m.f.*)   manager
gobierno (*m.*)   government
gotear   to leak
gracias   thanks
graduarse   to graduate
gran   great
grande   big, large
guía (*m.f.*)   guide
gustar   to please, to be pleasing

H

hablar   to speak
hacer   to do, to make; —— **calor**
    to be hot; —— **falta**   to need;

—— **frío**   to be cold; —— **sol**   to be
sunny; —— **viento**   to be windy
haragán, -ana   lazy
hasta   until
hasta luego   I'll see you later
hasta mañana   see you tomorrow
hay que . . .   one must . . .
hermana   sister
hermano   brother
hermoso, -a   beautiful
hija   daughter
hijo   son
historia (*f.*)   history
hombre   man
horrible   horrible
hospital (*m.*)   hospital
hotel (*m.*)   hotel
hoy   today

I

idea (*f.*)   idea
idioma (*m.*)   language
iglesia (*f.*)   church
impaciente   impatient
impermeable (*m.*)   raincoat
importante   important
impresionante   impressive
increíble   incredible
inflación (*f.*)   inflation
información (*f.*)   information
informe (*m.*)   report
ingeniero (*m.*)   engineer
inglés (*m.*)   English (*language*)
insistir (en)   to insist (on)
inspector, -a (*m.f.*)   inspector
instructor, -a (*m.f.*)   instructor
instrumento (*m.*)   instrument
inteligente   intelligent
invierno (*m.*)   winter
ir   to go
irse   to leave, to go away
italiano, -a   Italian

J

jabón (*m.*)   soap

jamás   never
jefe, -a (*m.f.*)   boss, chief
jueves   Thursday
jugar   to play (*a game*)
julio   July
junio   June
juntos, -as   together

L

la (*pl.* las)   the (*f.*)
la (*dir. obj. pron.*)   her, it (*f.*), you (*formal f.*)
laboratorio (*m.*)   laboratory
ladrón, -ona (*m.f.*)   thief
lápiz (*m.*)   pencil
las (*dir. obj. pron.*)   them (*f.*), you (*formal f.*)
lavar(se)   to wash (oneself)
le (*ind. obj. pron.*)   to him, her, it, you (*formal m.f.*)
lección (*f.*)   lesson
leer   to read
lento, -a   slow
les (*ind. obj. pron.*)   to them, you (*formal, pl. m.f.*)
levantar(se)   to lift, to raise, to get up
libertad (*f.*)   liberty
libro (*m.*)   book
licencia (*f.*)   license
límite (*m.*)   limit
limonada (*f.*)   lemonade
limpio, -a   clean
lo (*dir. obj. pron.*)   him, it, (*m.*), you (*formal m.*)
lo siento   I'm sorry
los (*dir. obj. pron.*)   them, you (*m. pl.*)
lugar (*m.*)   place
lunes   Monday
luz (*f.*)   light

LL

llamar   to call
llegar   to arrive
lleno, -a   full
llevar   to take, to carry

llevarse bien   to get along
llorar   to cry
llover (o:ue)   to rain
lluvia (*f.*)   rain

M

madre   mother
maestro, -a   teacher
mal   badly
maleta (*f.*)   suitcase
malo, -a   bad
mano (*f.*)   hand
mañana (*f.*)   morning
mañana   tomorrow
máquina de escribir (*f.*)   typewriter
martes   Tuesday
marzo   March
más   more, most; ——— o menos   about, more or less
matar   to kill
matemáticas (*f.*)   mathematics
matrícula (*f.*)   registration
mayo   May
mayor   older, oldest
me (*obj. pron.*)   me, to me, (to) myself
mecánico (*m.f.*)   mechanic
media hora   half an hour
medianoche (*f.*)   midnight
medicina (*f.*)   medicine
médico (*m.f.*)   medical doctor
medio, -a   half
medir (e:i)   to measure, to be . . . tall
mejor   better, best
mejorar   to improve
menor   younger, youngest
menos   less, least, fewer; a ——— que   unless
mentir (e:ie)   to lie
mes (*m.*)   month
mesa (*f.*)   table
meter la pata   to put one's foot in one's mouth
mi (*adj.*)   my

mí (*obj. of prep.*) me
miércoles Wednesday
milla (*f.*) mile
millón (*m.*) million
mineral (*m.*) mineral
mío, -a (*adj.*) my, of mine
mío, -a (*pron.*) mine
mismo, -a same
modelo (*m.*) model
molestar(se) to bother
momento (*m.*) moment
morir (o:ue) to die
mover (o:ue) to move
muchacha girl, young woman
muchacho boy, young man
muchas gracias thank you very much
mucho, -a (-os, -as) much (many); very
mucho (*adv.*) (very) much, a great deal, a lot
mucho gusto how do you do, much pleasure
muebles (*m.*) furniture
muela (*f.*) tooth, molar
mujer (*f.*) woman
mundo (*m.*) world
museo (*m.*) museum
muy very

N

nacimiento (*m.*) birth
nacionalidad (*f.*) nationality
nada nothing
nadar to swim
nadie nobody, no one
necesitar to need
negocios (*m.*) business
negro, -a black
nevar (e:ie) to snow
ni neither, nor
ninguno, -a no, none, not any
niña girl, child
niño boy, child
no no, not

noche (*f.*) evening, night
nombre (*m.*) name
norteamericano, -a North American
nos (*obj. pron.*) us, to us, (to) ourselves
nosotros, -as we, us
novela (*f.*) novel
noveno, -a ninth
novia girlfriend, bride
noviembre November
nuestro(-s), nuestra(-s) (*adj.*) our
nuestro(-s), nuestra(-s) (*pron.*) ours
nuevo: de —— again
número (*m.*) number
nunca never

O

o or, either
obra teatral (*f.*) play
octavo, -a eight
octubre October
ocupación (*f.*) occupation
ocupado, -a busy
oficina (*f.*) office
oficina de correos (*f.*) post office
ómnibus (*m.*) omnibus
otoño (*m.*) fall
otra vez again

P

paciencia (*f.*) patience
paciente (*m.f.*) patient
padres (*m.*) parents
pagar to pay
pantalones (*m.*) trousers
papel (*m.*) paper; role
paquete (*m.*) package
para to, for, by, in order
paraguas (*m.*) umbrella
pariente (*m.f.*) relative
parque (*m.*) park
pasado, -a last

pasaje (*m.*) ticket

pasajero, -a (*m.f.*) passenger

pasaporte (*m.*) passport

pasar to go by, to pass, to spend (*time*), to come in

payaso (*m.*) clown

pedir (**e:i**) to ask for, to request, to order

pelear(se) con to fight (with)

pelo (*m.*) hair

pelota (*f.*) ball

pensar (**e:ie**) to think

peor worse, worst

pequeño, -a small, little

perder (**e:ie**) to lose

perfume (*m.*) perfume

periódico (*m.*) newspaper

permitir to permit

pero but

perseguir (**e:i**) persecute

personal (*m.*) personnel

pescado (*m.*) fish

piano (*m.*) piano

piedra (*f.*) rock

pierna (*f.*) leg

piso (*m.*) floor, story

planta (*f.*) plant

plástico, -a plastic

playa (*f.*) beach

plomero (*m.*) plumber

pluma (*f.*) pen

poco, -a little (*quantity*)

pocos, -as few

poder (**o:ue**) to be able to

policía (*f.*) police (*organization*)

policía (*m.f.*) policeman, policewoman

pollo (*m.*) chicken

poner(se) to put, to put on

por around, along, by, for, through

por favor please

¿por qué? why?

porque because

portarse bien to behave properly

posible possible

postre (*m.*) dessert

precio (*m.*) price

preferir (**e:ie**) to prefer

preguntar to ask (a question)

premio (*m.*) prize

preocupar(se) to worry

presentar to introduce

presidente, -a (*m.f.*) president

prestar to lend

primavera (*f.*) spring

primero, -a (*m.f.*) first

primo, -a (*m.f.*) cousin

probar(se) (**o:ue**) to try, to taste, to try on

problema (*m.*) problem

prohibir to forbid, to prohibit

profesión (*f.*) profession

profesor, -a (*m.f.*) professor

programa (*m.*) program

pronto soon

próximo, -a next

puerta (*f.*) door

pues well, then

puesto (*m.*) position, job

Q

¿qué? what?

quedar(se) to be located, to stay, to remain

quejarse to complain

querer (**e:ie**) to want, to wish

querido, -a dear

¿quién? who?, whom?

química (*f.*) chemistry

quinto, -a fifth

R

radio (*f.*) radio

rápido, -a fast

recibir to receive

reciente recent

recoger to pick up

recomendar (**e:ie**) to recommend

reconocer to recognize
recordar (o:ue) to remember
refresco (*m.*) soda
refrigerador (*m.*) refrigerator
regalo (*m.*) present, gift
repente: de —— suddenly
repetir (e:i) to repeat
respuesta (*f.*) answer
restaurante (*m.*) restaurant
resultado (*m.*) result
reunión (*f.*) meeting
revisar to check
revista (*f.*) magazine
revólver (*m.*) revolver
rojo, -a red
romper to break
ropa (*f.*) clothes

S

sábado Saturday
sábana (*f.*) sheet
saber to know, to know how
sacar to take out; —— **copia** to photocopy
salir to go out
se (*reflex.*) (to) himself, herself, etc.
secarse to dry, to get dry
seguir (e:i) to follow, to continue; —— **derecho** to continue straight ahead
segundo, -a second
seguro, -a sure, certain; **estar ——** to be sure
seguro social (*m.*) social security
semana (*f.*) week
sentar(se) (e:ie) to sit, to sit down
sentir (e:ie) to regret
sentir(se) (e:ie) to feel
señor (*abr.* **Sr.**) Mister, sir, gentleman
señora (*abr.* **Sra.**) Mrs., Madam, lady
señorita (*abr.* **Srta.**) Miss, young lady
separado, -a separated
septiembre September
séptimo, -a seventh

ser to be
servir (e:i) to serve
sí yes
siempre always
silla (*f.*) chair
sin falta without fail
sistema (*m.*) system
sexto, -a sixth
siglo (*m.*) century
sillón (*m.*) armchair
sobrevivir to survive
sobrina niece
sobrino nephew
sofá (*m.*) sofa
solicitud (*f.*) application
sólo only
solo, -a alone
soltero, -a single
sombrero (*m.*) hat
sopa (*f.*) soup
su his, her, its, your (*formal*), their
suegra mother-in-law
suegro father-in-law
suéter (*m.*) sweater
sugerir (e:ie) to suggest
suicidarse to commit suicide
suyo(-s), suya(-s) (*pron.*) yours (*formal*) his, hers, theirs

T

tacaño, -a stingy
talonario de cheques (*m.*) checkbook
también also, too
tampoco neither
tan so
tarde (*f.*) afternoon
tarde late
tarea (*f.*) homework
te (*pron.*) you (*fam.*), to you, (to) yourself
té (*m.*) tea
teatro (*m.*) theater
techo (*m.*) roof
teléfono (*m.*) telephone
telegrama (*m.*) telegram

televisión (*f.*)   television
tema (*m.*)   theme
temer   to fear
temperatura (*f.*)   temperature
temporada de lluvias (*f.*)   rainy season
tener   to have
tener . . . años   to be . . . years old;
—— **calor**   to be warm; —— **frío**   to
be cold; —— **hambre**   to be hungry;
—— **miedo**   to   be   afraid;   ——
prisa   to be in a hurry; —— **razón**   to
be right; —— **sed**   to be thirsty;
—— **sueño**   to be sleepy
tener éxito   to succeed
tener que   to have to
tercero, -a   third
terminar   to finish
termómetro (*m.*)   thermometer
terraza (*f.*)   terrace
testamento (*m.*)   testament, will
tía   aunt
tienda (*f.*)   store
tierra (*f.*)   earth
tijera(s) (*f.*)   scissors
tintorería (*f.*)   cleaner
tío   uncle
toalla (*f.*)   towel
todavía   yet
todo, -a   all
tomar   to   take,   to   drink;   ——
apuntes   to take notes; —— **el sol**   to
sunbathe
trabajar   to work
trabajo (*m.*)   work, job
traducción (*f.*)   translation
traducir   to translate
traer   to bring
traje (*m.*)   suit
triste   sad
tropical   tropical
tu   your (*inf.*)
tú   you (*inf.*)
tuyo(-s), **tuya(-s)** (*adj.*)   your (*inf.*) of
yours
tuyo(-s), **tuya(-s)** (*pron.*)   yours (*inf.*
sing.)

U

único, -a   same
uña (*f.*)   fingernail
usar   to use, to wear
usted (*abr.* **Ud.**)   you (*form.*)
ustedes (*abr.* **Uds.**)   you (*pl.*)

V

vacaciones (*f.*)   vacation
vanidoso, -a   vain
vecino, -a (*m.f.*)   neighbor
velocidad (*f.*)   speed
vender   to sell
venir   to come
ventana (*f.*)   window
ver   to see
verano (*m.*)   summer
verdad (*f.*)   truth
verde   green
vestido (*m.*)   dress
vestir(se) (**e:i**)   to dress, to get dressed
vez (*f.*)   time
viajero, -a (*m.f.*)   traveller
vidrio (*m.*)   glass
viernes   Friday
visitar   to visit
viuda   widow
viudo   widower
vivir   to live
volar (**o:ue**)   to fly
volver (**o:ue**)   to come (go) back
vuelo (*m.*)   flight

Y

y   and
yo   I

Z

zapato (*m.*)   shoe

English — Spanish

A

a   un(a)
about   más o menos
accident   accidente (*m.*)
accountant   contador, -a (*m.f.*)
ache   doler (o:ue)
address   domicilio (*m.*)
administrator   administrador, -a (*m.f.*)
advise   aconsejar
afternoon   tarde (*f.*)
afterwards   después
again   otra vez; de nuevo
age   edad (*f.*)
airport   aeropuerto (*m.*)
all   todos, -as
alone   solo, -a
also   también
always   siempre
ambassador   embajador, -a (*m.f.*)
and   y
answer   respuesta (*f.*)
any   alguno, -a; cualquier, -a
anyone   alguien
application   solicitud (*f.*)
April   abril
Argentinian   argentino, -a
arm   brazo (*m.*)
armchair   sillón (*m.*)
around   alrededor (de), por
arrange   arreglar
arrive   llegar
article   artículo (*m.*)
ask (a question)   preguntar; —— for
   pedir (e:i)
aspirin   aspirina (*f.*)
assembly   asamblea (*f.*)
assistant   ayudante (*m.f.*)
at   en; a
at home   en casa
attend   asistir
attention   atención (*f.*)
August   agosto

aunt   tía
auto; automobile   auto (*m.*); automobile
   (*m.*); coche (*m.*), carro (*m.*)
avenue   avenida (*f.*)

B

bad(ly)   malo, -a (*adj.*); mal (*adv.*)
ball   pelota (*f.*)
banana   banana (*f.*)
bank   banco (*m.*)
barber   barbero, -a (*m.f.*)
bathe   bañarse
be   ser, estar; —— able   poder (o:ue);
   —— acquainted with   conocer; ——
   advisable   convenir   (e:ie);   ——
   glad   alegrarse (de); —— ready   estar
   listo, -a; —— cold (*weather*) hacer
   frío; —— hot (*weather*) hacer calor;
   —— windy   hacer   viento;   ——
   sunny   hacer sol; —— cold   tener frío;
   —— thirsty   tener sed; —— hungry   tener hambre; —— hot   tener
   calor; —— sleepy   tener sueño; ——
   in a hurry   tener prisa;   ——
   afraid   tener miedo; —— right   tener
   razón;   —— . . . years old   tener
   (cumplir) . . . años
beach   playa (*f.*)
beautiful   hermoso, -a
because   porque
bed   cama (*f.*)
bedroom   dormitorio (*m.*)
before   antes de
begin   comenzar (e:ie); empezar (e:ie)
behave properly   portarse bien
believe   creer
best   (el, la) mejor
better   mejor
bicycle   bicicleta (*f.*)
big   grande
bigger   más grande

bill cuenta (*f.*)
birth nacimiento (*m.*)
black negro, -a
blouse, blusa (*f.*)
book libro (*m.*)
boss jefe, -a (*m.f.*)
bother molestar(se)
bottle botella (*f.*)
boy niño, chico, muchacho
break romper
bring traer
brother hermano
build construir
building edificio (*m.*)
bus autobús (*m.*); ── **station** estación de ómnibus
business negocios (*m.*)
busy ocupado, -a
but pero
buy comprar
by por; para

C

cafeteria cafetería (*f.*)
call llamar
car carro (*m.*); coche (*m.*)
careful cuidadoso, -a
Catholic católico, -a
century siglo (*m.*)
certain seguro, -a
chair silla (*f.*)
champion campeón, -ona (*m.f.*)
check cheque (*m.*)
check revisar (*verb*)
checkbook talonario de cheques (*m.*)
chemistry química (*f.*)
chicken pollo (*m.*)
chicken and rice arroz con pollo
chief jefe, -a (*m.f.*)
child niño, -a (*m.f.*)
church iglesia (*f.*)
city ciudad (*f.*)
civilization civilización (*f.*)

class clase (*f.*)
clean limpio, -a
cleaner tintorería (*f.*)
close cerrar (e:ie)
clothes ropa (*f.*)
clown payaso (*m.*)
coat abrigo (*m.*)
cocktail coctel (*m.*)
coffee café (*m.*)
collide chocar
come venir; ── **back** volver (o:ue); ── **in** entrar
commit suicide suicidarse
complain quejarse (de)
concentration concentración (*f.*)
concert concierto (*m.*)
consulate consulado (*m.*)
continue seguir (e:i); ── **straight ahead** seguir derecho
contract contrato (*m.*)
contrary: on the ── al contrario
copy copia (*f.*)
corner esquina (*f.*)
cousin primo, -a (*m.f.*)
cover cubrir
cross cruzar
cry llorar
culture cultura (*f.*)
customer cliente (*m.f.*)
cut cortar

D

date fecha (*f.*)
daughter hija
day día (*m.*)
dear querido, -a
December diciembre
decide decidir
dentist dentista (*m.f.*)
deposit depositar
desk escritorio (*m.*)
dessert postre (*m.*)
develop desarrollar

dictionary diccionario (*m.*)
die morir (o:ue)
difficult difícil
dine cenar
dinner cena (*f.*)
director director, -a (*m.f.*)
discotheque discoteca (*f.*)
discover descubrir
divorced divorciado, -a
do hacer
doctor doctor, -a (*m.f.*)
document documento (*m.*)
dollar dólar (*m.*)
door puerta (*f.*)
downtown (*area*) centro (*m.*)
dress vestido (*m.*)
dress (*oneself*) vestir(se) (e:i)
drink tomar; beber
drive conducir
dry secarse

E

early temprano
earth tierra (*f.*)
easy fácil
eat comer
economics economía (*f.*)
eighth octavo, -a
either . . . or o . . . o
employee empleado, -a (*m.f.*)
end terminar
engineer ingeniero, -a (*m.f.*)
English (*language*) inglés (*m.*)
enter entrar
evening noche (*f.*)
exam examen (*m.*)
experiment experimento (*m.*)
express (*oneself*) expresar(se)

F

face cara (*f.*)

fall otoño (*m.*)
fall caer (*verb*)
fall asleep dormirse (o:ue)
fall in love (**with**) enamorarse (de)
falls cataratas (*f.*)
fantastic fantástico, -a
fast rápido, -a
father padre
father-in-law suegro
fault culpa (*f.*); defecto (*m.*)
favor favor (*m.*)
favorite favorito, -a
fear temer
February febrero
feel sentir(se) (e:ie)
feminine femenino, -a
few pocos, -as
fewer menos
fight (**with**) pelear(se) con
file archivo (*m.*); fichero (*m.*)
file archivar (*verb*)
fifth quinto, -a
find encontrar (o:ue)
fine bien
finish terminar, acabar
fingernail uña (*f.*)
first primero, -a
fish pescado (*m.*)
fit caber
fix arreglar
flight vuelo (*m.*)
floor (*story*) piso (*m.*)
flower flor (*f.*)
fly volar (o:ue)
follow seguir (e:i)
for por; para
for whom? ¿para quién?
forbid prohibir
fourth cuarto, -a
freeway autopista (*f.*)
French (*language*) francés (*m.*)
Friday viernes
friend amigo, -a
full lleno, -a
furniture (*pieces of*) muebles (*m.*)

G

generous generoso, -a
geography geografía (*f.*)
German (*language*) alemán (*m.*)
get obtener; conseguir (e:i); ——
along llevarse bien; —— **dressed**
vestirse (e:i); —— **near** acercarse (a); —— **off** bajar(se) de; ——
undressed desvestirse (e:i); —— **up**
levantarse
gift regalo (*m.*)
girl niña, chica, muchacha
girlfriend novia
give dar; —— **up** darse por vencido
glass vidrio (*m.*)
go ir; —— **to bed** acostarse (o:ue);
—— **away** irse; —— **by** pasar; —
out salir
good bueno, -a
good afternoon buenas tardes
good-bye adiós
good day buenos días
good evening buenas noches
good morning buenos días
good night buenas noches
government gobierno (*m.*)
graduate graduarse
grandfather abuelo
grandmother abuela
grandparents abuelos
great gran
green verde
guess adivinar
guide guía (*m.f.*)

H

hair pelo (*m.*)
half medio, -a
hand mano (*f.*)
happy feliz
hardly ever casi nunca
hat sombrero (*m.*)

have tener; —— **just** acabar de; —
supper cenar; —— **to** tener que
he él
head cabeza (*f.*)
her su(s) (*adj.*); la (*dir. obj.*); le (*ind. obj.*)
here aquí
hers suyo, -a, suyos, -as; (el, la, los, las) de ella
herself se
help ayudar
him lo (*dir. obj.*); le (*ind. obj.*)
himself se
his suyo, -a, suyos, -as; (el, la, los, las) de él
his su(s) (*adj.*)
history historia (*f.*)
homework tarea (*f.*)
hope esperar
horn bocina (*f.*)
horrible horrible
hospital hospital (*m.*)
hot caliente
hotel hotel (*m.*)
house casa (*f.*)
how? ¿cómo?
how do you do mucho gusto
how many? ¿cuántos?, -as
hurt doler (o:ue)

I

I yo
idea idea (*f.*)
impatient impaciente
important importante
impressive impresionante
improve mejorar
in en
incredible increíble
information información (*f.*)
inflation inflación (*f.*)
inside adentro
insist (on) insistir (en)

inspector inspector, -a (*m.f.*)
instructor instructor, -a (*m.f.*)
instrument instrumento (*m.*)
intelligent inteligente
introduce presentar
it lo (*m.*); la (*f.*)
Italian italiano, -a
its su(s) (*adj.*)
itself se

J

jail cárcel (*f.*)
January enero
job empleo (*m.*); puesto (*m.*)
joke chiste (*m.*)
July julio
June junio

K

kill matar
kind clase (*f.*)
kind bueno, -a (*adj.*)
know conocer; saber

L

laboratory laboratorio (*m.*)
language idioma (*m.*)
large grande
last pasado, -a
last night anoche
late tarde
later después
lawyer abogado, -a (*m.f.*)
lazy haragán, -ana
leak gotear
learn aprender
least menos
leave irse; dejar
lecture conferencia (*f.*)
leg pierna (*f.*)

lemonade limonada (*f.*)
lend prestar
less menos
lesson lección (*f.*)
letter carta (*f.*)
liberty libertad (*f.*)
library biblioteca (*f.*)
license licencia (*f.*)
lie mentir (e:ie)
lift levantar
light luz (*f.*)
limit límite (*m.*)
little chico, -a (*size*); poco, -a (*quantity*)
live vivir
look for buscar
lose perder (e:ie)

M

magazine revista (*f.*)
maiden name apellido de soltera (*m.*)
mail echar al correo
make hacer
man hombre
manager gerente (*m.f.*)
many muchos, -as
March marzo
marital status estado civil (*m.*)
married casado, -a
masculine masculino, -a (*m.f.*)
mathematics matemáticas (*f.*)
May mayo
me me (*dir. and indir. obj.*)
meal comida (*f.*)
measure medir (e:i)
meat carne (*f.*)
mechanic mecánico (*m.f.*)
medical doctor médico (*m.f.*)
medicine medicina (*f.*)
meeting reunión (*f.*)
midnight medianoche (*f.*)
mile milla (*f.*)
million millón (*m.*)
mine mío, -a, míos, -as (*pron.*)
mineral mineral (*m.*)

Miss; young lady señorita
model modelo (m.)
moment momento (m.)
Monday lunes
money dinero (m.)
month mes (m.)
more más
morning mañana (f.)
most más
move mover (o:ue)
movie (theater) cine (m.)
mother madre
mother-in-law suegra
Mr., sir, gentleman señor
Mrs., madam, lady señora
much mucho, -a, muchos, -as, (adj.);
  mucho (adv.)
museum museo (m.)
must deber
my mi(s) (adj.)
myself me

N

name nombre (m.)
nationality nacionalidad (f.)
near cerca de
need necesitar; hacerle falta a uno
neighbor vecino, -a (m.f.)
neither tampoco
neither . . . nor ni . . . ni
nephew sobrino
never nunca; jamás
newspaper periódico (m.)
next próximo, -a
next to cerca de
nice bueno, -a
niece sobrina
night noche (f.)
ninth noveno, -a
no; not no
no one nadie
nobody nadie
none ningún, ninguno, -a
North American norteamericano, -a
not any ningún, ninguno, -a
notebook cuaderno (m.)
nothing nada

novel novela (f.)
November noviembre
now ahora
number número (m.)
nurse enfermero, -a (m.f.)

O

obtain conseguir (e:i)
occupation ocupación (f.)
October octubre
of de
office oficina (f.)
often a menudo
older mayor
oldest (el, la) mayor
omnibus ómnibus (m.)
on en
only sólo
on time a tiempo
open abrir
or o
order pedir (e:i)
others, the los, las demás
our nuestro, -a, nuestros, -as (adj.)
ours nuestro, -a, nuestros, -as (pron.)
ourselves nos
outside afuera
over there allá

P

package paquete (m.)
pain dolor (m.)
parents padres (m.)
park parque (m.)
party fiesta (f.)
pass pasar
passenger pasajero, -a (m.f.)
passport pasaporte (m.)
patience paciencia (f.)
patient paciente (m.f.)
pay pagar
pen pluma (f.)
pencil lápiz (m.)
per por
perfume perfume (m.)

permit permitir
persecute perseguir (e:i)
personnel personal (m.)
photocopy sacar copia
physical físico, -a
piano piano (m.)
pick up recoger
place lugar (m.)
place poner (verb)
plane avión (m.)
plant planta (f.)
plastic plástico, -a
play (a game) jugar; (in a theater) obra
  teatral (f.)
please por favor
plumber plomero, -a (m.f.)
police (organization) policía (f.)
policeman policía (m.)
policewoman policía (f.)
position puesto (m.)
possible posible
post office oficina de correos (f.)
prefer preferir (e:ie)
present regalo (m.)
president presidente, -a (m.f.)
pretty bello, -a; bonito, -a
price precio (m.)
prize premio (m.)
problem problema (m.)
program programa (m.)
profession profesión (f.)
professor profesor, -a (m.f.)
push empujar
put (on) poner; ponerse; —— to bed
  acostar (o:ue)

R

radio radio (f.)
rain llover (o:ue)
rain lluvia (f.)
raincoat impermeable (m.)
rainy season temporada de lluvias (f.)
raise levantar
read leer
receive recibir
recent reciente
recognize reconocer

recommend recomendar (e:ie)
red rojo, -a
refrigerator refrigerador (m.)
registration matrícula (f.)
regret sentir (e:ie)
relative pariente (m.f.)
remain quedarse
remember acordarse (de) (o:ue); recordar (o:ue)
rent alquilar
repair arreglar
repeat repetir (e:i)
report informe (m.)
request pedir (e:i)
restaurant restaurante (m.)
result resultado (m.)
revolver revólver (m.)
rice arroz (m.)
right away en seguida
rock piedra (f.)
role papel (m.)
roof techo (m.)
room cuarto (m.)
rude mal educado, -a
run into chocar

S

sad triste
salad ensalada (f.)
same mismo, -a
sand arena (f.)
Saturday sábado
save (money) ahorrar
say decir (e:i)
school escuela (f.)
scissors tijera(s) (f.)
second segundo, -a
secretary secretario, -a (m.f.)
see ver
sell vender
separated separado, -a
September septiembre
serve servir (e:i)
service station estación de servicio (f.)
seventh séptimo, -a
sex sexo (m.)
she ella

sheet   sábana (*f.*)
shirt   camisa (*f.*)
shoes   zapatos (*m.*)
show   espectáculo (*m.*)
sick   enfermo, -a
sign   firmar
single   soltero, -a
sister   hermana
sit   sentarse (e:ie)
sixth   sexto, -a
sleep   dormir (o:ue)
slow   lento, -a
small   pequeño,   -a;   **smaller**   más pequeño
snow   nevar (e:ie)
so   tan
soap   jabón (*m.*)
social security   seguro social (*m.*)
soda   refresco (*m.*)
sofa   sofá (*m.*)
some   algún, alguno, -a, algunos, -as
someone   alguien
something   algo
sometimes   a veces
son   hijo
soon   pronto
sorry   lo siento
soup   sopa (*f.*)
Spanish (*language*)   español (*m.*)
Spanish (*nationality*)   español, -a
speak   hablar
special   especial
speed   velocidad (*f.*)
spend (*time*)   pasar; ——— (*money*) gastar
spring   primavera (*f.*)
state   estado (*m.*)
station   estación (*f.*)
stay   quedarse
stingy   tacaño, -a
stomach   estómago (*m.*)
store   tienda (*f.*)
street   calle (*f.*)
student   estudiante (*m.f.*)
study   estudiar
succeed   tener éxito
suddenly   de repente
suggest   sugerir (e:ie)
suit   traje (*m.*)
suitcase   maleta (*f.*)

summer   verano (*m.*)
sunbathe   tomar el sol
Sunday   domingo
sure   seguro, -a; **to be** ——— estar seguro, -a
surname   apellido (*m.*)
survive   sobrevivir
sweater   suéter (*m.*)
swim   nadar
system   sistema (*m.*)

T

table   mesa (*f.*)
take   tomar; llevar; ——— **notes** tomar apuntes
take out   sacar
tall   alto, -a
taste   probar
tea   té (*m.*)
teacher (*elementary school*) maestro, -a
telegram   telegrama (*m.*)
telephone   teléfono (*m.*)
television   televisión (*f.*)
tell   decir (e:i)
temperature   temperatura (*f.*)
tenth   décimo, -a
terrace   terraza (*f.*)
test   análisis (*m.*)
testament   testamento (*m.*)
thanks   gracias
that   (*adj.*) (*near person addressed*) ese, esa (-os, -as); (*distant*) aquel, aquella (-os, -as); (*pron.*) ése, ésa (-os, -as), aquél, aquélla (-os, -as); (*neuter*) eso, aquello; (*relative pron.*) que, quien
theater   teatro (*m.*)
their   su(s) (*adj.*)
theirs   suyo, -a, suyos, -as (el, la, los, las), de ellos, de ellas
them   los, las (*dir. obj.*); les (*ind. obj.*)
theme   tema (*m.*)
themselves   se
thermometer   termómetro (*m.*)
these   (*adj.*) estos, -as; (*pron.*) éstos, -as
they   ellos; ellas
thief   ladrón, -ona (*m.f.*)

think   pensar (e:ie)
third   tercero, -a
this   (*adj.*) este, esta; (*pron.*) éste, ésta; (*neuter*) esto
those   (*adj.*) (*near person addressed*) esos, esas; (*distant*) aquellos, aquellas; (*pron.*) ésos, -as, aquéllos, -as
Thursday   jueves
ticket   pasaje (*m.*)
tie   corbata (*f.*)
time   hora (*f.*); tiempo (*m.*); vez (*f.*)
tired   cansado, -a
to   para; a
today   hoy
together   juntos, -as
tomorrow   mañana
too   también
tooth   diente (*m.*); muela (*f.*)
towel   toalla (*f.*)
translate   traducir
translation   traducción (*f.*)
traveller   viajero, -a (*m.f.*)
tree   árbol (*m.*)
tropical   tropical
trousers   pantalones (*m.*)
truth   verdad (*f.*)
try; try on   probar(se) (o:ue)
Tuesday   martes
turn   doblar
turn off   apagar
twenty   veinte
type   clase (*f.*); tipo (*m.*)
type   escribir a máquina
typewriter   máquina de escribir (*f.*)

U

umbrella   paraguas (*m.*)
uncle   tío (*m.*)
understand   comprender; entender (e:ie)
unique   único, -a
university   universidad (*f.*)
unless   a menos que
unlikely   difícil
unpleasant   desagradable
until   hasta
us   nos (*dir. and ind. obj.*)
use   usar

V

vacation   vacaciones (*f.*)
vain   vanidoso, -a
very   muy
visit   visitar

W

wait   esperar
wake up   despertarse (e:ie)
walk   caminar
want   querer (e:ie)
wash (*oneself*)   lavar(se)
water   agua (*f.*)
we   nosotros, -as
Wednesday   miércoles
week   semana (*f.*)
well   bien, pues
what?   ¿qué?; ¿cuál?
when?   ¿cuándo?
where?   ¿dónde?
which?   ¿cuál?
white   blanco, -a
who?   ¿quién?; ¿quiénes?
whom?   ¿quién?; ¿a quién?
whose?   ¿de quién?
widow   viuda
widower   viudo
window   ventana (*f.*)
winter   invierno (*m.*)
wish   desear
with   con
without   sin
without fail   sin falta
woman   mujer
work   trabajo (*m.*)
work   trabajar (*verb*)
world   mundo (*m.*)
worry   preocupar(se)
worse   peor
worst   peor
write   escribir

Y

year   año (*m.*)

yes sí

yesterday ayer

yet todavía

you (*fam. sing.*) tú; (*dir. and indir. obj.*) te

you (*polite*) (*subj. pron.*) usted (Ud.), ustedes (Uds.); (*dir. obj.*) le, la, los, las; (*indir. obj.*) les, se

younger menor

youngest menor

your (*adj.*) (*fam.*) tu(s); (*formal*) su(s), de Ud., de Uds.

yours (*pron.*) (*fam.*) (el) tuyo, (la) tuya, (los) tuyos, (las) tuyas; (*formal*) (el) suyo, (la) suya, (los) suyos, (las) suyas; (el, la, los, las) de Ud., de Uds.

yourself (*fam.*) te; (*formal*) se

yourselves se

INDEX

(References are to page numbers.)